Y0-BZG-927

THE
OTHER
WAR

ADST-DACOR Diplomats and Diplomacy Series

Since 1776, extraordinary men and women have represented the United States abroad under all sorts of circumstances. What they did and how and why they did it remain little known to their compatriots. In 1995 the Association for Diplomatic Studies and Training (ADST) and Diplomatic and Consular Officers, Retired, Inc. (DACOR) created the Diplomats and Diplomacy book series to increase public knowledge and appreciation of the involvement of American diplomats in world history. The series seeks to demystify diplomacy by telling the story of those who have conducted our foreign relations, as they lived, influenced, and reported them. *The Other War: Winning and Losing in Afghanistan,* by Amb. Ronald E. Neumann (Ret.), is the thirty-second volume in the series.

Other Titles in the Series

Brown, Gordon, *Toussaint's Clause: The Founding Fathers and the Haitian Revolution*

Cohen, Herman J., *Intervening in Africa: Superpower Peacemaking in a Troubled Continent*

Cross, Charles T., *Born a Foreigner: A Memoir of the American Presence in Asia*

Grove, Brandon, *Behind Embassy Walls: The Life and Times of an American Diplomat*

Hart, Parker T., *Saudi Arabia and the United States: Birth of a Security Partnership*

Hume, Cameron R., *Mission to Algiers: Diplomacy by Engagement*

Kux, Dennis, *The United States and Pakistan, 1947–2000: Disenchanted Allies*

Loeffler, Jane C., *Architecture of Diplomacy: Building America's Embassies*

Miller, Robert H., *Vietnam and Beyond: A Diplomat's Cold War Education*

Parker, Richard B., *Uncle Sam in Barbary: A Diplomatic History*

Pezzullo, Ralph, *Plunging into Haiti: Clinton, Aristide, and the Defeat of Diplomacy*

Richardson, John, *A New Vision for America: Toward Human Solidarity*

Schaffer, Howard B., *Ellsworth Bunker: Global Troubleshooter, Vietnam Hawk*

Simpson, Howard R., *Bush Hat, Black Tie: Adventures of a Foreign Service Officer*

Stephenson, James, *Losing the Golden Hour: An Insider's View of Iraq's Reconstruction*

THE OTHER WAR

Winning and Losing in Afghanistan

Ronald E. Neumann
U.S. Ambassador (Ret.)

FOREWORD BY Bruce Riedel

An ADST-DACOR Diplomats and Diplomacy Book

Potomac Books, Inc.
Washington, D.C.

Copyright © 2009 by Ronald E. Neumann

Published in the United States by Potomac Books, Inc. All rights reserved. No part of this book may be reproduced in any manner whatsoever without written permission from the publisher, except in the case of brief quotations embodied in critical articles and reviews.

The opinions and characterizations in this book are those of the author and do not necessarily represent official positions of the U.S. Government.

Library of Congress Cataloging-in-Publication Data
Neumann, Ronald E. (Ronald Eldredge), 1944–
  The other war : winning and losing in Afghanistan / Ronald E. Neumann ; foreword by Bruce Riedel.— 1st ed.
      p. cm. — (ADST-DACOR diplomats and diplomacy series)
  Includes bibliographical references and index.
  ISBN 978-1-59797-427-1 (alk. paper)
  1. Afghan War, 2001—Personal narratives, American. 2. Neumann, Ronald E. (Ronald Eldredge), 1944– 3. Ambassadors—United States—Biography. 4. Afghanistan—Foreign relations—United States. 5. United States—Foreign relations—Afghanistan. 6. United States—Military policy. 7. Military assistance, American—Afghanistan. 8. Economic assistance, American—Afghanistan. I. Title.
  DS371.43.N48A3 2009
  958.104'7—dc22
                                                                2009028993

Printed in the United States of America on acid-free paper that meets the American National Standards Institute Z39-48 Standard.

Potomac Books, Inc.
22841 Quicksilver Drive
Dulles, Virginia 20166

First Edition

10 9 8 7 6 5 4 3 2 1

Contents

Foreword

Twice in the last quarter century the United States has squandered a great victory in Afghanistan by failing in the follow-through after success on the battlefield. In the 1980s America supported the Afghan mujahideen in their battle to liberate their country from the invading Fortieth Red Army of the Soviet Union. After enormous cost to the Afghan people, the Soviets were defeated and went home. The Soviet empire collapsed soon thereafter. But the United States walked away from Afghanistan, and civil war followed, leading to the emergence of the Taliban and ultimately to the al Qaeda attack of September 11, 2001.

Then history repeated itself. Again the United States scored a brilliant initial victory and toppled the Taliban's Islamic Emirate in a couple of months in late 2001. And again, U.S. attention wandered away from Afghanistan to another battlefield in Iraq. The effort to rebuild Afghanistan stalled; the Taliban regrouped in Pakistan and staged a comeback. By 2005 the war was all but forgotten by most Americans.

Ron Neumann has provided us with a unique view into this second tragedy. I have known Ron for well over a decade and have worked with him in many trouble spots. A distinguished diplomat with years of experience in tough places around the world, he reports in *The Other War: Winning and Losing in Afghanistan* how our diplomats and generals tried to get the resources they needed to secure our victory in Afghanistan but were thwarted by a White House that had become ensnared in a different war, ironically one it chose to start when it did not need to. Without the resources—troops and economic assistance—the Taliban became a threat it did not need to become.

Ambassador Neumann records this tragedy with a grace and eloquence that reflect his life and his dedication to his country. His father had served in Afghanistan years before the Soviet invasion and Ron's love of the Afghan people is clear. So too is his commitment to the Foreign Service. All American diplomats and aspiring ambassadors should read this book as a manual on what to do as an ambassador, both in general and especially in a war zone. Ron never stayed holed up in his office or in his embassy; he roamed the compound and the country knowing that only by direct observation and face-to-face discussion can you really know what is going on in a complex conflict.

The war in Afghanistan is also a coalition war with some forty countries now fighting with us in one of the North Atlantic Treaty Organization's largest missions ever. Ambassador Neumann provides many useful insights into the nature of coalition warfare and reminds us that our alliances are not just for show or publicity. In Afghanistan many of our NATO partners and other allies, such as Australia, have been in front, taking on the enemy for years, and have paid the price in blood.

The stakes in Afghanistan are enormous. If the Taliban consolidates its position in southern and eastern Afghanistan, it is certain it will again give al Qaeda safe haven to plot against America, expanding the sanctuary the terrorist group already has in Pakistan. There is no reason to believe Mullah Omar has broken with Osama bin Laden since 2001. Many, including the Saudis, have asked him to with no result. Indeed his rhetoric since 2001 has increasingly been that of a global jihadist, placing the Afghan Taliban struggle inside the global fight against NATO's "Crusader" armies. If Omar did not break with al Qaeda in 2001 after 9/11, when the survival of his Islamic Emirate was at stake, it is far less likely he will sever ties when he senses U.S. will is broken in Afghanistan. His goals are to drive the coalition out and impose the medieval hell he built in the 1990s back on the Afghan people.

Even more devastating would be the impact in neighboring Pakistan. A victory for the Afghan Taliban would encourage its new partner, the Pakistani Taliban, in its struggle to take over the world's second-largest Muslim country. Several Pakistani Taliban leaders have united their forces and proclaimed their allegiance both to Omar and bin Laden. Already on the march in Pakistan from the tribal frontiers to inside major cities like Karachi, a Pakistani Taliban further invigorated by its partner's success across the Durand line would be well positioned to take over much of the country. Al Qaeda's room for maneuver would be even greater, and it might well get its hands on the world's fastest growing nuclear arsenal.

The entire Muslim world also has a stake in Afghanistan's future. Jihadist terrorists, from Algeria to Indonesia and from Uzbekistan to Somalia, have been trained in Afghanistan in the past and will be again if the Taliban and al Qaeda triumph. Saudi Arabia and the United Arab Emirates have a special interest: they, like Pakistan, have longstanding ties to the Taliban. As we finally resource the struggle in Afghanistan properly after years of neglect, we should press our Muslim friends to do the same. It's their war too.

The NATO alliance, the most successful in history, will find its future decided in the Hindu Kush as well. Afghanistan is the alliance's first out-of-Europe mission. At stake is whether the alliance can be a global player in the twenty-first century. Failure in south Asia will probably limit the alliance to peacekeeping missions in the Balkans and training exercises in Europe.

Ignoring Afghanistan has cost our country a great deal. Now is the time to help the Afghan people, the vast majority of whom do not want the Taliban back, to build a national security force that can protect them. We cannot afford to make the same mistake three times. *The Other War* tells us just how critical this mission is for our country and the world.

National security strategy is not just about having a good plan. Indeed it is the implementation of the plan that is the hard part in most cases. Where strategy usually fails is not in the formulation but in the execution. Even the most brilliant strategy will fail if it is not given the resources to succeed. That is the message this book conveys so strongly.

Bruce Riedel
May 2009

Preface

The United States has been at war in Afghanistan since October 2001. It has been "the other war" written about only sporadically for long periods until it flames back into our political perceptions with some disaster. What little has been written about the situation besides news stories has been journal articles closely attuned to specialized issues or to discussions of broad policy, focused extensively on the period before or shortly after 2001. Very little has addressed more recent events in depth, and almost nothing conveys the complexity of the challenges. Debates focus on high policy with little understanding that many of our successes and failures are much more about how we implement policies than the policies themselves. The public has little understanding of any aspect of the conflict other than the military engagement, mostly at the tactical level, which makes for compelling stories but offers a limited view of a larger picture. Very few have any idea what the civilians do at war, yet they are major partners with the military in the armed struggle to build a nation that cannot be won by arms alone.

For almost two years I was in the midst of managing U.S. policy in Afghanistan as the American ambassador. More and more, as I worked my way through the fourth war that I have experienced up close, I was struck by how little either the public or senior policymakers understood the complex business of implementing policy. That lack is serious.

If we do not understand how critical implementation is, we are prone to starve it of resources. If we do not understand how much time is needed for accomplishment, we are drawn too often to give up ideas when we have only begun a process to put them into effect, and instead go charging off searching for new ideas whose realistic accomplishment time we also do not understand. Divorcing high-level policymaking from implementation leads us to ignore information from the ground level necessary to make policies work and prevents us from learning how to adjust policies when they do not. In short, making policy without paying attention to implementation is a bit like sailing near reefs without a lookout; the compass and map are not enough.

The complexity of implementation also poses a particular challenge for military and diplomatic leaders who are faced with the need to explain conditions on the ground. Noting too many problems can result in one being perceived as a defeatist, and worse—in a coalition environment—as critical of allies and undermining allied cohesion. With too much optimism or too little reporting, capitals lose clarity on the levels of sustained effort and the time needed to secure victory. In the end, I believe that professionalism requires honesty in reporting, whether it is welcome or not. But incomprehension of the complexity of implementation makes finding the proper balance between policy and operations difficult. Finding the right words to explain what is being attempted then becomes difficult also. Above all, inadequate understanding of the difficulty of implementing policy exerts a subtle but damaging pressure against policymakers' full understanding of what is needed.

This failure to comprehend implementation is neither partisan nor ideological; rather, I believe, it stems from a lack of the information and experience that would lead intelligent people to understand a complicated phenomenon they have never actually witnessed. And since very little is written about how the complex civilian part of counterinsurgency and armed nation building works, it is difficult to gain that understanding. I hope this book will help to fill this void.

The Other War's purpose is to recount how we in Afghanistan managed (or mismanaged, depending on your point of view) a very complex part of the struggle, how coordination with the military works, and how actions in the field sometimes shaped policy perceptions in Washington. It is an attempt to breathe life into words, like "complex" and "long-term," that are used so frequently by so many with so few having any idea what they represent. This book is a personal and not a scholarly account. It is a view from Afghanistan, and while it recounts some high-level encounters with Washington and my efforts to shape policy, it neither pretends nor claims to be an inside account of Washington policy deliberations.

I have attempted to recount honestly what I knew or did at given moments without too much shading of later thoughts. One benefit for history of my separation from my wife and family while I served in Afghanistan is that I wrote home extensively. This work drew heavily on those letters and personal communications to keep me honest. I had much help in trying to re-create this bit of history.

My former deputy Dick Norland, now an ambassador in his own right, made time to read and critique the whole work as did Thomas Johnson of the U.S. Agency for International Development (USAID), formerly supervisory program officer of USAID in Afghanistan. Doug Wankel, who has been in and out of Afghanistan with counterdrug efforts, also gave me the benefit of his recollections. Lt. Gen. Karl Eikenberry, who was my counterpart in so much of this story, kindly reviewed the text. As always his comments were highly perceptive. I am grateful also to Hilary Claggett and Julie Kimmel at Potomac Books for their labors to bring about the final shape of the manuscript. All have done their best to keep me honest, but I alone am responsible for any mistakes.

I owe a special debt of gratitude to my wife, Elaine. Her sense of duty and service, as well as her love, gave me much needed strength not only in Afghanistan but during our years of separation when I was in Algeria, Iraq, and, much earlier, Vietnam. When I questioned whether I should take up a new duty, she reminded me that I had certain talents that might be of use. And when I soared on the fascination and exhilaration of leading a large embassy in the midst of a war, she continued to keep the roof repaired and the bills paid and to tackle all the other drudgery of daily life without complaint. She was the first to tell me I should write this book. Eventually I paid attention. I believe she was right, but others will have to judge that for themselves after they read it.

Prologue

Helicopters are to me the sound of war, provoking heightened senses and a desire to look around quickly. This is odd because from the first of four wars I have experienced helicopters have always been on my side, first delivering me to possible battle as an infantry officer and later moving me as a civilian. Yet on August 6, 2005, as the big Chinook (CH-47) lifted off for my first trip outside Kabul, my first impression was of how much more relaxed security seemed in Afghanistan than in Iraq, which I had left only two months earlier. We would never have flown the Chinook in daylight in Iraq as it would've been too vulnerable to ground fire. There, the gunners loaded their machine guns and swung into position before we cleared the embassy compound. In Afghanistan, the crew seemed positively leisurely about the way they took position. The armored cars we were to use in Ghazni had driven down by road. So, after sixteen months in Iraq, life seemed both normal and improved. Five months earlier I had had no idea I would be in Afghanistan.

On a Tuesday in April 2005, I was in Amman, Jordan, coming out of Baghdad for a much needed break. Although I had not told anyone at our Amman embassy, the White House had given preliminary approval for my appointment as ambassador to Jordan. I had already completed the usual mountain of paperwork and was looking forward to being posted with my wife, Elaine, so that we could again be an ambassadorial team as we had been in Bahrain. As my departure the next day would be extremely early, I was reaching for the lamp at 9:00 p.m. to get some sleep when the phone rang. It was Bob Pearson, the director general of the Foreign Service, the State Department's senior officer for personnel. "I understand you'll be arriving in Washington on Wednesday," he said. "The secretary wants to see you on Thursday. It's about where you're going. It's not what you think, but I can't tell you anything more." And with that Delphic comment the call ended, along with any chance of getting to sleep.

Thursday morning I used my hours before my midday meeting with Secretary Condoleezza Rice to find out what was coming. After thirty-five years in State, I had some skill in snooping in the bureaucracy. I learned that President George W. Bush had agreed to a personal request of Jordan's King Abdullah to retain our excellent, long-serving charge in Amman, David Hale, as ambassador, a reasonable decision since the king was already comfortable with David. Instead of Amman my destination would be Kabul.

The prospect of further separation from Elaine was not pleasant but I was fascinated. Afghanistan had been my first experience in the Muslim world. Thirty-eight years previously my wife and I had traveled there to spend the time between graduate school and my reporting for duty in the army with my parents. At that time my father was ambassador to Afghanistan. For over three months we had traveled extensively in the country, visiting all of the major cities and driving through the center of the country from Herat through Bamyan to Kabul on unpaved roads. I had even gone by jeep, horse, and yak with a hunting party into the almost inaccessible mountains of northeastern Afghanistan and into the Wakhan Corridor, which juts out along the Amu Darya (Oxus) River to touch the Chinese border. We didn't go quite to the border but hunted in mountains with year-round glaciers. For me the trip began a cultural love affair that laid the ground for a career spent almost entirely in or working on the issues of Muslim countries.

It had also been our first embassy. I had earlier passed the Foreign Service entrance exam. Knowing that volunteering for the infantry was only a diversion for me (assuming I survived Vietnam), Elaine and I were entranced by everything we could learn about embassy life. Being able to see it all through my parents' eyes made for unusual insight into the role of the ambassador and his wife. We would draw on these lessons for many years.

Now I was flattered to be offered the chance to go back, to take my father's place in what had become the second highest profile diplomatic post in our service, and to try to apply to Afghanistan's problems a professional lifetime's experience often spent in difficult and conflict-ridden countries.[1] Also, during my first months in Iraq with the Coalition Provisional Authority (CPA), I had seen much I disagreed with, and this seemed an opportunity to draw on those lessons and perhaps to do better.[2] I quickly called Elaine to explain what was coming. Neither of us wanted a separation, but Elaine has an equally strong sense of duty and she instantly agreed.

By the time I met with Secretary Rice, my decision was already made, at least in my mind. Although I had been twice an ambassador, this was the first time a secretary of state had asked me personally to take an assignment. Not wanting to show I had advance knowledge of the offer, I asked for a day to talk it over with my family and called back to accept the following day. Secretary Rice and I agreed that I would go initially on a one-year commitment to see how the family withstood further absence. I would let her know in a few months if I would stay a second year.

Until the White House made the decision formally, few could be told. My replies to colleagues' questions were vague, although a few knew where I was headed. Some expressed surprise that I would go from Baghdad to Kabul. One told me I was "a great American," which I thought excessive for what I saw as an honor combined with an adventure. I was not too focused on my remaining consultations about Iraqi matters and happily departed for a week's vacation with my mind spinning with new ideas. All too soon I was back in Baghdad.

The work in Iraq was intense. It was difficult to find time to think about anything else, and as much as possible, I tried not to. But from time to time Afghan matters intruded. First, there was the huge mound of paperwork that had to be redone, even though it had all been completed only a few months previously and nothing had changed except the name of the country of assignment: security forms going back fifteen years, the narrative for the Senate, the background paper for the White House lawyers, and the dreaded financial disclosure form that seems to grow more complicated every year and always turns up some entry that needs additional explaining.

Thankfully, the bulk of the typing fell to Alene Richards, my extraordinarily competent secretary (office management specialist, OMS, in State Department speak). The only secretary and executive assistant in the ten-person Political-Military Section, Alene managed to support everyone to some degree. Moreover, she was a principal source of our good morale, looking out for every officer, organizing parties, working long hours, and transcribing my Dictaphone recordings at lightning speed. Her inevitable remark at staff meetings—"Just happy to be here"—was even emblazoned on T-shirts made for the section. I was delighted when she accepted my invitation to go with me to Kabul; many would have considered a year in Baghdad enough.

The ambassador in Kabul rated a special assistant, something I had never had in smaller embassies. Most of my experience with staff aides was formed by watching junior officers in the position grow insufferable as they exercised their authority to give orders on the ambassador's behalf and fought with the more experienced but lower-ranking ambassador's secretaries. I wasn't sure I wanted a special assistant.

Alene suggested I ask Bill Paton from our section to take the assistant job. Although technically a junior officer, Bill had worked for ten years as a civil service officer in State before joining the Foreign Service. He was shaping up well and bringing maturity and a willingness to take risks to his reporting on Iraqi police training.[3] Knowing that Bill planned to get married, I doubted he'd want the job, but Alene assured me he'd be delighted, and so it proved to be. It was an inspired decision for which I claim no credit. Bill subsequently defined the job and took enormous loads off me in Kabul. His excellent relations with Alene were to make our "front office" one of the happiest I have known.

One further personnel selection was that of my deputy, the deputy chief of mission (DCM). The secretary had advised me to make a change. I had to proceed by e-mail and telephone calls since personal interviews were not possible from Baghdad. I needed someone who could manage our large embassy, keep morale high under difficult circumstances, and make critical decisions when I was away.

Experience had taught me that while regional knowledge is important, I had to have an officer who could understand the political complexities of Washington and keep the government's confidence when I was away. The greatest experience in the world in a foreign country is useless if it is transmitted in a way that leads Washington to believe U.S. domestic political realities are not understood. Once that confidence is lost, every judgment and recommendation from post is suspect, and the ambassador can never truly get away.

Because I needed an officer who could handle Washington, I chose Dick Norland over several more senior officers who had more experience in Afghan or regional matters but lacked time in the home bureaucracy. Dick had served for three months in the northern Afghan city of Mazar-i-Sharif, but most of his service had been in European postings. However, he had served in Defense and on the NSC and came strongly recommended by two senior (and demanding) officers whose judgment I trusted. It was a great decision. We made a fine team. Dick was one of the two finest DCMs I have known and went onto an ambassadorship in his own right.

The one other Afghan matter that needed attention in Baghdad was a rumor that Zalmay Khalilzad, then the ambassador in Kabul, who was going to Baghdad, would retain the title of special envoy to Afghanistan. Zal had done a fine job of handling many difficult issues in Afghanistan, had a well-established rapport with Afghan president Hamid Karzai, and, as a naturalized American of Afghan origin, had an unparalleled knowledge of the country. But, rightly or wrongly, he was seen by many Afghans as the real ruler in Afghanistan. With new institutions coming into being, it was time for the Afghan government to come into its own and to try for a slightly lower American profile. And if there were a special envoy as well as an ambassador, there would always be a question about who spoke for the American government.

I called Undersecretary for Political Affairs Nick Burns and said that if officials in Washington wanted more than one ambassador, that was their decision. But they could not have two and have me be one of them. If the special envoy role was to be continued, I wanted to withdraw while I could do so quietly and without a fuss. Burns called back soon to pass on Secretary Rice's decision that there would be no special envoy.

The time in Baghdad drew quickly to a close. Our last adventure came with a sandstorm that closed the airport and helicopter landing zone the day Alene and I were to leave Baghdad. All day we sat in the office watching clouds of yellow dust blow by while visibility was reduced to a few hundred yards. I read my briefing material for my upcoming Senate confirmation hearing. No planes were arriving in Baghdad, so none were leaving.

Then we learned that Gen. George Casey would leave in the evening (his plane was already in Baghdad, and takeoff in a sandstorm was less chancy than landing), and if we could get to Baghdad Airport, we could leave with him. We hastily organized an armored convoy and departed on the dangerous airport road. Sand blew in the open turret of the Humvee. The turret gunner swiveled to cover the top of every overpass we drove under. But the terrorists must also have been waiting out the sandstorm. Nothing happened. We spent another five hours at the airport waiting for a late-night flight. General Casey was most gracious, as always, and we finally staggered to our beds in Kuwait sometime around 3:00 a.m. My hosts in Kuwait, Ambassador and Mrs. Richard LaBaron, had long gone to bed but thoughtfully left me directions to a cold dinner and excellent wine in the refrigerator. Baghdad was behind; Kabul ahead.

But first there was vacation. I had promised myself and my family a month off. I needed it, they deserved it, and I had made clear to the department that I must have the break. We interrupted vacation only for my Senate hearing on June 15. The taxi arrived half an hour late, and I barely slid into my seat at the hearing table as the chairman's gavel opened the proceedings. Since I am regrettably often late to meetings, Bill and Alene told me that it was perfectly in character. After the taxi problem, the hearing was easy.

Vacation was excellent—a time to reconnect with my brother in

Los Angeles, son in Virginia, daughter and her family and daughter in Tennessee, and Elaine's sister in Wyoming. The time flew by. I resisted pressures to cut the vacation short and get to Kabul, but the compromise was to shrink my consultations in Washington to eight days. For seven of them I had an hour of early morning Dari lessons that slowly began to uncover a bit of the once fairly decent Farsi I had long buried under layers of struggles with Arabic.[4]

One critical predeparture appointment was with President Bush. He was particularly interested in the progress of women in Afghanistan, an interest strongly shared by Mrs. Bush. The president told me that I should ask for what I needed.

While on vacation, I noted the testimony of administration officials on Afghanistan. The figures given for numbers of soldiers and policemen trained and the expected completion dates for the new army and police turned out to be wildly optimistic and have not been reached as of this writing.[5] At the time I was only mildly questioning of this good news story. I was to learn that such inflated expectations were all too prevalent, and I suspect that they had given the president an exaggerated sense of progress.

Back home I scrambled to put together a few things I believed I would want in Kabul: a few pictures from the basement, extra clothes, and other bits and pieces. Late at night, after being in consultations all day, the little pile grew, stacked helter-skelter in the dining room to await the packers. The wine came in handy. Many of the books took months to get to, and the computer war game remained untouched for lack of time and energy. At least it didn't weigh much.

A week of consultations having zoomed by and the Senate having duly confirmed my nomination, I was sworn in by Secretary Rice on July 27. The swearing-in ceremony is one of the better traditions of the Foreign Service. The ornate rooms of the department's eighth floor are decorated with colonial period antiques, all given by charitable donations, and provides a fitting location for ceremonial events, which the bureaucratic corridors of the rest of the building lack. It is a time to invite friends and to thank the many senior officers, some retired, who have mentored and helped one along the way. The spouse is always on the stand with the nominee, with the family grouped to one side and champagne and refreshments (paid for by oneself, certainly not the government) waiting behind.

The ambassador of the receiving country is present. The newly minted ambassador is aware that his or her remarks will be carefully perused by the receiving government, so it is a time to be nice and hope to get off on the right foot. Remarks are generally written with multiple audiences in mind. For the Afghans, I needed to make the point that I intended to listen to Afghans and support them. I restated the U.S. determination to remain fully engaged in Afghanistan.

My late father and I were very close, and I reflected on his influence on me and my pleasure at returning to Afghanistan. While this was very heartfelt on my part, it was also a way of reminding Afghans that I had a personal connection to the country—something they value greatly.

Mission morale would be important, and I knew my future staff would also be reading my words. Because of the dangers of Afghanistan, I made a point of pledging to do everything I could to keep my staff safe, keep "their morale high, and ensure that they receive all the support they deserve." I emphasized that I would be leading an excellent team; this was not going to be a one-man show.

It is a tradition at swearing-in ceremonies to thank one's spouse. I wanted to go beyond the routine—and hence devalued phrases—and say something special to my wife:

> Elaine, without whose love and support my life could not possibly have unfolded as it has . . . In nearly forty years of marriage we have never liked being separated. But she understood and supported me when I asked to go to Vietnam. She supported me in Algeria and humanized my leadership of my first embassy through her counsel from a distance. When I pondered the decision to remain in Baghdad, she helped me make that decision by reminding me that I had some particular talents that might be of service at a difficult time.
>
> I have long believed that the sometimes ritualistic thanks we pay to spouses left behind is inadequate. We who go to far-flung and sometimes dangerous posts have the professional fascination of the work and the adrenalin stimulation of excitement

to keep going. They get to keep up the bills, the house, and the family. It is all critical, but it is not exciting. We know most of the time that we are safe; they have always to wonder. I think Elaine's job is harder than mine. I could not do mine without her support; and for that [turning to her], for your love and your strength, thank you, darling.

I meant every word of it. What I did not know until much later was that these words made a considerable and favorable impression on my staff in Kabul and later helped some others to decide that they wanted to join us. Sometimes good intentions do bring a reward.

The next night I left for one day's consultations in London and then an overnight stop in Dubai. The UN runs a special flight open to diplomats, journalists, aid workers, and Afghan government officials, so security is good. Seeing no need for ceremony, I took a taxi to Dubai's Terminal Two, a considerably less flashy place than the main terminal but from which all flights to inauspicious places like Baghdad and Kabul depart. The UN flight supervisor, having been used to a motorcade driving over from the VIP lounge, was most surprised to see me walk in with my own bag. I was comfortable with the impression I was making.

Two hours later I walked down the ramp and was met by my bodyguards and a convoy of three armored Chevy Suburbans in Kabul. It was time to go to work.

Afghanistan

— International boundary
-·-·- Province (velāyat) boundary
★ National capital
⊚ Province (velāyat) capital
⊢—⊢ Railroad
—— Road

| 0 | 100 | 200 Kilometers |
| 0 | 100 | 200 Miles |

Lambert Conformal Conic Projection, SP 29 N / 39 N

Boundary representation is
not necessarily authoritative.

Base 802986AI (C00362) 6-03

1
First Days

From the moment I arrived I had endless questions. Some I would be asking for a long time for Afghanistan is one of those places where detailed knowledge of complexity often reveals contradictions that make generalization about the situation harder rather than easier.

Yet certain things had to come first. I needed to present credentials, that is, my letter of appointment from President George W. Bush and the letter of recall of my predecessor. This is a diplomatic practice going back to the days when ambassadors were really the personal representatives of one sovereign to another. The process is formalized in diplomatic practice: one first calls on the chief of protocol; then the foreign minister, to whom one gives a copy of one's credentials; and finally the head of state. Until an ambassador hands the credentials to the host nation head of state, the ambassador is not really official and in many countries is limited in the official appointments he or she can make. In some cases ambassadors can wait months to do this, and in the days of vast bureaucracies the practice is often a bit silly as well as a waste of much time for a busy president. In my case, the embassy had already set up an appointment, and I was able to present credentials on

August 1, 2005. I had a short chat with President Hamid Karzai, and we agreed to get together for a longer and more substantive meeting after he returned from the funeral for Saudi King Fahd, for which Karzai was about to depart.

President Karzai is a fascinating, sympathetic, and enigmatic figure destined to play a pivotal role in Afghan history. I was to spend many hours with him. I understand the frustration of those who think he should take this or that action, and sometimes I urged such action, but I also understand the enormous conflicting pressures on this one lonely leader. I retain deep respect for him despite his occasional flaws.

Two priorities are normal for taking over any diplomatic mission even in a war: early calls on ministers and fellow ambassadors and getting to know one's own staff. Ministers or ambassadors who are ignored for too long can get into quite a snit, so I embarked early on endless rounds of meetings, which were often very interesting but also time consuming.

Getting to know one's own staff is critical but not easy in a mission that at the time involved over three hundred American staffers and almost as many Afghan and third-country national employees. I spent part of one day walking around the chancery shaking hands and talking to personnel.[1] Really getting to know them as people would take longer.

Once rather grand, the chancery was showing the signs of having been empty for many years, then occupied by U.S. Marines (who had left some fairly artistic graffiti in the basement), and then crammed to overflowing with American staff members. Everything was dingy and worn, but since a new chancery was under construction, there was no time to spruce up the old building that was due for reconstruction once we moved.

My office was similarly dingy but spacious, while much of the staff was crammed into large bays. I had trouble remembering the building's former layout, but with the help of a 1967 fire plan that had been preserved, I worked out that my father's old office was now the political section and my office was around the corner. The front looked much as I remembered it except for a few bullet holes, but the plaque commemorating my father's opening of the building was still in place. My wife and I had been there when it was dedicated.

The once stately line of trees I remember sweeping up the driveway had been cut down by a zealous security officer and replaced with hooches, specially made container-like structures, some used for housing and others for offices.

The empty field across the street that I remembered from thirty-eight years earlier was now a separate compound housing the U.S. Agency for International Development (USAID), several other offices, and many more housing containers as well a cafeteria, maintenance and motor pool facilities, and a rocky volleyball court baking in the summer sun. A tunnel bored under the public street dividing the heavily guarded compounds provided secure access between the compounds.

Two not-so-traditional tasks I faced when I arrived were understanding our security conditions and getting out into the countryside. The ambassador is responsible for security but is advised by a security chief, called a regional security officer (RSO, from the days when there were only a few and they really were responsible for regions), and his staff. There is often tension between the two. The RSO tends to want to err on the side of caution, and the ambassador, who has a broader responsibility, wants to get out, move, and learn as much as possible.

While an ambassador is a little king in his embassy, he must be mindful of the steady flow of e-mail traffic home. If the staff, particularly the RSO, feels the ambassador is taking too many chances, the ambassador may find his credibility gone and Washington interceding to overrule his decisions. When I first became an ambassador, I was cautious about maintaining my credibility and put up with some decisions I felt were unnecessary. After numerous dangerous posts, riots, and security threats, I had developed what I thought to be a pretty good ability to differentiate between specific threats and "school solutions."

I wanted to start on a different footing in Afghanistan. Over time I explained to my RSO that as far as possible I needed him to find ways for me to do safely what I had to do, not tell me not to do it. If I had such cooperation, he could be sure that I would pay attention if he really opposed something. If he said no to everything, I would pay less attention and make my own decisions.

The security staff was surprised when I asked to walk the whole interior perimeter of the two compounds. I asked questions about fire hydrants (I once watched a piece of Embassy Baghdad burn because we didn't have one), cameras, reaction procedures, armament, why we didn't have razor wire on some walls, and more. My purpose was simple: I had been through mob attacks and experienced how limited the vision is from inside, even with cameras, once a building is locked down. Having a good mental picture of the surroundings in advance makes a world of difference in a crisis. And if we had to make a decision someday to use lethal force (other than in immediate self-defense, in which case it is always authorized), I intended to make that decision myself.

None of the security staff had ever encountered an ambassador who asked such detailed questions. They were a bit confused and came to see if I needed more briefings; I didn't. But I did explain why I wanted to know, and they seemed to go away comforted. The assistant RSO said he had been a bit surprised by my questions on the perimeter walk but had finally decided that I just knew more than the average ambassador and that the questions were sensible. This is what he told his staff. It was all rather amusing. In the end, we got on very well, and my personal protective detail, first from DynCorp and most of the time from Blackwater, did an outstanding job of protecting me while helping me do my job and trying not to anger the Afghans. I had excellent RSOs. Their job is difficult, and first Jim McDermott, then Scott Moretti, and finally Marty Kraus were outstanding officers with good judgment and steel nerves.

Starting to Learn

Another priority was to start moving around the country to see and learn for myself. I was determined to keep up an active schedule, traveling once a week unless weather, leave, or cabinet-level visitors got in the way; all other meetings would have to fit around the travel. Unless one is firm about this, it is all too easy to find weeks have flown by and one has not left the capital. Then information shrinks to staff reports and endless PowerPoint briefings from the military that have passed through multiple hands and judgments.

And so, a week after my arrival, I was on a helicopter heading for Ghazni, southwest of Kabul. The governor was Sher Alam, an old warlord of uncertain literacy who, while pleasant to me, seemed lethargic. It was difficult to learn much from the formal meetings that in this case and so many later were held in rooms full of people. However, the chief justice of the province was interesting. Sher Alam stuck to me like glue, making a frank conversation with the chief justice impossible until I learned he had been educated at Al-Azhar University in Cairo. Then we switched to speaking in Arabic. While my Arabic is not of first quality, it was enough to understand a litany of complaints: corrupt judges, inadequate administrative support, and a complete absence of legal records and Afghan laws were the essence of the problem, along with constant interference by the governor. We had built an attractive new court building. It was a start, but the justice situation wouldn't get better without a lot of work on the other problems.

Franker assessments came from the commander of the provincial reconstruction team (PRT) and the State and USAID officers assigned to the PRT. From first to last in my travels, I always came back feeling that I had learned new things, not only the answers to questions I went with but things I didn't know about at all. I began on this first trip a practice I continued throughout my tour of meeting separately with the State and USAID officers to hear their frank views. While they were part of the team, they were in my chain of command, not the military's. I was responsible for their well-being and depended on them for insight into their provinces that was often available nowhere else. If they had complaints, I wanted to hear them. If they had views different from those of the military, that too was important. Generally cooperation was good, but I was to learn how much the two cultures, civilian and military, had to learn to work well together.

One point that had bothered me since my time in Iraq was that State Department communications equipment was designed for use in embassies and was not easily deployed. As a result, we could not keep our officers properly informed of goings on in Kabul that were classified. One of the delights of being in charge is that occasionally one can fix something. I talked the problem over later with Lt. Gen. Karl Eikenberry, the commander of Coalition Forces Command–Afghanistan (CFC-A), and he promptly offered the use of military communications. Although I offered to purchase military laptops if necessary, he provided all that we needed. A problem that had gone on for years was solved with one conversation that for some reason had never been held.

Allied Operations and New Issues

My first months on the job were a mixture of endless meetings, new issues, and a gradual focusing in on some of the large problems that would dominate much of my tour. One of these issues was the planned handover of military operations to the NATO-led International Security Assistance Force (ISAF) in Afghanistan.[2] Initially confined to Kabul because of then–defense secretary Donald Rumsfeld's desire that U.S. forces retain a free hand in hunting terrorists, ISAF had gradually taken responsibility for the north, center, and west of Afghanistan. There was little fighting in those areas.

But in 2006 ISAF was to take real responsibility for the war, first in the south and finally in the whole country, including eastern Afghanistan, where the bulk of U.S. forces were engaged.[3] In a brief stop in London, I had started consultations with the British, who would take command of a combined UK, Dutch, and Canadian force in the south the following year. Fortunately, UK prime minister Tony Blair's special representative for Afghanistan was British lieutenant general John McColl, with whom I had worked closely in Baghdad. I had some concerns about whether British forces would be properly equipped and whether the UK government had the will to fight.

NATO had no mandate for "counterterrorist" operations, which often involved raids and targeted killing of terrorists. The counterterrorist mission was often carried out by U.S. forces not under NATO/ISAF command but operating in the same area, sometimes without coordination with units in the field. These issues of command and control needed to be addressed correctly; getting them wrong could imperil the future chances of success. One concern revolved around the way NATO did business: by consensus. For many years U.S. diplomats to NATO have tried for what we wanted but often settled for what we could get in order to reach decisions and move on. Under normal political circumstances, this is a correct judgment. But now we had a war. It would be better not to have an agreement than to have a bad one. It was well into 2006 before I felt comfortable recommending that the transfer to NATO proceed.

While some considered the ISAF handover to be a military issue of no mind to diplomats, I took the view that losing the war would be a political issue and hence of legitimate concern to the ambassador. I came away from London somewhat reassured about the British but with many questions still unanswered.

Another issue of ongoing concern was the disarmament of illegal militias. The heavy weapons disarmament was successfully completed before my arrival; tanks and artillery had been turned in, major units disbanded, and the creation of the Afghan National Army begun. However, it was estimated that some eighteen hundred illegal armed groups of various sizes remained.

Parliamentary elections were due in September. Candidates who retained armed militias were to be barred according to the election law. An extensive system of vetting candidates had been set up and involved an Afghan body headed by Masoom Stanekzai in cooperation with international officers under the UN Assistance Mission for Afghanistan (UNAMA).

On paper the system was very thorough. In practice it was something else. Evidence was often circumstantial, and the conflicts between law and political reality were extreme. On August 16 I participated in the second high-level meeting on the subject since my arrival. Jean Arnault, the head of UNAMA, was a superb official, an activist with great political sensitivity whom I came to like and respect. Stanekzai struck me as an intelligent man trying hard to do a good job but under heavy political pressure. Others in the meeting included the Canadian ambassador Chris Alexander (subsequently the deputy head of UNAMA), who had been in country for some time, and Francesc Vandrell, a Spanish diplomat who was then the personal representative of the head of the European Union and who had been engaged in Afghan matters for many years, including the original conferences that created the Afghan governing structure. These and others were first-class representatives of their nations and organizations. They were serious, informed, and as wise as the difficult circumstances and limited information permitted.

I kept pushing to have a sufficient number of candidates disqualified to maintain some credibility in the process. However, I would not advocate for or against specific individuals as the final result had to be a matter of Afghan decision and not arranged by foreigners. My foreign colleagues generally agreed with this approach. They seemed to appreciate my efforts to demonstrate real collaboration.

The discussion was fascinating. Some of the potential candidates controlled large armed forces. One was characterized as, "Yes, he has forces, but he fought the Taliban and the Islamists. He's obedient to government orders and left a senior position when ordered to do so. He leads a whole tribe, so how can you take him off the list?" In another case there were four or five different tribal and ethnic divisions in one province. Pulling only two candidates off the list would have destabilized the election in the whole province because supporters of the absent candidates wouldn't have a chance to be represented in the election.

There was great tension between Western insistence that the rules be followed and recognition that Afghanistan was still largely controlled by armed groups and was not about to have an election completely decided by one man, one vote. International troops could keep order on Election Day, but there were real risks to longer-term stability if major groups were disenfranchised. Additionally, the Afghans around the table, while representing the government, often had unspoken agendas of their own. Finding the balance was not easy.

The decision was left somewhat in the air. I followed up two days later in a private meeting with President Karzai. These discussions went on subsequently, but very quietly, as Karzai needed to be, and to be seen as, the final arbiter. In the end, a few candidates were delisted. Some credibility was established, although perhaps not enough. On the other hand, had we pushed for a more pure result we might have created more problems than we resolved.

Evenings often found me working late, finishing reports or reading either in the embassy or at home. Home was two and a half containers strung together in the shape of an *H*. On one side I had a small living room and bedroom. A kitchen and entrance way were in the middle, and on the other side was a study and equally small dining room. Eight people could just fit, if we tucked in tightly to let the servers get by between our chairs and the wall.

Often I was asked how I liked my "doublewide," as my abode was called. The questioners usually seemed to expect some complaint, as the dwelling was of somewhat less than ambassadorial proportions. I think they were often surprised when I told them it was positively palatial next to the one room in half a trailer with a shared bathroom that I had lived in for sixteen months in Baghdad. Besides, I had a small garden of grass with roses growing around the fence. No matter if it was practically in the middle of a construction zone; it was private and a delightful place to sit in the dry and temperate evenings that followed the heat of a summer day at six thousand feet in Kabul.

As we looked forward to the election the following month, it was apparent that Taliban strategy was different from what it had been during the preceding presidential election. Then it had made a major effort to stop the election using threats and attacks. This time it seemed the efforts were halfhearted. The Taliban had killed some officials, but there was little evidence of a concentrated campaign to stop the process or to threaten death to those who voted. Why the change?

One answer seemed to be that having failed previously, the Taliban was smart enough not to set itself up for a media failure a second time. Another theory to which I was gradually becoming persuaded was that it had a much longer-term strategy of trying to prevent the Afghan government from establishing authority in much of the country and intended to wait us out and attack harder, later.

Writing in 2009, when the lack of effective local governance is broadly accepted by Afghans and foreigners alike as a major weakness in counterinsurgency, it seems strange to look back at how tentative our understanding of this problem was in mid-2005. In an August 12 letter home, I wrote that the evidence was still inconclusive for the theory that the Taliban strategy was to hold back while it built strength and then to overwhelm a weak Afghan government. "But if [the theory] is correct then it would follow that *the critical task is not the military confrontation with the Taliban, important as that is, but the establishment of governmental authority* [emphasis added]." My letter noted that I had mentioned this theory to Secretary of State Condoleezza Rice as a "hypothesis for discussion, not a clear fact." She seemed to find the idea interesting. Six months later I would be more certain that the critical need was to expand provincial governance.

Drugs and Economics

Two further and immediate preoccupations were reformulating the counternarcotics strategy and evaluating recommendations for the next year's economic assistance budget. The previous year's effort to reduce opium poppy cultivation had not worked well. Equipment for eradication arrived late, the national eradication force was just getting started and had not performed well, and farmers and Afghan governmental officials alike believed we were not meeting our commitments to provide alternative assistance.

A problem that recurred in many areas was that our matrix for measuring progress was too focused on bureaucratic output such as delivery of equipment. Under this approach, if a fire department had a standard of a fifteen-minute reaction to a fire, they would score a success if they arrived in fourteen minutes—even if the house burned down. We were under considerable pressure from Washington to provide a new plan. Drafts were whizzing about and meetings were frequent.

I was ably assisted by the head of our counternarcotics office, Doug Wankel. A longtime Drug Enforcement Administration (DEA) agent, Doug had been in Kabul in 1979 when Ambassador Adolph "Spike" Dubs was assassinated during the Russian storming of the hotel room where the kidnapped ambassador was held. Doug was the first American into the room. He had returned to Kabul on a contract after the war. When I arrived he had already been there a year and had an extensive network of Afghan and foreign contacts. I shared his view that we had to be realistic about what could be done.

Such realism sometimes clashed with Washington's demands for rapid progress. We believed that the strategy of working on agricultural development, justice, arrest of higher-level traffickers, public information, and eradication was sound. The problem was that most parts of the strategy would take years to work. As I had told President Bush in our meeting before I left for Afghanistan, it was essential to try to coordinate our narcotics and counterinsurgency strategies. At a minimum we had to avoid having the two strategic priorities pull against each other. For now we were hopeful that with better equipment, training, and funding, we could eradicate enough to keep Washington happy while buying time for other elements of the strategy to begin taking hold.

Over the next two years we were fairly successful in insisting on realism, less so in reducing poppy growth. What we saw as insistence on reality would later be seen in some parts of Washington as stubborn adherence to our own views. Other proposals since Doug's and my departure have not been noticeably more effective. But that was for the future.

Our USAID budget submission was due in September. We were looking at a multibillion dollar program that some thought was required. My initial sense was that we had a long list of important tasks we should be doing, but no agreed sense of priorities. The Afghan government had few qualified people to run its ministries or settle issues of priorities. Thus, I told my staff, our sense of priorities would be particularly important when we considered which issues I should take to President Karzai.

The embassy had a generally capable but very diverse group of people working on economic issues. USAID was responsible for managing programs. The Afghan Reconstruction Group (ARG) was composed of highly qualified people from the American private sector who had been brought in to advise on various issues. Tension between ARG and USAID was high. And then there was the embassy's Economic Section, which produced reports but seemed to have little policy function. I asked all three to consider what our top priorities should be for the next year.

All these issues were before us by mid-August, and I had been in Afghanistan for only three weeks. Yet it was exciting and fun (albeit that is probably rather egocentric) to be leading, teaching, and trying to solve complex problems. So far as I could tell, the mission was reacting well. I was getting feedback that the staff felt empowered and directed rather than beleaguered by the new requests. One person told me that the staff felt it was getting clear orders and a lot of responsibility for carrying those orders out. Of course, if the reaction had been bad, I would probably have been the last person to be told directly.

Getting Out of Kabul

I had kept the trip to Ghazni quiet as I had doubts about the governor and didn't want to be forced by a press contingent either to criticize him publicly or to express support I was not yet ready to give. Thus it was my second trip, to Mazar-i-Sharif in the north, that was treated by the press as my first provincial trip. I began the practice of having a "morale seat" on each trip.

Some of the officers in State and USAID had jobs that took them out into the capital and in some cases into the country. But many, especially those doing administrative jobs, never had an opportunity to leave the compound except to travel to the airport. Hence one seat on my trips was reserved for whoever was on the top of the list of volunteers who had no other chance to get out. I could not work my way through all the candidates, but I did help a few see something of the country.

And a spectacular country it is. On the way to Mazar we flew over miles of the sharp-ridged, arid mountains of the Hindu Kush, gazed down on small, steep valleys where trees lined plunging watercourses, and traveled across verdant fields and stark brown plains before the plane settled into the great bowl that holds Mazar, an historic city on the old Silk Road of the caravans.

The city had far more electricity than Kabul because it could be purchased cheaply from Uzbekistan across the border. New shops and streets were bustling. Governor Mohammad Atta was making progress in rebuilding the province of Balk and its capital city of Mazar.

Atta had one foot in the modern world and one in Afghanistan's turbulent past. He was a war commander whose tanks and artillery had fought the Taliban and, more recently, the Uzbek commander General Abdul Rashid Dostum, until they had been surrendered to the government. Some thought that Atta had ties to the drug trade, but these ties were unproved, and he subsequently suppressed poppy cultivation in the province. He also had investments in Asia and a modern business sense. He had the authority to run his province but seemed loyal to Kabul. Trim, always in fashionable suits, with a small black beard (which some wags pointed out had been quite a bit longer during Taliban times) and shined shoes, I found him emblematic of the powerful and intelligent people we needed to bring fully into the system if a new country was to emerge.

The Afghan press coverage of my trip was interesting. I received good marks for visiting the famous Blue Mosque, showing interest in Afghan culture, and talking about my earlier visit to the city many years ago. Some of the press felt that I lacked my predecessor's language and cultural familiarity and would be overshadowed by him. Others noted charges that he had intervened too heavily in Afghan politics and maybe I would be different. There was much speculation but no real hostility. As Afghans have been taught by their violent past to always search for hidden meaning and purposes, a willingness to wait and see was a reasonable attitude.

In Mazar the PRT was under British command but would soon be handed over to the Swedes when the British deployed southward. We had a U.S. State Department officer with the PRT while our USAID representative was further east in Kunduz with the Germans who commanded the region as a whole. To make matters more complicated, the ISAF PRTs reported to their national capitals, not the ISAF military command, and the civilian political and developmental personnel reported to their own ministries, not to the military command and in some cases not even to their embassy in Kabul. The U.S. chain of command was messy, but it looked positively idyllic by comparison. Still, much good work was going on, and the British PRT commander and UK political officer were balanced in their judgments and as effective as they could be with the limitations under which they operated. They were responsible for a large area of several provinces and often patrolled for a week at a time to show the flag in remote areas.

Back in Kabul, it was time for my first formal press conference. Afghans have lived with years of disinformation and have learned to look to actions rather than words for a sense of policy. The diplomatic task in such circumstances is to try to articulate clearly what one is doing, to explain constantly, and to keep pointing out that actions and words are pointing in the same direction. This task is never finished and needs constant attention.

My main themes in this first press conference were three. First, I restated our determination to stay in Afghanistan. Many Afghans feared that the NATO expansion signaled U.S. plans to withdraw. The United States and most of the world had forgotten Afghanistan after the Soviet withdrawal, and Afghans approach paranoia in concern that they will be abandoned again.

Second, I urged Afghans to participate in the forthcoming election and to vote for the people they felt best represented them, secure in the knowledge that the process would be secret and honest. The point here was to distance myself from the assumption that the United States would back particular candidates or allow vote rigging.

My third theme, very much tied to the second, was that the United

States would support whatever electoral results emerged. Several of the questions turned on the issue of whether I would interfere in internal politics as my predecessor had. Not wanting to get into this invidious and largely useless question, I told the press this was a bit like the old question, "Do you still beat your wife?" Yes is wrong and no is an admission that you used to beat her. That got a laugh. How long the good press would last was an open question.

August flew by. On the twentieth I traveled to Farah in western Afghanistan. I began there a policy I continued throughout my tour of taking the press with me whenever I traveled. I wanted them to see that I was moving about as a sort of physical confirmation of U.S. determination to remain engaged. And press attention to each trip gave me numerous opportunities to emphasize points I wanted to make. My repeated statements that the United States would not withdraw were widely publicized.

In Farah I ran into my old friend Mike Metrinko. A retired Foreign Service officer of great experience, Mike had taken my old job of consul in Tabriz, Iran, and ended his term there as one of the hostages when our embassy was seized. Despite that experience he continued to be fascinated with the Islamic world.

An excellent Persian speaker, Mike had been in and out of Afghanistan for several years on contract with various organizations. He had covered the constitutional *loya jirga*, helped investigate and pacify the situation after an Afghan wedding party was bombed by mistake, and been with the PRT in Herat. Bearded and rotund, never in a tie, cynical but realistic, he had a profound knowledge of the country. His willingness to help was matched only by his disdain for bureaucracy. It was a pleasure to talk with him again, and he was to become one of my most useful advisers.

I prowled around a massive mud fort of uncertain history. Room after room was full of leftover Soviet ammunition. Rockets and mortar rounds were stacked in boxes and tumbled about on the dusty floors. A small U.S. Army team was hauling out several small truckloads a day for destruction. When I asked if giving me a Soviet helmet as a souvenir would cut into their stock they said, no, they had fourteen thousand of them. This was only one example of the problem we had with munitions leftover from the years of war.

The small PRT was the only coalition force in the province. To the south lay Nimruz Province, which bordered both Pakistan and, as did Farah, Iran. The local police were corrupt and largely untrained. The governor had once been convicted in the United States for heroin trafficking. There were no Afghan army soldiers present in either Farah or Nimruz, and the Italian army in Herat rarely ventured that far south. The problem of a lack of security was clear, although at that point it was more a matter of criminal gangs than of insurgents.

On August 21 a group of ARG personnel were hit by a roadside bomb just outside of Kabul. They were lucky in that the bomb was detonated a fraction of a second early so that much of the explosion went into the engine. The vehicle was totally destroyed, but they survived. When I visited them in the hospital, they were in good spirits and remarkably cheerful. However, Brig. Gen. Pat Maney, USAR, in civilian life a judge from Florida, suffered brain injuries that took a long time to heal. We remained in contact, and he continued to work from the United States on issues of medical care for personnel injured in Afghanistan.

We had two other incidents of bomb attacks around the country involving embassy staff in the PRTs. There was no clear pattern. In one case it was not even certain if we were the intended target, but the incidents were a reminder that our jobs had real risks.

I traveled to Khost in eastern Afghanistan. Although the town was frequently rocketed, nothing happened when I was there. In the east we had the bulk of U.S. forces, and I could begin to see the difference that was possible when larger security forces were in place. Still, we were too thin for all the tasks at hand.

Taking Stock

Not everything I did was so serious. I began to play volleyball, both for my own enjoyment and to encourage the staff by example to get out of the office on our one-day weekend. I attended the Afghan Special Olympics. I went as though it were a routine attendance of the sort ambassadors are expected to make and found that not only was I the only ambassador in attendance but I was also expected to make a speech. So I stood on the reviewing stand and waved and applauded as the various handicapped athletes came by. Some gave me big smiles in return. My staff was slightly appalled that they hadn't known I had a speaking part and hadn't prepared any remarks. As speaking at the drop of a hat was a long acquired habit of mine, I couldn't see what the problem was.

At the end of the month I joined a meeting of the Afghan cabinet so that I could support the decision to have President Karzai sign a new decree putting in place a military justice law. Every modern army must have its own ability to administer justice in order to maintain discipline. The justice minister wanted to keep all judicial enforcement in the civil system. Given the widespread corruption and incompetence of the civilian courts, this was a recipe for disaster. After a vigorous discussion President Karzai accepted the need for the new law. I had intervened, but in the end, it was an Afghan decision.

The military justice law was an interesting example of the difficulty of bringing about change. General Eikenberry told me that the Afghans had first started drafting the law in 2002. It had to be brought into conformity with Afghan concepts, translated into legal Dari and Pushtu, and signed into law. That was only the beginning. Judges had to be recruited and trained, a prison built, and correctional staff trained. Afghan officers had to receive training in the new law and procedures different from the traditional harsh and unregulated ways of maintaining discipline. The first court-martial under the new law occurred only in 2006—four years of work to implement a single law, but given the problems that had to be surmounted, that was what it took.

Management issues continued to take time. With one-year duty tours, almost the whole embassy staff was turning over during the summer, a kind of institutional frontal lobotomy of lost experience. We recommended to Washington various ways of improving the situation: tours linked with Washington jobs so that two officers would rotate back and forth and the staggering of some jobs so that rotation would occur in the winter and spread out the loss of critical knowledge. Nothing happened.

General Eikenberry and I began to have regular meetings and private dinners to harmonize our operations. Karl, having had a previous tour in Afghanistan, had broad experience. We were each aware that there could be no "lanes": no pure division between what was military and what civilian. The two areas constantly interacted and affected the other. Karl had great understanding of many of the political, economic, and social issues I had to face and was willing to listen to me on military questions. We began a relationship that remained effective, genuinely and mutually respectful, and pleasant despite the stresses. When we had differences we were usually able to sort out a decision. Months later one officer told me on his departure that what he noticed particularly was that while Karl and I had very different personalities and temperaments, we each worked hard to make our partnership work. We did. It worked.

By the end of August, I wrote home that I was starting to develop clearer notions of what had to be done:

> The structures of this [Afghan] government are still very fragile and its reach into the provinces is weak. . . . The notion of the country in transition is one that affects all of our programs and policies. Over the last few years we have had to scramble just to move forward with the basic milestones of the political process: getting the president elected, standing up the interim government, selecting governors, registering voters, beginning a disarmament process and so on. Each step has been hard and has taken a great deal of time. . . .
>
> Now we need stocktaking and need to think about where we are going for the next few years. Our aid and narcotics programs need to be multiyear, in conception if not in funding. Our pressures and work for economic reform need clearer prioritization. . . . Also our security activities have been very closely linked to our political purposes. NATO is a military, and not a political, organization. We need to think through how the military and political efforts will be joined as NATO takes a larger role.

As the first month of my tour ended, I ordered USAID to delay submission of our budget to Washington. Under the direction of the very gifted and experienced director, Alonzo Fulgham, the budget was well conceptualized and supported, but I felt we were asking for too little. The numbers needed to go up. Little did I know that I was starting a bureaucratic battle that would last over a year.

2
Elections and More

Afghanistan's parliamentary elections of September 18, 2005, required a massive effort from the international community in partnership with the Afghan government. This was to be the last major step of the Bonn process, the agreement and subsequent decisions and conferences that in 2002 had mapped out the process for organizing the Afghan state.[1] The first parliamentary elections would be a major milestone in Afghanistan's potential to return to being an organized state.

The election security efforts had begun months before my arrival. In March Maj. Gen. Jason Kamiya, commander of Task Force 76 (TF-76, under General Eikenberry's overall command), had launched Operation Determined Resolve, a series of patrols and operations to set the conditions for a secure election. This was followed starting in August by Operation Vigilant Sentinel, which also involved eleven thousand ISAF troops.[2]

With mixed feelings the international representatives had accepted President Karzai's decision to use a fairly rare electoral system called the single nontransferable vote (SNTV). Under this system all candidates would run as individuals. Voters would cast ballots for individuals, and the highest vote-getters for a province would win seats at large from the province. Thus, for example, if a province was entitled to thirty seats, the top thirty candidates would be elected, even if some had ten thousand votes and others only two thousand.

Although Afghanistan had over sixty registered parties, no candidate would be identified on the ballot as a member of a party.[3] There were several reasons for this decision and multiple consequences. The very word "party" had a negative connotation. For many Afghans, "party" was associated with the various communist parties that had taken power in coups and Islamist and ethnic parties that had records fully as bloody over the years of struggle as the Communists had. President Karzai shared the view of many of his countrymen that they had had their fill of such parties.

Tribal allegiance remains a powerful force in Afghanistan's complex political structure. The largest ethnic group, the Pushtuns, have historically been the dominant element, but Tajiks, Uzbeks, and Hazaras compete vigorously for their share of political power. Each magnified its size and significance in conversation and probably believes at least some of what it says. None ever feel they are properly treated. Yet the sense of nationhood remains strong; in all the years of war, no group has fought to found a separate state.

Had Afghanistan moved directly to a proportional election system, it would have almost certainly favored the entrenchment of parties based on ethnic and tribal divisions. The moderates and liberals had no single party of their own. Divisions between potential leaders and the shortage of time made it unlikely that any such party could have achieved significant results. In the end the SNTV did lead to a weakening of militia and factional leaders, but it also resulted in a parliament of shifting personal alliances based on personal relations, payoffs, and favors. Single district representation was rejected because the lack of a census precluded agreement on drawing electoral districts. In any event these decisions had all been reached before I arrived.

President Karzai himself refused to sanction the creation of a party of his own supporters. As he told me in one long meeting, if he had a party then all who were not in it would be in the opposition. He wanted to rule as the leader of all Afghans. He also believed that, while Afghans would be divided in the search for personal advancement, they would unify around the objectives of reconstruction and foreign policy. I suggested that while his view was laudable, it might stem from too kindly a perspective of human nature. Every major policy decision and law would advantage some and disadvantage others. I doubted the rallying he foresaw would come about. In retrospect, Parliament was more responsible than I had predicted and far less unified than he had hoped.

Security was well in hand. I had been in Baghdad for the successful elections of January 2005. It seemed to me that the level of violence in Afghanistan was far lower than it had been in Iraq. From a security perspective I was confident that the elections could be carried out.

The logistics were another matter. The SNTV ballot itself was a cumbersome product. The one for Kabul province alone had 120 candidates. Because many voters were illiterate, each candidate had a symbol randomly generated by computer (to prevent any candidate having an advantage from a particular symbolism but also resulting in the symbols being largely meaningless), his or her picture, name, and a number. The resulting ballot required four pages measuring 13 ½ by 19 inches.

The ballots were so large that they could not be accommodated in the ballot boxes used for the presidential elections. New transparent ballot boxes had to be manufactured, shipped into the country, and distributed. Forty million ballots had to be printed outside Afghanistan, shipped in, and distributed. After the elections the ballots would have to be secured and moved to thirty-four province centers for counting.[4] Eighteen massive cargo planes and nine helicopters, along with 1,247 donkeys, 306 horses, and 24 camels, were required for this effort. And everything had to get where it was supposed to be for Election Day and be secured throughout the process.

Overseeing this huge effort were 197 international observers; 2,200 independent Afghan election monitors, who were trained in their duties by the internationals; and another 30,000 candidate representatives, who would also witness the polling and vote counting. The planning for this had gone on for months. The training effort alone was a major undertaking. Those involved were inspired by the willingness of literally thousands of unpaid Afghans to travel to training centers at their own expense and often over difficult terrain.

A further effort led by the State University of New York was in progress to train the staff of the new parliament so that once seated the deputies would have a somewhat competent staff to support them. USAID alone was spending over $40 million for the project, which all told would cost over $100 million by the time it was completed.[5]

International and Afghan nervousness about how this would all work was widespread. On September 1, I gave a telephonic press conference with reporters in the United States to show our confidence in the process. I said I was confident that violence would not derail the election, although I expected that there would be some incidents. I was careful to avoid suggesting that the election would be a culmination of rebuilding Afghanistan; I called it a milestone but not a destination. "This is part of a much longer process of stabilizing Afghanistan both as a nation and as a democracy. . . . It involves the development of a political culture, the establishment of a democratic government that has never been seen in this country, the building of an economy that people can live off of, and the reabsorption into society of people that have been fighting each other for twenty-five years." In saying this, I wanted Americans as much as Afghans to understand that success in the election would by no means imply we were finished or could reduce our aid to Afghanistan.

The United States was heavily involved in the preparations "without ever forgetting that at the end of the day this is an Afghan process. We are the strongest supporter, but we don't dominate it." I noted that election observers working together under UNAMA supervision were present from the European Union, the Asian Network for Free Elections, Human Rights Watch, and many other organizations registered with the international and Afghan Joint Electoral Management Body.

Some of the resulting headlines had nothing to do with the election. At the end of the press conference I was asked about a recent kidnapping and whether it was safe for international observers and others to do their jobs. Not wanting to sound like I was sugarcoating the situation I said that security was "something of a gray environment." The country was unruly. There was crime as well as terrorism. But, I concluded, "If you take reasonable security precautions, you can probably live and work pretty safely. If you insist on being an idiot, you can suffer the consequences."

Some of the journalists tried to suggest I was saying that the kidnapped individual had been an idiot. I said, "No, don't put words in my mouth. But I know foreigners who say things are safe, 'I can just walk around.' If people do that they can get in trouble."[6]

Some stories exaggerated these remarks. No particular damage resulted, and my military colleagues were delighted that I had pointed to the need for individuals to act responsibly. The political adviser with TF-76 sent me a doctored photo in which my scowling visage had been placed on a uniformed body with the caption, "Life is hard but it's harder if you're stupid." I was delighted and kept the picture in the office. My secretary, Alene, later put this version of my remarks on a T-shirt.

Travel and Consultation

I continued my provincial travels, both to learn and to publicize our involvement to Afghans. The central province of Bamyan had become internationally known when the Taliban destroyed the magnificent carved Buddhas that had stood for centuries in the red cliffs alongside its valley. Stepping out of the plane on December 5, 2005, I was surprised at how much of the scene I recalled. Except for the empty niches where the Buddhas had stood, the valley was much as I remembered it.

The province now had Afghanistan's only woman governor, and interest in the national election was high. Several young local political leaders assured me they would have no reservations about voting for competent female candidates, and this later proved to be true. I used my visit and the press coverage to continue emphasizing the same themes that I had covered in my press conference. In a culture where words are received with doubt, constant repetition is essential.

What I had not anticipated was the welcoming ceremony from the New Zealand troops who ran the PRT. Their practice was to greet visitors with a traditional Maori ceremony. As the sergeant major and I slowly walked toward some thirty soldiers in ranks, a bare-chested "warrior" came out from one side of the formation brandishing a spear. Then another warrior appeared from the other side. Following my briefing I ignored these distractions and gazed at a third warrior in the center who brandished his spear and advanced with many flourishes, kicking up dust and making threatening noises before finally laying on the ground a green leaf of greeting, which I duly picked up.

After the ceremony we were led to benches in front of the soldiers, who, after the colonel's welcoming speech in Maori and English, sang several songs. I was told that when they finished, I was supposed to sing a song but that if I didn't want to they would sing a song for me. I decided that if I was supposed to sing I would do so, quality not being a requirement. So there I stood, in the dirt in front of all these folks, singing, "I've Been Working on the Railroad"—the first thing that came to mind. The defense attaché, the USAID director, and a few others joined in, and while it felt a trifle silly, everybody seemed to be having fun. It had never occurred to me that someday I would be standing in the bright Afghan sun singing an American folk song as part of a New Zealand ceremony. There is just no telling what an ambassador may end up doing.

I toured an impressive USAID training program for midwives. Afghanistan has one of the highest infant mother mortality rates in the world. I was impressed by the care taken to ensure that the husband or family of each woman in training had agreed in advance that she would be permitted to work in her new trade and in her home community after completing the training. Over time the Health Ministry, with strong American support, is reducing these many unnecessary deaths.

On our return flight the plane lost an engine. It was impressive to see how calmly the U.S. Air Force crew handled the situation. I learned that if the engine blades do not stop spinning, their turning in the wind flow can be a problem on landing. The crew very professionally reviewed their procedures, checked manuals, adjusted air speed, and consulted with the tower in Kabul while circling. We had press on board who sensed a story in having the ambassador aboard when the plane lost an engine. Feeling it necessary to tamp down exaggeration, I remarked that I had never felt threatened, the crew was professional, and I had gone to sleep for a while. This was all true but came out as perhaps a bit too much bravado. Regardless, it seemed to reassure my own staff.

A one-day trip to Islamabad with General Eikenberry allowed for extensive consultations with our embassy there and some meetings with the Pakistani government. Relations between Pakistan and Afghanistan were badly strained. The Afghans were convinced that Pakistan supported the Taliban and that the Pakistanis could stop the violence if they choose. The Pakistanis denied this and pointed out that they had lost over four hundred soldiers in fighting in the tribal areas.

Getting to the bottom of the situation was difficult. The tribal areas had never been under firm control, either by the British or the successor Pakistani government. During my consultations in Washington with various intelligence agencies and senior officials, I had found uncertainty about how to handle the situation. There was no doubt that the insurgents had bases as well as command and control centers located in the Pakistani tribal areas. But doubt existed about whether this was a matter of Pakistani policy or the result of Pakistani inability to exert control. No one accepted the Afghan belief that violence could be shut off by a simple Pakistani decision.

Washington policy was to press Pakistani president Pervez Musharraf in private to do more but to avoid public criticism that only seemed to anger Musharraf and reduce assistance in combating the insurgents. The problem was complicated by the fact that the Pakistani government was cooperating in apprehending al Qaeda leaders even though there was little success in getting the Pakistanis to move against the Taliban. Also, we depended a great deal on Pakistan for the movement of military supplies. A one-dimensional policy was impossible, but over time we would find little success with our approach either.

Embassies Kabul and Islamabad had a reputation for feuding in the press over the claims of their respective host governments about Pakistani support for the insurgency. This public display of disunity was contrary to policy and professionalism, yet I had to be careful that I did not become identified in Afghan eyes as being pro-Pakistani. Ambassador Ryan Crocker (then in Islamabad and later in Baghdad) was an old friend, and bringing our staffs and ourselves together to discuss the situation helped establish a coordination of public positions and private views that we maintained throughout our tours.

I wanted to get away from generalized pressure to "do more," which only seemed to produce deadlock. I favored an intensified intelligence effort to work with the Pakistanis to target specific Taliban targets. Crocker and I discussed ways to advance this approach. On my return to Kabul, I was careful to quickly provide President Karzai with a briefing on our discussions.

In Kabul the forthcoming elections dominated everything. Politicians of every stripe were shameless in seeking U.S. support. I continued to assert our neutrality but doubted anyone believed me. In a long dinner with a leading opposition politician I found him nervous about what we would do. I assured him we would not take sides. He, in turn, assured me that he would respect the outcome of the election.

A Promise in the Panjshir

A September 10 trip to the Panjshir Valley, where the late Northern Alliance (NA) leader Ahmad Shah Massoud had held out against the Soviets and then the Taliban, gave me a chance to reassure these Tajik leaders that we would not forget them.[7] We had depended heavily on Northern Alliance troops during the war, but since 2002 they had lost many positions of influence to Pushtuns. The trip was on the occasion of a large ceremony to commemorate Massoud's death.

Flying to the valley, we crossed barren brown ridges thrusting up from the plain, a once fertile area now desolate owing to the many Soviet mines that had not yet been cleared. Then we passed beyond the mine belt; green fields suddenly spread out until they stretched for miles across the valley. Trees, corn fields bordered by narrow, flowing irrigation ditches, and mud-brown houses and villages here and there passed below our helicopters. We flew through the Lion's Gate, the narrow entrance to the valley, along a rushing river between stark brown hills rising above us with occasional side glimpses into fertile narrow side valleys.

After landing in a grassy field beside the river, we visited Massoud's tomb and then adjourned for tea and a visit with the governor and various local leaders. The situation in the valley was a bit tense. Heavy weapons had been surrendered, but the Panjshiris were refusing to let small arms and ammunition be moved out of the valley without a quid pro quo of economic development. We were starting several projects and would do more, but I had to avoid a direct linkage between disarmament and economic assistance as the precedent would have led to unmanageable demands all across the country. The British and Japanese ambassadors who were on the trip, as well as the deputy UN representative, explained this to the governor in detail. I stressed the $31 million the United States was putting into the valley. Over time we made progress on removing these munitions.

USAID had decided before my arrival to build a paved road into the Panjshir. In my speech I announced this as a personal promise. One great satisfaction was that a year later I was able to drive into the valley on this very road, which by then was nearly completed.

From the governor's simple house our cars crept down the dirt road five miles to where the ceremony would be held. The road was thronged with cars and foot travelers heading for the tomb. Security was nonexistent, but the Panjshiris were solidly anti-Taliban and well able to control who entered the valley. I was not worried.

We were ushered into a huge nylon tent with vivid panels of blue, green, yellow, and red standing in a broad meadow beside the river. The tent was colorful but hot. Its sides were soon rolled up to admit a breeze that disappeared as quickly as it came, as the further crowd of standing spectators once again walled in the tent. So there we sat in a press of people and steamed our way through a long line of speeches from a brother of Massoud, me, the British and Japanese ambassadors, the defense minister, at least three poets, plus a mullah to start the proceedings and another to conclude. I made notes. I tried to stay awake in the heat since somebody always seemed to be taking my picture. I felt the sweat trickle down inside my shirt but did not take off my suit coat because all the other officials kept theirs on. UK Air Vice Marshal Paul Luker, coalition deputy commander, passed me a note: "Damn this war. Damn this endless poetry. Two more to go." I tried not to smile.

Finally it ended. Another slow drive through small villages and along cliffs and green fields backing onto stark, rocky mountains brought us to the delightful house of Foreign Minister Abdullah.[8] Lunch awaited us in a garden full of roses. We dined on mats in the shade of an arbor. Conversation, food, and a pipe revived me. A quick drive took us back to our helicopter. On the way back we learned that a Russian-built helicopter ferrying guests to the memorial event had crashed on landing. We flew over a heap of melted slag and a plume of smoke and bright orange flame at the center of a green meadow. Miraculously, no one was killed.

Cell phones did not yet work in the valley, and we had been out of touch with the embassy for six hours. News of a helicopter crash had gotten back. There had also been a shooting at Kabul International Airport. No one was certain that neither incident involved us, so we were greeted with relief.

The shooting was typical of the confusion that often arose in

Afghan matters. Initially we heard several stories in quick succession: two soldiers had had an argument, six soldiers had been involved, it was an assassination attempt on the defense minister, it was not, four were arrested, none were arrested, and more. In the end it turned out to have been an argument with no political purpose.

Two days later I was in Gardez, still learning, showing confidence for journalists, and getting my own impressions of people and of our programs. In an example of the pace of change, Gardez had a new videoconferencing system installed for the governor to talk to Kabul, but the central city depended on a switchboard that could have come straight from a 1920s movie with the operator pulling and pushing cables to connect calls.

A BBC reporter who was on the trip seemed intent on finding something negative to write about. He questioned me about the difficulty of following in my better-known predecessor's footsteps. I told him it was not an issue because as the American ambassador I spoke for my government. He tried the same question on a group of tribal sheikhs when I was not around. My press officer told me that an old bearded Afghan with a big turban told him that it didn't matter who the ambassador was; what counted was U.S. policy. Others answered another negative question by saying that only the United States was really helping and they wanted us to stay. I doubted any of these positive comments would appear on BBC.

Conversations with tribal leaders and local notables were beginning to raise doubts in my mind about the way we were handling police training. Others reassured me that taking money from Pakistan to build a road was perfectly acceptable; this was not what I was hearing from the Kabul government. Governor Hakim Taniwal expressed it eloquently: "We want the apple. We don't care what tree it comes from."[9]

With the election coming close I kept up the media work in Kabul. Print journalists, ABC, National Public Radio, and various Afghan media all figured in the mix. A frequent question was whether too many "warlords" would end up in Parliament. I always responded that while it was possible, it was an Afghan decision. Our job was to see that the election was honest and the results respected.

At the embassy our organizational efforts were going into high gear. We had organized an interagency group to coordinate activities with the U.S. and international military and the Afghan government. Deborah Alexander from the ARG had been longest in country and had well-established ties to the whole panoply of international and Afghan groups involved in the election. I put her in charge of the mixed military and civilian group, and she did an excellent job. Every day brought fresh issues: of security, of funding, of coordination. The team handled most without my intervention.

We put in place procedures to get rapid reports from provinces where we had political officers. A stream of telegraphic and e-mail reports kept Washington up to date and assured them that we were on top of things. Preemptive information is often the best way to avoid unwanted instructions from headquarters.

Accurate reporting is a core skill of professional Foreign Service officers, but it needs constant emphasis and teaching to balance quality and speed. Shortly before the election one of our provincial officers sent the embassy a draft cable about the transfer of a governor. If the story were true, it raised some problems, but I thought the author of the cable seemed to base too much of the report on only a single source from an interested party. I held the cable and was able to discuss the subject with the interior minister and later with a very knowledgeable British source. In the end we had a more nuanced report. It was only through such painstaking work that I could begin to learn the level of details about militia and political leaders and about devious maneuvers of various groups necessary to understanding Afghan politics. I doubt any foreigner can ever master it all; in Afghanistan the "great game" still lives. The big change is that the regional states have moved from being pieces on the board to being players themselves.

Afghanistan is full of fascinating people. One evening I broke from the endless round of meetings and consultations for a private dinner with Massoud Khalili, then the Afghan ambassador to India (now the ambassador to Turkey). Khalili was one of Ahmad Shah Massoud's close advisers and had been injured in the attack that killed Commander Massoud, as Khalili always called him. He recalled the incident in detail: the long argument with the purported reporters and the strange smile of the leader just before he detonated the bomb. Khalili lost sight in one of his eyes and needed many months to recover. These sinister reminiscences were balanced with the philosophical wisdom and gentleness of Khalili, who has translated his father's poetry, has turned his home into a cultural haven, and has a wife who paints in an arresting mixture of traditional and oriental styles.

Election Day

Election Day was tense. We had organized a massive effort involving most of the embassy. Eight teams of observers would cover multiple polling places. To field them we used all our own security personnel, extra personnel brought in from outside, USAID's contract security, and agents from the Drug Enforcement Administration. Additional State Department volunteers from other posts supplemented our people in Kabul and the provinces. Volunteers came from every section of the embassy, and the military loaned us additional body armor.

An operations center collated information from all sources and fed reports to Washington throughout the day. Not counting my own security detail, some 130 people were involved. I was up at 4:00 a.m. to see our first teams of monitors out the gate.

Even though I knew all the numbers and figures, it was surprising to see the long line of vehicles stretching back to the corner of the compound road. In the predawn darkness it seemed as though I were back in the army. The armored vehicles lined up, the armed men walking back and forth, the light spilling out of a large room where people were putting on equipment, having a last cup of coffee, and heading out—it all felt familiar.

I saw our first teams out, had breakfast, and left at 7:00. During the day I made three rounds in different parts of the city and toured eight polling centers. Each center had multiple voting rooms. Men and women voted separately, although not far apart and in many cases simply on different corridors or different floors of the same building.

We talked with many of the election workers. All seemed enthusiastic and to understand their jobs. The day passed quietly, perhaps a bit too quietly since turnout was lower than we had hoped. There seemed to be many reasons for this: confusion over the large ballot and some measure of election fatigue after three elections (constitution, president, and parliament) in three years, for example. Several election officials told us they had expected more progress after the presidential election and that the low turnout reflected some disappointment. The good news was that fear did not seem to play an important role in reducing participation. Turnout in the provinces seemed to be better. Overall the results were not bad.

As I moved about I found myself doing a running press commentary. I spoke to reporters from England, France, Denmark, Poland, and Belgium as well as American and Afghan journalists and finished with a press conference for about eighty foreign and Afghan journalists. The mood was upbeat. Despite many white-knuckle moments, the day passed without too much violence. Across the country fifteen people, including one French soldier, died in several small incidents, but there were no large attacks, a tribute to the great efforts of coalition and ISAF troops and leaders. We finished the night with a pizza party for all our election workers. I was able to stop by after a night meeting with President Karzai, who was well satisfied with the day's events.

Many of our security people were not able to get to the party, so on the suggestion of my aide Bill Paton, I threw a two-hour open bar later in the week. Wow, did they turn out for that. The bar overflowed into the patio, and then that filled up. In two hours they managed to put away $500 worth of beer, but the short time kept anyone from getting really drunk. Too rarely do we recognize the risks and responsibilities of our security people. They had done a great job, and I felt satisfied with the thanks I received and the loyalty I knew I was building in the teams.

The election's results would take several weeks to tabulate, but we were confident that things had progressed well. National Security Adviser Stephen Hadley wrote a nice note to Secretary Rice saying, "In the run-up to and on the day of the elections, Embassy Kabul's support for the electoral process was superb. Ron Neumann and his staff provided insightful, timely analysis of key election issues and, on September 17–18, kept my staff linked directly to late-breaking field reporting on voter turnout, security conditions, and Afghan management of the process." I shared the note with the whole staff along with renewed thanks for all their hard work. Our success was very much a team effort. Now we could get back to all the other issues.

3
Fall 2005

Throughout the fall we were preoccupied with how to organize the international community for the post-Bonn reconstruction effort and how to expand our own assistance efforts. We succeeded in the first and failed in the second, a failure for which we paid substantially later. Preparations for the seating of Parliament raised many issues. Security, the turnover to NATO, relations with Pakistan, counternarcotics efforts, and a range of other issues kept the pace intense but will be reviewed later.

Reaching Agreement: The London Compact

Even while we were absorbed in electoral preparations, we had begun to look forward. The international effort to this point had been focused on the steps of the Bonn process. With the completion of the elections we would have run off the map. New direction would be needed. Without agreement on goals there would be much time wasted with repeated discussions of what to do next. Talk about a post-Bonn process had circulated among capitals. Washington had written and debated, but nothing much seemed to be happening and what was debated seemed too general. We needed specific commitments attached to specific timelines on both economic and governance issues.

The diplomatic corps in Kabul progressively took the lead under the direction of the UN Secretary General's special representative, Jean Arnault. His creativity, dynamism, and endless patience have not been sufficiently recognized.

Jean and his UNAMA staff provided a draft of the cover declaration to be issued at an international conference scheduled for January 2006 in London. We duly sent this back to Washington and proceeded to let the various capitals deal with multiple drafting suggestions. I viewed this effort as largely hortatory: the declaration would be quickly forgotten after the conference closed. What concerned me was the annex of benchmarks.

Who first suggested having specific benchmarks I cannot now remember. Perhaps it had several authors. The discussions of the concerned ambassadors unrolled over many meetings and working dinners. We each stimulated the thinking of the others. Whatever its origin, I seized on the idea of benchmarks as the centerpiece of my own efforts. I began to elaborate the idea with Jean, and with a core group of ambassadors and then Afghan ministers, we sketched in the details.

The benchmarks and timelines would be the real road map that would guide international and Afghan efforts over the years to come. Because of the detail involved, the benchmarks could be developed only in Kabul. I kept Washington generally informed of what we were doing and periodically sent back drafts. However, the process, with its multiple layers, needed to be kept moving, and there was no time (nor, to be honest, much desire on my part) for specific instructions. Some of the ambassadors played their hands in the same way. Others either wanted or were required to have somewhat tighter instructions from their home capital.

The benchmark drafting process was already moving by September 23, when I explained in a letter to my family that what we were doing was consistent with Washington's policy but well ahead of any instructions. I knew there would be a few areas in which Washington would have to make decisions, but for the rest I would, as I wrote, "just drive on with the group, report as we go along, and see if Washington can catch up. . . . It is not that we are ignoring instructions but, rather, that we are creating them through our actions."

The process took several months, but early on several points were clear. We did not expect that the benchmarks would produce any automatic follow-through. Rather we saw them as levers to be used to lift us all over difficult problems. In some cases the levers—that is, the fact that there would be broad international agreement—would help to harmonize international pressure on the Kabul government. In some cases it might be the Afghans who would in the future use the levers to prod the international community to fund and live up to its commitments.

We expected that issues of corruption and efficient government would seriously strain Afghan political will in the future. Some of the benchmarks, such as the creation of a nonpolitical commission for senior government appointments, were phrased as dry administrative steps but their intent was deeply political: we were doing nothing less than taking a politicized appointment process out of government control. Other such issues were touched on in a similar way.

Some mechanism would be needed to manage the process. An annex eventually provided for the setting up of the Joint Coordination and Monitoring Board (JCMB), but neither Jean nor I ever believed that this formal body could be kept small enough to be effective. Many months later I noticed that as he and I explained our intentions to Jean's successor, we were virtually finishing each other's sentences and thoughts as we outlined how we expected a more informal process to be needed behind the scenes.

The whole body of benchmarks had to be coordinated with a much larger Afghan development plan. This plan, called the Afghanistan National Development Strategy (ANDS), was still being written in a multiyear effort coordinated by the World Bank and the UNAMA staff with the Afghan government. It would not be finished in time for the conference. It was far too large and in some cases too vague to be folded into an international agreement. Yet the two had to be kept parallel to avoid future conflicts. The trick would be to excerpt the most important points from the ANDS while not letting its grandiose nature overshadow our more political purpose.

Finally, we had to keep in mind that the London conference would also be an occasion for donors to pledge money, although it was not technically designated as a pledging conference. We needed to allow

time after completing the documents for them to influence governments' individual decisions about funding. This is never fast for any
government. We needed many to come through with funding. And we
were aware that the many senior Western officials' departures for Christmas vacation would create a dead period of several weeks in which nothing serious would be decided. We agreed that we needed to wrap the
process up by mid-December.

The details, and even some of the central ideas, evolved over four
months. Francesc Vandrell, the special representative of the EU who
had been involved in early UN efforts to mediate in Afghanistan, participated in the Bonn Conference, and stayed involved ever since, was
particularly active in keeping the justice sector in focus. How hard one
could push accountability for war crimes had to be balanced against the
tenuous political circumstances. Often small groups would meet to work
out differences. Then new language would be suggested to the larger
international and Afghan group.

While we were making progress, it soon was apparent that we
needed a way to bring capitals to closure faster than could be done by
sending drafts and having sometimes contradictory suggestions come
back days later. A conference on regional relations was already scheduled for early December 2005. Since it would include all the main players, I suggested that the delegations hold separate meetings in the margin
of the conference to try to resolve the remaining issue of the benchmark annex. The others agreed.

Our delegation, headed by Deputy Assistant Secretary of State
Maureen Quinn and Anthony "Tony" Harriman from the National
Security Council (NSC), arrived on December 1. Both had long experience in Afghan matters, and Maureen had been chargé briefly before
my arrival. Maneuvering around the necessary briefings for a congressional delegation that arrived the same day, we held an initial organizing
meeting at the German embassy. From then on progress was steady but
grueling. On December 3 we had an all-day negotiating session. On
December 4 the Regional Conference met in the day. We returned to
negotiations at 4:00 p.m. and carried on until midnight.

To try to get the agreement of delegations from Japan, the major
European states, the World Bank, the International Monetary Fund

(IMF), and the Afghan government on some forty benchmarks and timelines was a tough job. Everyone had his or her favorite piece. On the Afghan side, Hanif Atmar, the minister of rural development; Anwar-ul-Haq Ahadi, the minister of finance; Ishaq Naderi, President Karzai's senior economic adviser and titular head of the Afghan delegation; and Foreign Minister Abdullah were articulate spokesmen for Afghan interests. They negotiated hard with one eye on costs and another on the political message that what we were now coming to call "the London Compact" would send to Afghans.

A particularly contentious issue was whether the benchmarks were too ambitious. Some felt that we should reduce them to ensure performance, and indeed some would later criticize the result for overreaching. If it was clear that even with full funding something could not be achieved in the time proposed, the goal had to be scaled back. We did not want to set ourselves up for failure.

However, when the issue involved political will or was simply going to be difficult, I argued strongly that it was better to be ambitious, daring even, and fall short than to dumb down the goals so that we could claim success from inadequate achievements. We needed to be audacious in calling for the changes that we knew were needed. I was very pleased that this intervention was broadly accepted and we were able to move on.

Some delegations seemed more interested in endless statements of principle than in getting down to specifics. Sometimes the debate verged on fantasy. One argued that help for the handicapped must be stated in terms of "rights" rather than needs—and this in one of the poorest countries in the world with a shattered economy, where the burden of just getting the essentials in place would take years and billions of dollars. Handicapped "rights" is a Western idea and a noble goal but is still gaining acceptance as a matter of international law and practice. The discussion was not a big deal but was symptomatic of what had to be debated, sometimes at length.

An annex to reorganize the donor community and coordinate efforts on the ground took a lot of time. We needed an agreed-to mechanism to push when individual ministries weren't keeping up the pace and donors couldn't or wouldn't make needed progress. There were legitimate concerns that we not set up a parallel bureaucratic structure that would overload the Afghan government's limited resource of qualified people. The resulting document was less than a page long but required hours of negotiations.

The Afghan ministers did an effective job. They knew what they wanted and argued their political and economic positions with force and logic. This helped convince other delegations that the compact really was becoming an Afghan document, an important step in having the Afghans take responsibility for the work in the future.

Jean Arnault did a superb job of chairing the sessions. He never showed frustration, although some of the time I was twitching and almost grinding my teeth waiting through some particularly turgid presentation. In such a meeting the chairman has a difficult job. He has no authority to overrule a sovereign representative or an Afghan minister. And yet he must know when and how to cut off discussion, summarize a conclusion, and move on. A chairman who tries to be too autocratic will produce rebellion and breakdown. One who is too timid will never steer the meeting through its work. Jean was brilliant in sensing how long to let discussion run and when he could step in to cut it off, state an agreement on some point around which we were circling, and move on. I greatly admired his sense of timing but doubted I could match it.

Finally, after some fifteen hours of intensive negotiations and many more hours preceding the "pre-conference," we had most of the issues settled. Final agreement would come from capitals, but most of our work was done and nations could now address the resulting need for funding and pledges when the documents were signed in London in January.

In January 2006, I went back to Washington for consultations on the budget (discussed later). I was happy to be with my wife to celebrate our fortieth wedding anniversary, but then it was back to work. I was able to join Secretary Rice on her plane for the flight to London—a very comfortable way to travel allowing opportunity for extensive discussions.

In one sense the London conference was anticlimatic. All the documents had already been agreed to and that part of the conference was finished after the first hour in which Prime Minister Blair and Secretary Rice were present. Sixty countries pledged a very satisfactory $10 billion dollars, somewhat more than we had expected and good news for the Afghans.

Since Secretary Rice had to rush back for the State of the Union address and two undersecretaries with her each had a number of side meetings, I found myself in the U.S. delegation chair for nearly half the conference with the dubious pleasure of listening to a great many speeches. The discussions at the conference were actually statements of governments' positions rather than negotiations.

It was amusing to see various chairmen try to control the length of the interventions. The officials of governments and international organizations were each determined to have their say. At some point the chairman would loudly rap the gavel and the speaker would hunch his shoulders, ignore the gavel, and just keep talking. The Russian went further, announcing that what he had to say was important and that he didn't intend to pay attention to time limits. After this announcement he proceeded to give a lengthy restatement of Russian views with no new content.

But if the speeches were boring, the setting, dating from the grandeur of the height of the British Empire, was gorgeous. Lancaster House had a room at least two hundred feet long in which we assembled between white walls set off with gilded plasterwork. Above the central part of the hall, the ceiling soared fully one hundred feet covered with a long mural, all framed in yards of gold-leafed wood or plaster. Oil paintings adorned the walls. It was a suitable place to be making history, and we hoped that we were doing so. Months of work had gone into the documents that we hoped would keep us on track in building an Afghan state. But a lot of money was going to be needed.

Increasing the U.S. Assistance Budget

Intertwined with work on the compact was labor to increase our budget. Of course, we were never doing just one thing at a time. In addition to budget and London conference work, October brought a visit from Secretary Rice, the extradition of a narcotics trafficker, earthquake relief for Pakistan, State Department inspectors, frustrations with equipping the police, the relocation of our quarters, and even a desultory rocket attack. At least no one had time to be bored.

Administrative issues take surprising amounts of time even in a war. Embassy Kabul had grown helter-skelter in response to crisis and needed to stabilize. Poorly attended to, support problems irritate people and lower morale. Our effort to normalize embassy operations, far from being the reflex of stuffy State Department bureaucrats, was part of an effort to raise efficiency and spirits. ARG coordination with the Economic Section allowed us to give single, clear policy messages to the Afghan government. The deputy chief of mission (DCM) supervised such coordination, and he was usually able to settle intramural turf struggles without them consuming my time.

Just moving into the new apartments was a chore. More spacious and blast-resistant than the containers, they boosted morale. But staff growth had outpaced planning, there were only enough apartments for half the staff, and our gifted administrative counselor, Rosemary "Rosie" Hansen, was needed to manage a transparent, fair process that would avoid leaving agencies or individuals feeling slighted and nursing resentments.

On October 7, I was in Jalalabad, my seventh provincial visit in nine weeks in country. On the eighth a serious earthquake struck Pakistan, and USAID had to divert some efforts to support their colleagues in Islamabad. More striking was General Eikenberry's rapid decision two days later to deploy U.S. and, with Afghan consent, some of the few Afghan army helicopters to aid in the relief effort. While there was some impact on combat operations, the decision brought immense goodwill in Pakistan and temporarily smoothed relations between the fractious neighbors.

On October 11 a rocket struck several hundred meters from the embassy but did no damage and fortunately did not scare off the arrival the next day of Secretary Rice. It was lucky that her lead agent was a veteran officer whom I had known in Baghdad and who was calmly able to distinguish real threats from the background noise incidental to a war.

But as we dealt with one issue or event after another, our focus was on the budget, a five-month struggle whose bureaucratic defeat would cost us dearly. Because the war in response to the 9/11 attack began quickly, there had been no time for careful advance planning of assistance programs. Initial efforts were in humanitarian assistance. Afghanistan was suffering first from winter cold and then drought. Refugees returned and needed assistance. Washington's original focus on hunting terrorists and avoiding entanglement in nation building also resulted initially in resistance to large assistance commitments.

Development theory worldwide has changed since the United States built roads, dams, and canals in Afghanistan in my father's day; the focus has shifted to education, social services, and the like. USAID had gotten completely out of the road-building business. All these factors combined to delay strong efforts to rebuild, or in many cases to build, since there had been little existing infrastructure in Afghanistan.

Serious development budgets had been appropriated only in fiscal year (FY) 2004.[1] In FY 2005 a large appropriation of $1.673 billion had thrust us forward. In theory, 2006 was to return us to a normal budget process with little or no supplemental. Although approximately $970.58 million was to be allocated, it soon became apparent that we were underfunding both for war and development.[2]

The poppy problem was getting worse, but because of limited funding we were ignoring non-poppy-producing provinces for agricultural development. Therefore, as poppy spread to additional provinces we had no way to even keep pace, still less to get ahead of the problem by providing other sources of sustainable rural income. The fighting was getting worse. The need for visible results in the countryside was pressing. But the budget proposal I had inherited added little new funding for agriculture and would be stretched even thinner by the addition of new PRTs. But above all we were missing the bigger picture of critical bottlenecks that would continue to affect security and development alike.

The first priority was roads. We who live in the modern world can scarcely imagine the impact of medieval transport on every aspect of life. The forty-mile journey from Washington to Baltimore that we can drive in an hour is in most parts of Afghanistan a five-hour bone-jarring effort. Few crops can move economically to market over such roads and fragile or perishable ones not at all; tomatoes shipped on such a journey turn to mush, and melons are smashed into fragments. Government officials avoid such trips if possible, so a fragile administration has even less reach than it might. The insurgents' task is eased when security forces cannot move quickly.

In short, roads had to be the backbone of revitalizing the still largely rural Afghan economy; we were building few and were not proposing to do more. The draft 2006 budget would add only $37 million for roads, all committed to finishing existing projects, not starting anything new.

If roads were critical, so was electric power. The dark of Kabul's unlit nighttime streets was a potent political symbol of a lack of international progress. But more important was the economic impact. Power in Afghanistan came from a few dams, mostly silted up and deteriorating after the neglect of the war years. Diesel-powered generators provided some power but at a cost six times higher than in neighboring Pakistan or Iran. Without comparably priced power, Afghanistan could not add even the value of simple agricultural processing industries. It would continue to grow tomatoes and import tomato paste, grow wheat and import flour. And without industry, there would be little employment for the men beyond opium poppy harvesting and few new taxes for the government to rebuild the country. Electricity was a key bottleneck that we needed to break through, but we were not planning to expand beyond our large project to bring electricity from Central Asia to Kabul.

I was no economic genius suddenly illuminating a dark landscape with my intellect. These problems stood out clearly in the careful briefings USAID and our economic team in the ARG and embassy provided. I was fortunate that Alonzo Fulgham had directed the USAID Afghanistan office in Washington before arriving as USAID mission director in Afghanistan at the same time I arrived. We had already begun a partnership even before leaving the States. Going over the prospects, I decided we had to do more. Alonzo and his team built the budget, gradually working up a three-year plan for power and another for roads. Later we would come to see even these plans as inadequate, but already they were a major expansion in scope and change in direction.

Throughout September USAID had refined figures, enlarged projects, consulted with me, and gone back to the drawing board with more guidance as I was able to focus on different issues. Alonzo and I debated strategy and projects with his team. His USAID mission was staffed primarily to implement existing projects rather than to formulate a whole new plan and was understrength even for that. The additional workload was considerable, but they carried on with enthusiasm.

What emerged was a request for a $600.9 million dollar supplemental for fiscal year 2006—virtually a doubling of the budget already passed by Congress. This was not going to be an easy sell in Washington, which was already dealing with the twin fiscal blows of escalating fighting in Iraq and the repair of damage from Hurricane Katrina. President Bush had told me before I left to ask for what I needed, but there was many a hoop to get through before a final budget decision would go to him. I had worked a good many issues through the U.S. bureaucracy and interagency process over the years, but the size of this budget proposal made it clear I was playing in the major leagues for the first time and needed to feel my way.

Springing a surprise on Washington, especially one costing money, is definitely not the way to get what one wants. We needed to build support. When Secretary Rice arrived for a five-hour visit October 12, 2005, we insisted on preserving one hour for a briefing to lay out our proposal. Alonzo took the lead. Rice wanted more details on the longer-term picture but supported our coming in with our proposal. She explained her strategy of gradually trying to increase the regular aid budget over several years while using declining supplementals to bridge between what was needed and what would be acceptable in the regular budget.[3]

I alerted Assistant Secretary Christina Rocca to what we were going to propose and also called then–USAID administrator Andrew Natsios to gain his support in advance. Andrew had long overcome his early aversion to road building in Afghanistan and became a strong supporter of our efforts. Finally, after much drafting and rewriting and having gained as much advance support as we could, we sent our formal request for an additional $600.9 million on October 18, 2005.

A summary cable laid out the problem (a second telegram spelled out the details of each project). Roads, power, and agriculture were interlocking roadblocks to economic progress. In the wake of successful Afghan elections, it was important to understand that Afghan popular expectations were not being met and would now be focused heavily on a new government completely without resources to respond to the demand.

We pointed out that under the planned regular budget we would not build one new kilometer of road; all new money was committed to finishing existing projects. We reviewed Washington decisions made earlier and reported that the "comprehensive strategy approved by the Deputies cannot be implemented and sustained without additional funding," and we explained why, including aspects of a multidonor effort.[4]

Our telegram noted that while poppy production had declined in

2004, it was now (2005) increasing in several other provinces not targeted for agricultural, rural development, and alternative livelihoods efforts. We specified five provinces in which this increase was happening and four more where we felt it might happen. We explained the demonstrated value of improving rural conditions before poppy took hold and noted that under the current budget we would not be able to work in any of the provinces we listed.

Without new PRT funding, we would "cut down the ability of our PRTs to support developing governance just as the new provincial councils take office." Our joint civil-military teams were the only tool we had to work collectively on governance, security, and development. We pointed out that at the previously decided level for the budget, we would be able to do an average of only two projects per existing team, "a sum that will not provide significant leverage."

A large new U.S. effort would "galvanize international donors, shore up President Karzai and lay the groundwork for self-sustaining government in Afghanistan." We sought $223 million for roads, primarily for a few large roads, including new work in neglected northeastern Afghanistan (by the next year we would be seeking three times that amount). Power required $152.9 million heavily devoted to building the Kajaki Dam in the south to triple electric power, building a new transmission line to carry that power to the cities of Kandahar and Lashkar-Gah, and expanding agricultural production by increasing the dam's capacity. Agriculture and rural development would get $125 million for expansion into additional provinces; we considered this figure low but it was as small as we thought made sense. For USAID efforts in the provincial reconstruction teams we sought $100 million.

We had made our case in print. Our unclassified recommendations had gone in a formal telegram that would be widely read in Washington.[5] My team had given me all the help and data it could. Now I had to push the effort myself.

I returned to Washington for intensive consultations as well as a brief break. Contrary to what one might suppose from academic writings, few policy decisions are made in a single meeting or by deliberate consideration of a single document. Rather, support for policy change has to be built incrementally, through reports, conversations, and individual meetings, where the advocate can argue his case, elicit the doubts of others, and build the arguments and political support to overcome the doubts.

As I made the rounds I found understanding and strong support in the policy parts of State and the NSC. Defense was also supportive in principle but seemed unwilling to play any role in agitating for sufficient resources for the civilians to be full partners to the military. But the budgeteers were another matter.

In State budget offices and even more so in the Office of Management and Budget (OMB), I found mostly doubts and questions.[6] There had been a large supplemental the previous year. Why must there be another when little of the money had been spent? Wasn't there a full fiscal "pipeline," and couldn't we just reprogram if we wanted to change priorities?

With the help of my USAID colleagues, I responded that the fiscal 2005 money had only begun to be available for obligation in late calendar 2005. While obligating such large sums took time, we knew where the money was going, the program was sensible, and we needed substantial increases to expand into new areas. Thomas Johnson, from USAID Kabul, who had been invaluable in constructing our case and came from Kabul specifically to join me for the OMB meeting, pointed out that congressional requirements (known as earmarks) for spending on humanitarian and other areas considerably limited the funds actually available for reprogramming to the areas we recommended. Along with "Mac" McLaughlin from the Afghan Reconstruction Group, who had a long relationship with OMB, we pointed out that we had carefully negotiated a number of agreements with the Afghan government on how portions of the existing budget would be used; these commitments should be maintained. OMB officials seemed unpersuaded.

I argued the urgency of the situation. They replied with explanations of budget procedures. To my mind we were dealing with a war and that ought to demand a different kind of consideration. The answers I received seemed to focus on the rules governing "normal" economic development. I thought I was making an articulate case and came away with the sense that our arguments would at least get a hearing. As my team and I compared notes we all felt we had scored some points. We might not get all we wanted, but we felt that surely we would have a large additional hunk to advance the work. In this deluded state I returned to Kabul on November 9.

Fall moved into winter. Preparations for London absorbed us. I traveled extensively in the countryside. General Eikenberry was reasonably optimistic that the separate recommendations he had made for increases in police and army equipping and training would be supported in the supplemental. We moved into our new embassy office building and suffered from days without telegrams or e-mails as the technicians grappled with the technical problems of the move.

We brought the whole embassy community together for a Thanksgiving dinner in the new embassy. December brought days of intensive negotiations with donors and Afghan officials preparing for London. We were bombarded with questions from Washington about our budget. OMB wanted minute details: Which roads were to be built? It was in our documents, but we answered again. What was the multiyear plan for power? We gave more details. Why couldn't we give a full five-year spending plan for Afghanistan development?

We resolved to meet this request, although we had to point out that we continued to have new insights about the country given that there had been so little time for planning before we jumped in. Also, some sixty donors were operating in Afghanistan, and while coordination was slowly improving, any five-year projection would be something of a plan in a vacuum without knowing what the out-years would bring from other donors.

Nevertheless, by December 5 we were able to send back a ten-page detailed projection over the succeeding two years. We argued that a "surge investment" would close the road loop, making Afghanistan a land bridge between the Indian subcontinent and Central Asia. For roads, power, and agriculture we recommended an additional $873 million over two years (fiscal years 2007 and 2008). These sums were detailed project by project and were over and in addition to the notional totals already in Washington calculations for these budget years. We knew Washington was going to have sticker shock, but they had asked us for answers and we provided them in page after page of details and rationales.

A favorite Washington response when asked for money is to suggest getting it from other donors. This provides an ostensible decision at no immediate cost. The problem is that it usually doesn't work. For this reason I added to the cable the notation that up to that point we had not been able to get funding from donors for our priorities. We needed to budget "to protect our interests, not bet on hope."[7]

E-mails sped back and forth. Washington seemed always to have more questions, some of which we had previously answered. We groused to each other in Kabul that OMB seemed to lack a sense that we were at war and snidely asked each other why Eisenhower wasn't asked in 1943 to prepare and stay within a multiyear spending plan for the war in Europe. But we tried to stay civil to our Washington colleagues in our communications.

Meanwhile, one congressional and senatorial delegation after another came through the embassy, and each received a detailed briefing on what we proposed. Invariably they were supportive. Congressman Jim Kolbe (R-AZ), the head of the relevant House appropriations sub-committee,[8] was initially displeased and shocked that we were proposing large increases. But he listened closely, probed deeply, and before he left offered to support if the administration put forward our proposal. I reported to State our continuing successful building of support as one congressional delegation after another came and went.

One congressional delegation was grounded by snow, so I drove them from Bagram Air Base to Kabul. Shocked that only one road in Afghanistan, the ring road around the circumference of the country, was better than the potholed, rundown, two-lane highway that threaded its way across a bleak snowy plain, they went away most supportive of our budget proposal.

As December moved along we focused on a replacement for the UN top job. Multiple issues were coming at us. Drugs were heating up. We had to get agreement on where to base counterdrug helicopters, and I had to engage with ministers and NATO commanders to clear away obstacles. There were new problems in the police-training program, but I wasn't sure how to fix them. One day I had nine meetings. We were getting budget questions from Washington that seemed to suggest some of our colleagues didn't have the stomach for a budget fight in a tough budget year. I kept reminding them that we were at war; regular developmental procedures couldn't apply.

I visited Herat in the west, where the Italians hosted the PRT. We opened a burn center. In the speeches one official quoted a sura from the Koran that says if someone takes a life it is as though they have taken the life of all humanity.[9] It struck me how alike this was to John Donne's sentiment that "no man is an island."

I moved into the new penthouse apartment that had replaced my old containers and wondered why State would construct a lovely building but send out some twenty table lamps with plugs that didn't fit the sockets they had installed. All the apartments had table lamps with the wrong plugs. Congressional visitors were coming so quickly on each other's heels that we seemed to be turning into a permanent tour office, but the budget briefings continued to be well received. If the administration would push for what was needed, I was confident of bipartisan congressional support for the Afghanistan part of the budget.

Memories of better conditions in the Afghanistan of my parents' days sometimes flickered into focus. I visited the old ambassador's residence where we had stayed years ago. Buried memories awoke. As I gazed at a desolate expanse of weeds and bare ground, I suddenly saw a green lawn with elegant people and my father standing on the steps to greet guests for the Independence Day reception. In the back of an old safe, Dave Newell, the counselor of embassy for management, found a guide on hikes and picnic places near Kabul that my mother had edited. I wondered when such peaceful and secure days would return. Also in the safe was a pamphlet she had written on the history of the residence. It allowed me to identify a large eighteenth-century French mirror that had miraculously survived years of war and now hangs in the new ambassador's apartment.

Fighting cooled a bit from the summer months but not as much as in previous years. General Eikenberry and I were meeting privately at least once a week, staying in e-mail contact, and coordinating closely. We were bothered by periodic rumors from Washington that we were not getting on personally—a complete lie but one that we could never drive a stake through.

Electoral complaints were finally all dealt with. Extensive preparations culminated in a brief visit by Vice President and Mrs. Dick Cheney for the opening of Parliament. The parliament building was in town and without many of the security features the Secret Service would have liked. Fortunately the Afghans cooperated, right down to letting us bring our own explosives-sniffing dogs into the building before the deputies assembled. Literally hundreds of Afghan soldiers and police were assembled to keep all secure, and American forces were out of sight but ready to move in if needed. As we helicoptered into Kabul from Bagram on December 18, I told Cheney that Parliament contained a great mix of people, including some thugs and crooks. Chaney replied that it didn't sound too different from the U.S. Senate.

The vice president heard my abbreviated budget briefing during helicopter rides. He seemed to think we were proposing something sensible. I was encouraged.

On December 20 we were advised that our supplemental request was being reduced by State to just under $400 million. I talked to Secretary Rice and came away feeling that she wanted to support us but believed that $400 million was as high a figure as she could push through. We were disappointed, but with two-thirds of our request much could still be done, and after all Rice was my boss and responsible for making such decisions.

State sent a long list of detailed questions about how we would reallocate the reduced amount among our priorities. They demanded a response in two days. With many of the critical USAID personnel absent for Christmas leave, this was an impossible request. The State budget people were not interested in our problems, and I had to request from Rice an extra week to work. The staff worked late into the night for days even with the extra time. I was proud of their effort and told them so.

Two days after the Cheney visit Secretary of Defense Donald Rumsfeld was with us. It was a strange visit, not quite hostile but not particularly warm either. He was correct that Afghanistan was plagued by corruption and bad governance. He was impatient. I had the feeling that he thought General Eikenberry and I should have been able to solve these problems much faster, but he didn't say so or suggest how this miracle might be achieved.

There was a long argument with his staff over a border control program that Eikenberry and I agreed had been wrongly started and pursued without involving the Afghan government.[10] All the Defense staffers could see was that a year had gone by and we were starting over.

Some of them finally accepted that their original concept was flawed, but I doubt they communicated that to Rumsfeld. At least Eikenberry and I were in agreement.

Christmas came. I had a Christmas Eve open house with mulled wine and food. The Embassy Employees Association contributed twenty-five bottles of wine; we went through it all, and I added another ten bottles. It was a clear success and an early evening. Later that night a small group going to Christmas Eve mass at the Italian embassy got stuck inside our embassy when a small rocket attack across town led the security officer to keep everyone locked down.

All in all Christmas passed quietly. I gave everyone the day off. We cleaned a light snow off my patio. It was black with the flakes of whatever they burn besides diesel in Kabul in the winter—probably goat and sheep dung. Some days you could taste the air. I was missing home. The budget fight was suspended until Washington staffers returned from their Christmas vacations and decided to think about a war besides Iraq.

We had a "black tie or whatever you've got" dance for New Year's Eve. Half our staff was gone, and the rest was working long hours to cover; it was a lonely time of the year, spending the holidays away from home. The dance in the dining hall seemed good for morale. The women brought out dresses instead of pants and the heavy shoes demanded by the combination of Afghan social habits and unpaved muddy streets. Everyone had a good time.

January 2006 and still no budget decisions. A congressional delegation was snowed in, and we housed them somehow.

I visited Uruzgan Province, where we would soon turn over command to the Dutch. A suicide bomber blew himself up at the police station while I was in another part of town. The security people wanted me to rush back to the PRT, but that would have looked cowardly to the Afghans, the bomber was blown to pieces (unfortunately along with some children), there was no real threat to me, and there didn't seem ever to have been one. We carried on for lunch with the governor.

Congressman Jon Porter (R-NV) came on January 6 with seven other congressmen. He asked me to write up my oral briefing, which I did. It provides some record of the message I was giving to everyone in Congress and the Executive Branch.

The war was not won by any means. Our first priority was security. The second was establishing the government in the provinces. I went over the priorities for the budget. I told Porter that with active military support and a breakthrough strategy in economics we could revitalize a sense that Afghanistan was moving forward. "Without that, we risk a growing Afghan public belief that help is not coming at anything like the pace they consider promised or central. We are still fighting a war and we need to look at the commitment of resources in terms of what is necessary to win, not as a developmental priority in competition with other needy areas of the world. Because it is a war, if we do not pay adequately now, we will very probably pay a stiffer price later."[11]

Porter praised the briefing and was solidly supportive. Two days later I received word that the Fourth Brigade of the Tenth Mountain Division would not go to Afghanistan as programmed for later that year. We would have to fight with fewer troops than expected. Those of us in Afghanistan did not think the reduction a wise decision. Still no word on the budget.

On January 11, I arrived in Washington for leave. A State Department car met me at the airport and whisked me off for a 5:00 p.m. meeting with Secretary Rice. She had no big news; she just wanted to see me before I went on leave. We talked about the upcoming London conference and developments in police training and army development. I was critical of our police effort, but we were still working out solutions. I went on leave and rejoined the secretary at the end of January to fly with her to London for the conference described earlier. Then it was back to winter in Afghanistan.

In Dubai, on the way back to Kabul, I got the news: OMB had cut out virtually all supplemental aid for Afghanistan. It did not make for a happy flight back to Kabul.) OMB had decided that neither roads nor power could qualify as "emergencies" for a supplemental. (This totally bogus argument vanished a year later when both were included in the 2007 supplemental.) OMB was also pushing its view that the money in the pipeline was sufficient for our needs.

I felt that OMB had lied to me, in substance if not in specifics. None of our discussions had indicated that a supplemental couldn't be entertained. What was the point of the endless questioning, the requests for details that had consumed my staff's days and nights, if the decision did not even consider the value of the projects proposed? I believed then and suspect now that the decision was driven by the desire to avoid too large a budget; Iraq and hurricane relief won and we lost. The reasons OMB gave for the decision were rationalizations at best.

I talked to Secretary Rice in the evening from Kabul. She seemed to believe that she could not buck OMB's main decision but was not clear about her reasons. I did not push as we were speaking on an open telephone line with the assumption that half the world's intelligence agencies were probably enjoying the call. Rice was prepared to support a request for a puny $140 million for agriculture and PRTs. I wanted those projects, although not as much as I wanted the roads and power. At midnight I briefed Assistant Secretary Rocca. We would write a telegram appealing OMB's decision.

On the good news side, we did seem to be getting other funding that we had asked for to deal with embassy operations, security funding to protect ourselves, and USAID operating expenses. At least I wouldn't have a management crisis.

On February 6 we sent our cable of objection. I tried to be polite, but the cable was stiff in tone. It said that the budget decision "will make narcotics worse . . . slower to build the ANA [Afghan National Army], [the] margin of victory tighter and the Taliban's role easier." It made no difference. In the end, OMB even rebuffed Secretary Rice's smaller effort. We received only $32 million in additional economic assistance over the already programmed base budget plus $11 million in an accounting transfer to offset the forgiveness of Afghan debt.

Secretary Rice challenged me to reprogram within our budget to meet the needs we believed were key and assured me that she would work to find money from other nations to meet some of the unfunded priorities. We did do a major reprogramming (discussed later), but it met only some of the needs for roads and power and none in agriculture and the PRTs. It exhausted our flexibility so that when new needs arose we could not shift money to meet them. Although Secretary Rice and others did make efforts with the Italians, Kazakhs, and others, none of the unfunded priorities were met by other nations in the succeeding year.

4
Wake Up, Washington

Issues rushed at us incessantly as winter snows gave way to gentle spring and then the heat of the Afghan summer in 2006. Yet among the constants was Washington's slowness to act on our predictions of worsening security conditions. Although more troops were needed, the answer was never to be found only in deploying foreign soldiers. The security issue was always intertwined with needing economic assistance, budgeting for the creation of the Afghan police and military, fighting drugs, expanding NATO's competence, shoring up the Afghan government, and structuring a more efficient international response. Surely Afghanistan was not a place for those who wanted to concentrate on one problem at a time.

After the initial successes of 2001, Washington believed that the war was won. What remained was mopping up and hunting terrorists. A series of attacks by larger Taliban groups in the spring of 2005 were surprising but were easily repulsed by airpower. The Taliban faded back into pinprick attacks, which the forces on the ground apparently could manage. Washington and many allied capitals were comfortable with the overall military situation when General Eikenberry and I arrived within weeks of each other in Afghanistan in 2005.

As we moved toward 2006, military, intelligence, and State reporting increasingly noted disturbing trends, although fighting had slowed in the cold winter months. Yet, as Karl and I conferred regularly throughout the fall and early winter,[1] it seemed to us that Washington's perceptions were stuck in an increasingly unrealistic appraisal of the situation. Individual reports were not registering. With Karl's full support and active cooperation, I prepared a written overview to try to wake up headquarters. We expected a bloody summer.

I spelled out the reasons for this prediction. Poppy eradication in 2005, while largely a failure, was a warning to the drug traffickers that more was coming. We were seeing signs of increasing cooperation between traffickers and insurgents in the south and expected more. NATO nations were engaged in highly public domestic political squabbles over their troop commitments, and this generated a perception of NATO political weakness. We concluded that this would encourage the Taliban to strike hard to try to break NATO's will to remain in the fight.

We had never had adequate forces in the south so that in much of the region the mixture of criminals and insurgents had been relatively undisturbed. Clearly they were going to be disturbed as thousands of additional British, Canadian, and Dutch forces arrived. The Taliban were no fools. They could be expected to strike hard before NATO could become well established on the ground. The Afghan administration was still very weak, and few Afghan forces would be available to support the allies.

Finally, there was a widespread Afghan perception that the United States was preparing to withdraw and leave the fight to NATO/ISAF. This perception had been reinforced by Washington's decision, against our advice, in December 2005 to reduce U.S. combat forces in the south from three to two battalions. We believed, based on both intelligence and logic, that the insurgents would see ISAF's expansion and the U.S. contraction as the moment to rekindle the war.

General Eikenberry was taking what measures he could to mitigate these problems, reinforcing ISAF with available U.S. conventional and special forces drawn from Regional Command East. In the end he was able to prevent the withdrawal of one additional battalion from Zabul Province, and this was added to ISAF's area. However, these actions would not be enough to prevent a Taliban offensive, nor would they be visible enough to remove the public perception of weakness.

The intelligence community was paying some attention to the reports. At the end of February, Lt. Gen. Michael Maples, the director of the Defense Intelligence Agency (DIA), testified to Congress that the insurgency was growing and would intensify in the spring.[2] Both General Eikenberry and I continued to use every channel available to us to alert Washington to what was coming. In doing so we had several purposes. First was the simple professional responsibility to report our best judgment of the situation. Second, I wanted to avoid surprise. The administration and the public needed to be braced as far as possible so that surprise would not lead to political panic. If people understood that we were experiencing something that we had predicted and in some measure were dealing with, we would be more likely to maintain support in a tough time. Finally, I wanted Washington to agree to supply additional troops and money early to position us better to confront the expected Taliban offensive. General Eikenberry and I both used public statements and briefings of senior officials to get our message out.

President Bush Comes to Town, but Riots and Issues Continue

President Bush's first visit to Kabul gave us an opportunity to be heard. I was informed of the visit by secure telephone two weeks before, but only a tiny handful of people in the embassy were allowed in on the secret per explicit White House orders. Many of the preparations fell on the military. The large base at Bagram could hide more preparations than the embassy could.

The logistics of a five-hour visit were minutely scripted, often by me and National Security Adviser Hadley directly when the DCM, the only other embassy officer authorized to handle the matter, couldn't get agreement. The White House agreed to have the president dedicate our new embassy chancery as a highly visible symbol to the Afghans of our determination to remain strongly engaged. The most difficult aspect was arranging a lunch. The White House wanted a standard, fast drop-in, including a meeting with President Karzai, a press conference, the embassy dedication, and a speech to our troops.

I had to explain that in Afghan culture refusing the hospitality of a meal would be a major insult to President Karzai and, through him, the Afghan people. It was not important that President Bush eat, but he had to sit at the table. Getting this across took a special call to Hadley. What I didn't tell Hadley was that I knew Karzai would insist on enlarging the Afghan guest list. I reckoned Karzai would make that point in his meeting, and Bush would accept. That is what happened, and Bush gracefully went along.

The White House advance team insisted on secrecy. Although the tour of the embassy grounds attracted the attention of some of our senior staff members who knew the president would be traveling in the region, we avoided questions and everyone pretended to know nothing.

Even so everything was tightly controlled. As instructed I officially told President Karzai of the visit only the night before, although I had given him earlier hints that he well understood to make sure that he would be available. Only on the morning of the visit were our security people allowed to brief Karzai's security people.

While all these preparations were going on, we had plenty of other business. I was called to the palace with two hours' notice to be present when the king, Zahir Shah, presented medals to two departing Americans. The event was slightly surrealistic with the old and now powerless king sitting in a room designed in eighteenth-century fashion, a ramrod stiff officer behind his chair, the sweet but ninety-year-old and very deaf king speaking in a whispery voice, and translations bellowed back and forth in French and Dari.

There were numerous meetings with the UN secretary general's special representative and new head of UNAMA, Tom Koenig, who had replaced Jean Arnault and was trying to arrange the composition of the Joint Coordination and Monitoring Board agreed to in London. Every country seemed to share two points of view: the group should be small and they should be on it. Various ambassadors came on short notice for "urgent" meetings to press their country's case for inclusion; I was happy to let Washington take the heat for this.

And in the midst of all this we had a riot in the major prison outside

Kabul. Although it was mostly an Afghan affair, Americans were also serving time in the jail for having run an illegal prison and torturing prisoners. Two of the American prisoners had managed, through bribery, to obtain weapons, and were actually running an Internet site, on which they posted reporting that politicized the riot. The reporting on this website had the potential to set off trouble elsewhere in the country. In fact, Afghan prisoners had seized much of the prison and were holding some Afghan guards as hostages. The early reports were confusing, but by the second day we learned that the Afghan army might attack to settle the matter. We had visions of a bloodbath right before President Bush landed. A still bigger concern was that a large number of Taliban prisoners might escape and rejoin the insurgency. I wanted to head off an attack but not at the risk of a mass escape.

Under cover of checking on the well-being of the American prisoners, I sent the defense attaché, Col. Mike Norton, and Consul Adrianne Harchick to scout the situation, a somewhat risky task but one that they accomplished with prudence and efficiency accompanied by our assistant security officer and a considerable security detail. They reported that the Afghan army had a very secure perimeter around the prison. Knowing a breakout was unlikely, I was free to weigh in strongly against an attack. The matter was settled peacefully shortly thereafter, and the Afghan government closed down the illegal Internet connection from the prison.

Notwithstanding riots and visit preparations, we showed up at a three-day Afghan government seminar on national security strategy, continued to struggle with how to reprogram the USAID budget, and were deeply engaged in preparations for poppy eradication (discussed below). Finally, the day before the president arrived we had a visit from the secretary of commerce. Normally a cabinet visit is a big deal for an embassy and involves most of the mission's resources. For us it had to be a minor blip on the radar. Somehow we found the resources for site preparation, briefing papers, note takers, and security escorts. The secretary spent the night at my residence and flew out the next morning unaware that his boss was landing a few hours later. Fortunately he left just before the embassy started sprouting a grandstand and flags in front of the chancery in the morning.

Only at 9:00 that morning did I inform the full senior staff of the embassy dedication. Many knew from the news that the president was in the region. I told them that anyone who didn't understand what I was really saying didn't deserve to be in a senior position. There were grins all around the table, but I could still report with a straight face that I had not said the president was coming. At 11:00 we told the rest of the embassy that we were dedicating the embassy at 3:00, and they were ordered to cancel any conflicting meetings and show up.

I flew out to Bagram with General Eikenberry. Our only chance to brief the president would be in transit, so we wanted again to review our script of main points. The helicopter crew was new and had forgotten to bring radio headsets for the passenger compartment. It was impossible to talk over the noise of the rotor blades and engines, so we were reduced to writing notes to pass each other through an aide who gripped them firmly to keep the wind from blowing them away in the air blast from the open gun ports. All the main points came out right, including forceful warnings of what the summer fighting would look like and what we needed.

President Bush had brought with him a full delegation, including Secretary Rice, National Security Adviser Hadley, Mrs. Bush, Chief of Staff Andrew Card, and bunches of others. The president had long wanted to see Afghanistan. As we flew over mud-walled compounds to Kabul in the clear March day, we had views of snowcapped mountains behind brown plains. The president was intent on the scenery, so it was a good thing we had reduced our briefing to the essentials, but he did pay attention.

We landed in a flurry of dust in a grassy field and hurried to cars for the short drive into the palace grounds. We were met by an honor guard turned out in brown overcoats and hats that looked patterned after the old German army, and perhaps they were, since the Germans helped create the first modern Afghan army before World War II. A short private meeting was followed by lunch in the king's dining room (which was more elegant, Karzai felt, than his own). Dark walls in a French style set off the polished wood table covered with platters of Afghan food, including the delicious *kabuli palau* of brown rice, raisins, cinnamon, and tiny strips of sweet carrots all heaped over large chunks of lamb.

The conversation was light, but the president managed to work in all the themes we wanted: our plan to support NATO and not leave, the need for strong counternarcotics policy, support for girls' education, and the example a democratic Afghanistan could be to the region. They were all familiar themes, but it was important that he said them. Mrs. Bush ate separately with Mrs. Karzai and a women's group. We had made sure that the Secret Service had women agents so that we would not have to insert men into the women's quarters.

After lunch and a short press conference, we dashed down the street to the embassy. The new chancery had rather strange mustard-yellow paint. As we pulled in Bush gazed on it and asked, "Who picked that baby-shit yellow?" His description was all too apt. With a straight face I replied, "Sir, Secretary Rice owns that building."

We held inside the embassy for a few minutes in order to allow President Karzai to arrive with the foreign minister and others. Dedicating the embassy was going to be as high-profile and symbolic an event as we could make it. Much of the staff had suspected that the president might show up, but when he was joined by his wife, Secretary Rice, and President Karzai, the applause was thunderous. In my introductory remarks I made reference to my father, who had dedicated the old embassy. In his speech Bush quipped that he thought it was just fine for a son to follow his father, a reference to his own father that brought down the house. More importantly, he stressed America's determination to remain strong in Afghanistan. He was gracious in thanking our Afghan and third-country-national employees for their service. The ribbon was cut, and Bush and the senior Americans worked the rope line. Then it was back to the helicopters and Bagram for a meeting with troops, and then they left. We were on schedule. All was well.

Coming back we had helicopter problems, and General Eikenberry and I ended up having an unplanned dinner at Bagram and a late-night flight back. At least everything that went wrong happened after the official party was airborne.

Security Worsens: Is NATO Ready?

If the visit was good, the security situation was not. The signs of impending large-scale fighting were increasing and a prolonged debate in the Dutch parliament over the decision to deploy troops added to Afghan worries and doubts about the willingness of Dutch troops to fight once they arrived. NATO and U.S. officers assured me that while the deployment decision was contested, there was no reason to worry about the political will to fight once the Dutch troops arrived. I hoped this was true, but there was no way to assuage Afghan doubts until they could see a more determined reality.

In fact, both Eikenberry and I were concerned that not enough NATO troops would show up. We thought that the British, Canadian, and Dutch battalions would perform well but were not convinced that this would be true of Romanians, whose will to fight was not matched by adequate equipment. Their armored personnel vehicles were not suitable for extensive off-road movement in the Afghan countryside. They were not bringing artillery support, and they had no interoperable communications with the American forces they would have to call on for fire support or medical evacuation. In the end, a U.S. element was added to provide communications and one extra U.S. infantry battalion, previously slated for withdrawal, was retained in the south.

In mid-March, I was back in the United States and made more public my expectations of coming trouble. In a March 21 speech at Georgetown University, I said that despite progress, violence in Afghanistan would get worse before it got better. I gave the same reasons for my analysis that I had conveyed in my reporting. This will "be an extremely bloody year." NATO forces would push into areas not previously under government control, and this would increase combat. The perception of NATO weakness would embolden the insurgents. So would drug eradication, and I pointed out that our drug efforts had to be balanced with an increased effort to develop the entire rural economy of Afghanistan, not with simple crop substitution.[3] I had briefed Washington officials on what I intended to say and found no resistance to my public comments. But neither did this seem to produce any conversations about the need for much greater resources for the war.

Drug Policy Dominates Policy Debate
Instead, Washington was much more focused on the counterdrug campaign. In 2005 opium poppy production had begun to surge. In early

2006 we had analyzed the problem and realized that almost every element of the strategy had failed but that the failure had been in implementation rather than conceptualization. Afghan government policy decisions had been made late in the previous poppy-growing cycle and our decisions were late as well, as I told one newspaper.[4] Our funds and equipment had been late in getting to the field, so that while we had pressed for more eradication by local governors we were able neither to assist with equipment like tractors nor to repay penniless governors for tractor rental. Public information efforts had been weak, and many farmers who had refrained from growing poppy felt that promises of economic assistance had not been kept. In short, with such a dismal record of operational performance, it was at least premature and possibly wrong to say that the strategy itself was at fault.

We believed that the basics were sound but that there needed to be a renewed effort of implementation. Washington accepted this, and new resources were coming into the country, although slowly. We would be in better shape for eradication, but as we had warned in our failed appeal for a supplemental, we were not going to be making all the efforts in agricultural development that we should. We warned also that many farmers would likely see the previous poor performance in eradication as reducing the risk of eradication in 2006, so more farmers would choose to grow poppy. The Afghan government was making the right policy noises at the top but not communicating much of anything to the countryside. We proposed to create special communication units with foreign and Afghan staff to help but were aware that staffing and mobilizing this effort would be difficult, and we would be able to operate in only a few provinces—far less than the countrywide effort needed.

The full drug strategy involved multiple parallel efforts, often referred to as "pillars." These included developing an efficient police force to arrest drug traffickers, creating a special judicial system to get major cases out of the corrupt local courts and make conviction more likely, going after higher-level traffickers, and continuing efforts at eradication, agricultural development, and public information. The problem was that most of these elements take years to bear fruit.

The Drug Enforcement Administration was training an Afghan force to go after higher-level drug dealers, but everything had to be built from scratch. Even in America, building legal cases against high-level dealers can take years, and Afghanistan was only starting to draft some of the necessary laws for wiretaps, to train the investigators, and to build the prosecutorial system. Afghans with DEA support were busting heroin labs, but we were several years away from delivery of the helicopters needed to support the force, and meanwhile military helicopters were already in short supply.

The State Department was building a national-level eradication force, but not all its equipment had been delivered and additional aircraft to support the operation were only starting to arrive in country with the necessary expanded contractor support. New facilities had to be built to station the new helicopters and planes, and agreement on location was still being worked out with the military.

A new court system had been enacted but was less than a year old. Judges were beginning to hand down convictions, but the court lacked its own buildings or protection for the judges and key witnesses.

Simple crop substitution would fail unless new crops could get to markets, and we lacked the roads as well as the packing and wholesaling facilities and access to outside markets, all of which had yet to be built. At one point in May, I was told that Secretary Rice had seen a telegram about counternarcotics success in part of Pakistan and wondered if we couldn't use the same ideas. The cable noted that a critical factor was the building of four hundred kilometers of roads in two frontier agencies of Pakistan. I asked my staff to calculate the density of these roads to land area in the two agencies and tell me what it would mean for Afghanistan. The answer: 72,225 kilometers of new roads. I passed the figure back to Assistant Secretary for South Central Asian Affairs Richard Boucher, who enjoyed it.[5] In fact, the calculation was an illustration of what was needed for agricultural success to counter poppy: nothing less than the building of an entire Afghan rural economy would work. This would take years, even if we were not deprived of the proper funding.

So progress would take time, and meanwhile poppy production was expanding every season to the vast discomfort of the administration and Congress, which were both pressing for faster eradication. Congress had already placed restrictions on the use of economic development funds unless the administration certified that national and local Afghan authorities were fully cooperating with eradication. There was a provision for a waiver that the administration was forced to use, but the congressional pressure to increase restrictions was real. Both our war-fighting and development efforts could be endangered if we did not make enough progress to keep these restrictions from being triggered.

Some scholars and military officers argued that we should avoid eradication until we had managed far more development. They believed that eradication would alienate farmers whose livelihood was being destroyed and push more support to the insurgency.

I thought this argument deficient on several grounds. First, the main drug support for the insurgency came from large drug barons and tribal and militia leaders who were making fabulous profits. They wanted to protect their illicit income and cared little whether the farmers were better provided for, so development would make little difference to their opposition to drug control and the expansion of Afghan governmental authority.

Second, the money from drugs fueled enormous corruption and provided funding for the insurgents.[6] This illicit flow would continue to rot any effort at building an efficient government far faster than we or the Afghans could possibly build. To try to fight and develop while ignoring drugs would be to construct an unsustainable isometric exercise in futility.

And finally, the argument to wait simply ignored the foreign, especially American, political realities of pressure to contain drug production. We had to make enough progress in eradication to contain our own political pressures and keep our drug and counterinsurgency strategies from coming into direct conflict, a danger against which I had warned President Bush in our first meeting.

But while we could not do without eradication, making it work and not conflict with military operations was also going to be difficult. Afghans high and low counseled against aerial eradication. Years of merciless Soviet bombing of civilians and destruction of their farms and villages had created an intense Afghan resistance to anything that looked like aerial eradication. The risks of major increases in support for the insurgency were too great. I also felt that to substitute foreign for local judgment on such an issue was the kind of arrogance that had landed us in big trouble in more than one war already.

So eradication would have to be done by manually. In most provinces this required getting the local governor to take the matter in hand. There would be problems of corruption and great pressure from President Karzai on down would be necessary. In a few areas where the insurgents were strong, we would have to bring in the national Afghan Eradication Force (AEF) to supplement the governor's effort and might need military protection and backup.

In February, I visited the AEF camp near Kabul International Airport. They would shortly face their greatest test to date. Mick Hogan, an ex–Special Forces soldier in charge of the unit, seemed to have a real gift for training and leadership, an impression constantly reinforced in operations over the next two years. New equipment had arrived and the unit was practicing how to rapidly load its numerous trucks with everything from tractors to camp equipment to deploy several hundred men anywhere in the country. The Afghan leadership seemed a touch weak, and complaints about the quality of their rifles sounded like excuses. After checking with Hogan about the issue, I told the commander that when I was being shot at by similar weapons in Vietnam they worked fine, so he should spend more time cleaning the AKs than complaining about them.

One bizarre feature of U.S. policy was that because the AEF was classified as police, we were not then allowed to provide them with weapons heavier than rifles. Since they could end up in a sizable fight, we had to pay for contract Gurkhas to man machine guns. Despite the problems, planning for a major AEF deployment to Helmand was well on track, and the force was already deep into examining target areas and bivouac locations. Our operations were being closely coordinated with the British both because they were still the lead nation for counternarcotics and because we would have to operate closely with British forces in Helmand.

As we tried to work our way to sensible solutions, Washington constantly hammered us for more information and progress reports. My small drug office was getting so many e-mail requests for information, often redundantly from different sources, that in February 2006 I had to insist that my staff use my name to refuse requests unless they came through my office, if meeting the request was getting in the way of actual operations. I did not want to restrict information, but the time devoted to this had to be controlled or we would do nothing else. This produced some resentment at Washington working levels but helped control the problem.

Afghanistan was not a place for those who like to pursue policies in neatly separated intellectual boxes. One goal was imprisoning drug traffickers. Another was supporting President Karzai. In late April 2006, I had to walk a fine line to balance the two. Karzai had talked to me about tribal pressure he was under for the release of Haji Bashir Noorzai, a leader of the Noorzai tribe awaiting trial in the United States on multiple drug charges. Catching him in a sting operation had been one of DEA's major successes before I arrived. On April 27 the palace called to ask me to meet with tribal leaders from three southern provinces. Before the meeting President Karzai called to say whatever I did I should avoid a flat turndown.

I went with Doug Wankel, my ex-DEA drug chief who had long experience in Afghanistan. We met the elders in a long building on the palace grounds, old in style with a series of domes each held on four intersecting arches. White and unadorned, the hall held over a hundred tribal figures at a table that seemed to stretch to where I could barely make out the rugged faces in the distance. I was accompanied only by Doug, the palace protocol chief, and my translator.

Several spoke. They included tribal leaders, members of Parliament, the Kandahar Provincial Council (Karzai's home base), and even one businessman with investments in California. They never claimed that their compatriot was innocent. Rather they spoke of the years of war, how many people had committed many crimes but we were reconciling former Taliban so why couldn't we show mercy and release this person. Noorzai had great influence in his tribe, and they promised that if released he would use his influence to stop drug smuggling and fight insurgents. The cultural clash was fascinating. Westerners live in a world of hard and fast rules. The case was in the courts and must run its course. The Afghans lived in a world where justice is corrupt, the will of the victor counts for everything, and talking of rules would sound like making excuses, which could be refused.

I tried to frame my answer in Afghan style. There were issues of dignity and form to consider, so the answer was long. Giving only the essence of my argument would have seemed harsh and abrupt to the Afghans. I talked about my feelings for Kandahar and my visits there years ago, about seeing Afghanistan first through my father's eyes, and about how drug money would rot the new Afghanistan. I told my audience a bit about the case and how evidence would be presented in open court. I said I understood the importance of what they were telling me and that I would report carefully what they told me. By prearrangement with Doug, I concluded that if the prisoner would actually work against drugs, it might be possible to do something. It went off reasonably well. Nothing was resolved, but neither was there a crisis or a breakdown in support for Karzai from a key tribe.

By March the poppy was ripening in many areas and eradication was in force in many provinces. This time we had money to reimburse governors for tractor rental and fuel but lacked either banking or Afghan government mechanisms to move the money. Doug Wankel had to fly around the country with bags of dollars to make payments; sometimes he carried well over $100,000 a trip. To maintain accountability we insisted on paying against receipts, a new concept in Afghanistan, where neither the governors nor the tractor owners had ever seen paper receipts or had any idea why we wanted these strange records. Sometimes we had to refuse payment until receipts were produced. Then the governor would run out of money, and eradication would stop until the problem could be solved. Everything had to be done locally, so Doug, his small staff, and the equally small State staff of the Bureau of International Narcotics and Law Enforcement (INL) would grab weapons, don body armor, and head off once again to resolve the problem.[7] Generally they succeeded, but it was hard and frustrating work. We depended on UN-run efforts to validate the governors' figures of acreage eradicated.

Fraud was a constant problem. The governors lacked the force to eradicate against strong resistance, so there was constant negotiation with villages to allow eradication to proceed. Wealthy farmers made payoffs to avoid having their fields cut, and this built resentment from the poorer farmers whose crops were destroyed. In 2005 many such complaints were documented and aerial photography showed some areas in which the patterns of eradication could be explained only by corruption. We did what we could to reduce the problem, but so long as we had to proceed through "negotiated eradication," corruption would be an issue, and we lacked the force to operate any other way.

Trying to Coordinate War and Eradication

The end of February reduced our military operations somewhat as the troops and headquarters of the 173rd Airborne were replaced by a brigade of the Tenth Mountain Division commanded by Maj. Gen. Benjamin Freakley. The large forces in Iraq (roughly five times larger than the U.S. forces in Afghanistan) were able to rotate units and still maintain an intensive operational tempo, but with the much smaller numbers deployed in Afghanistan, major troop rotations inevitably caused a loss of momentum no matter how carefully the commanders planned. Freakley's headquarters, under General Eikenberry's overall command, included troops from the UK, Canada, Australia, New Zealand, Holland, the French Special Forces, and others.

On February 21, I flew to Bagram for the change of command. The day was beautiful and sunny, but it was still winter and I remained wrapped in my overcoat in the cold hangar where the ceremony was held. Defense Minister Abdul Rahim Wardak made an elegant speech full of gratitude to the troops for having come to his "poor and rocky land" and promising that someday Afghanistan would not only stand on its own but would repay America's help by sending Afghan forces to help with peacekeeping in other states. General Wardak is a large man who proudly wears the insignia of U.S. ranger and airborne training, which he earned in his younger and thinner days. He is an eloquent speaker in English, Dari, and Pushtu.

General Freakley would soon be heavily involved with us in eradication planning. In Helmand we would have to send the AEF to back up the governor's efforts. The fighting could get so heavy that regular military forces would be needed for support. Therefore they had to be involved in the planning from the beginning. General Eikenberry accepted the essential backup role of coalition forces. The need for extensive planning brought about the first time the Afghan Ministries of

Defense, Interior, and Counternarcotics cooperated in joint operational planning with coalition forces and the AEF. Our police and military training command, under Maj. Gen. Bob Durbin, were of enormous help in this effort since the Afghans still lacked the staff structures to bring willingness together with planning capacity.

At the same time, the heavy injection of our military colleagues into the operation brought many new perspectives and some disputes. From our perspective, the lack of Afghan capacity meant that we had to walk individual governors as well as ministers through a lot of complicated coordination. Karl Eikenberry and I never did completely agree on the optimum staff structures, but we did agree on all essential points for the operation while maintaining cordial personal relations, and that is what counted. Strong-willed people, including both our senior staffs and ourselves, will never see every issue identically, but it is imperative to keep the disputes professional and to solve the operational problems effectively. I believe we did that, then and later.

Eradication in other parts of the country was going reasonably well despite all the hiccups. Helmand would be the big test. That was where poppy cultivation was the heaviest, governance the weakest, and the threat the most severe. In mid-March, after several last-minute delays, the AEF deployed to Helmand. On March 12, I flew to Helmand to get a sense of the operation.

Helmand's former governor had been replaced after intensive international pressure. His successor, Mohammad Daoud, was making a serious effort to upgrade administration but was seriously hampered by the lack of adequate numbers of police. The police chief at the time was corrupt, politically well connected, and allied to the previous governor. It would be several months before the police reform process brought about his removal, so Governor Daoud had to work with him. Daoud knew as well as we did that by trying to bring legitimate government into the area we would stir things up. The comparative quiet was the result of the lawless mix of drug traffickers, criminals, and Taliban being left undisturbed except for the disruptive tribal maneuvering of the previous governor.

The British were preparing to take over the PRT and the military role in the province and were legitimately concerned that these changes would provoke conflict just as they arrived. I felt we had no choice. Another year of expanding drug activity and Taliban control was not going to make things easier.

I arrived at a time of serious disagreement between the governor and our people. Daoud wanted to let the deputy governor and police chief start cutting poppy in the far south of the province along the Helmand River and work north to meet the AEF in central Helmand. The poppy in the south was comparatively light, however, and our people and the AEF wanted to concentrate in the center and south of the provincial capital of Lashkar-Gah, where the growth was heavier.

Daoud was concerned that if the AEF started eradication without the deputy governor present, we would increase local resistance, and he wanted us to wait until the local southern force joined with ours. We did not want to wait, partly because we didn't want to lose time and also because, after all the expense of organizing the AEF, we would face serious congressional criticism if the force was not employed. From an efficiency standpoint our people were correct. However, there was value in showing government authority in the virtually lawless south: we needed to balance our eradication goal with our objective of building Afghan government authority. In the end, we found a compromise. Part of the AEF would move farther south and one of Daoud's people would join the force to interact with the locals. All parties seemed satisfied.

Later on there were probably correct charges that serious corruption in selecting which fields to eradicate had marred the southern operations of the deputy governor and police. Whether we would have been better off to insist on a foreign-prescribed solution I do not know. In such situations one has to make what seems the best call and move on. There was no time to wait for perfect information.

I flew over miles of poppy down to the AEF base camp. Touring the base I was proudly shown an unexploded rocket that had missed and landed just outside the perimeter the previous night. There had been a few other small shooting incidents. The Afghan commander of the AEF was hesitant to split his force as my compromise with Governor Daoud required. The commander insisted this division would weaken him too much to withstand a massive attack. On the basis of our intelligence and my own instinct, I believed the threat was limited to mines and harassing fire, not a large ground attack, so I pressed hard for and got agreement to the move. Our mentors, with a strong Special Forces background, were comfortable with my call and the move went ahead later.

While in Lashkar-Gah, I went to the opening of a "stone road" we were building as an experiment. Stone roads had been successfully constructed in Bolivia using smooth riverbed rock and mostly hand tools. The result was much cheaper than asphalt, used much more local labor, and was supposed to be capable of handling loaded trucks at speeds up to thirty miles an hour. I wanted to drive on the road and see if it shook my back teeth as I feared. In fact, I was impressed by the smoothness of the ride on the short trial strip. The Bolivians we had brought in to teach the new skill were getting along in a mixture of Spanish, English, Pushtu, and sign language. All the villagers working on the project seemed very proud of their work as well as content with the new income. Later we were to build hundreds of miles of these stone "farm to market" roads in other parts of the country to stretch our dollars and increase the use of local labor. Afghans really want paved roads and the stone roads are sometimes criticized, but without maintenance pavement will deteriorate until eventually the highway is worse than a dirt road. Until the Afghan government has sufficient resources to handle all its maintenance problems, stone roads make sense in low traffic areas because the villagers can repair them with minimal government support.

The short ceremony to open the trial stretch of road was held in the shadow of the ruins of the old castle of Qala-e-Bost at the confluence of the Helmand and Argandab rivers. I guess ambassadors are supposed to be either too decrepit or too dignified to walk, so there seemed to be some surprise when I climbed rapidly up the small hill to look at the view and the ruins. I remembered walking there with my wife years earlier when she had found an ancient coin on the top. I also had good talks with the USAID and State officers in the PRT, the fourteenth I had visited.

Countering an Offensive

The security situation continued to be difficult, especially in the south. There was one serious fight in Helmand, but it was beaten back and eradication continued. What was striking to me was that the attack by Taliban forces seemed to have been without any special new support from local farmers; we still seemed to be avoiding a major backlash from the eradication.

Fighting was picking up in the old Taliban core area of Kandahar Province. In the eastern provinces, U.S. troops had the situation fairly well contained but were stretched too far to add much to civilian security. A traditional infiltration corridor from Pakistan through the mountainous province of Nuristan was wide open because there were no troops to send. Between U.S. forces in the east and the arriving British and Canadian troops in the south, we had a largely unpatrolled border except for small detachments. Stories of infiltration were picking up.

We were doing what we could. In mid-winter we had started a province-by-province review to devise actions to improve our position in six provinces we considered most under threat from the anticipated spring offensive. The meetings included the coalition command, the UN and EU, the ambassadors of the countries with major forces in the south, the Afghan security chief, and the ministers of defense, interior, and some others as well as me or my DCM. The Afghan national security chief, Dr. Zalmai Rasoul, chaired the meetings. Our focus was strictly short term: actions we could take to strengthen the government before fighting picked up.

There was an interesting dynamic to the meeting. The Afghans were making progress in planning and working together but were still politely hesitant to ask directly for what they needed from the foreigners. The diplomats would often talk up to the edge of a plan but were reluctant to pronounce on military subjects. The military had senior officers present but not the top commanders, and while they would frequently put forward ideas or plans if they were asked, they were hesitant to speak to the political issues and were properly cautious about proposing military solutions to problems that often needed politics and aid as much as force. In short, everyone was a little hampered by working outside their comfort zone. For whatever reasons of background (military, more war experience) or hubris, I was reasonably comfortable on both sides of the equation. Thus I often found my role was not so much to lead as to be a catalyst to bring together into proposals the pieces and ideas that others were putting forth. Also, as the United States was the largest aid donor, I had special leverage. I tried to be careful to put forward ideas for discussion and not to give orders. It struck me that with the retirement of the Vietnam generation, we have few senior officers in our diplomatic service who have seen combat and are comfortable making military judgments.

We accomplished a few things. We were able to get a few poorly performing police commanders moved, some police reinforcements were sent to bad areas, and we scratched up some money for a few projects. The main problem was that, without more force, with the Afghan army still building, and with most of the new military and police equipment still waiting on delivery or even manufacture, what we could actually do was less than we knew we needed to strengthen the government for the coming fight.

The lack of civilian personnel was as bothersome as the limitations on force. In early May the commander of the U.S. Central Command (CENTCOM), Gen. John Abizaid, was visibly disappointed on a visit to Jalalabad by a long gap in staffing of our one embassy officer with the PRT. I wrote him to explain that with only one officer per PRT, usually assigned eight to twelve months in advance, we had been gapped by a combination of illness and the resignation of one officer from the Foreign Service. We had created new PRTs and political officer positions with the regional commands at the military's request, but the personnel system could not find and forward new officers to keep up with even the handful of additional new positions. The result was triage; Washington sent State and USAID officers where they were most needed and left other positions empty. It was not a satisfactory response, but I wanted him to know we were trying our best with what we could get Washington to give us. John wrote back in an unclassified e-mail, "I do not believe you or your great folks on the ground are at fault. . . . My concern is that the Government of the United States needs to be in the field to its full capacity everywhere if we expect to win this war. That we have fallen short for nearly five years is a disgrace."[8]

I could only agree. The problem was not just the State Department but the lack of civilians from the Departments of Justice, Agriculture, and others. To mobilize the needed resources, the administration needed to put the country on a war footing, not only by ordering other cabinet departments to participate but by finding the funding for them to do so. That was not happening.

The Afghan pace was also slow, not through intent but because they had few qualified people to work on the problems. Often the best ministers had only a handful of qualified subordinates. The war years had killed or driven out much of the old, educated bureaucratic elite and destroyed the educational system so that few qualified graduates were produced to fill the gap. The ministers frequently had to be their own staffs and action officers, and they still had the rest of their business to attend to. They tried. We tried. The results were not impressive. We would have to work with what we had.

There were some creative actions. The campaign plan that Generals Eikenberry and Freakley devised involved a series of operations. In May they delayed the departure of one Marine battalion to provide the extra force for Operation Mountain Lion, an attack into Nuristan Province to contest what had been an open infiltration route for three years. Civilian projects with military and some USAID funding and medical teams would begin immediately after the operations, although there would be few Afghan forces available to hold what we took and only a few road projects would have long-term impact.

After Mountain Lion, forces were quickly shifted south for Operation Mountain Thrust in Kandahar, Uruzgan, and Helmand provinces. ISAF cooperated with blocking forces in Farah to the west. There was no way with the small numbers of Afghan forces available that we would really be able to stabilize the area, but the operation did disrupt the Taliban offensive somewhat and bought time and space for the beginning of the NATO deployment.

Operation Mountain Fury later in the year pushed down into Ghazni Province in east-central Afghanistan, where conditions had steadily deteriorated since my last visit. Each new operation required shifting troops from other areas and then often returning them. It was creative. It made gains. In May 2006 an editorial in the *Washington Post* referred to "a crucial battle for control of the south."[9] We were not losing, but neither were we able to build on what we took or make Afghans feel safer. The problem was not the strategy, which I thought made brilliant use of what assets we had, but the lack of sufficient forces and qualified Afghans to follow up successful actions and lock in our gains. I wished devoutly that Defense had not withdrawn one battalion in December.

In late May a sharp fight in Kandahar Province resulted in a number of civilians killed by our bombing. This had happened before and would again. It was a constant worry for Karzai, who saw clearly the potential for losing civilian support. In some cases the reports of civilian deaths were the result of agile Taliban propaganda and efforts to contact reporters who would print before verifying. In this case, however, the causalities were real and probably unavoidable since the bombs were dropped in direct support of troops that had been attacked while on patrol. We expended a good bit of effort to calm the matter. President Karzai went to Kandahar on May 25 on short notice to meet with tribal elders and see some of the civilians in the hospital. He came back somewhat reassured. The civilians had told him that under the circumstances the strike was the right thing to do. Yet mounting civilian deaths were one more sign of problems.

So too was infiltration across the Pakistani border. To get a sense of the border situation, I visited the remote border outpost of Shkin. We flew down at night to avoid being a target. It was my first experience flying with night-vision goggles, gazing out at a weird but detailed green landscape. The post was often shelled, although it was within eyesight of a Pakistani border post. I was told that the actions of the Pakistani forces varied greatly depending on the Pakistani commander of the moment. Some would engage insurgents trying to cross the border. Others would do nothing: they would fail to alert the Americans or even answer radio calls. It sounded to me more like disorganization than deliberate policy. Nobody fired at us, and I returned the next night more aware than ever of how insecure the border was.

On May 14 we had trouble on the western border when one of our border trainers was killed in an attack in Herat City. FBI agents subsequently fired on a civilian car that appeared to be trying to ram into the guards protecting the site of the first attack. We were able to calm the inhabitants with rapid apologies and payments, but the new threat level forced us to suspend the regular trips to the border to work with the Afghan customs post.

Trying to Solve Police Problems

All the security problems were making President Karzai suitably un-happy. By May he was extremely concerned for security, especially in the south. We were trying various ideas but not achieving security for normal Afghans in their villages in the south and parts of the east. Karzai felt popular support slipping because his government could not respond to the delegations of worried Afghan tribal leaders that beat a regular path to his door. The international community was pressing him to take more actions to make government effective: firing poor perform-ers, promoting officials on merit alone, moving some of the ignorant and conservative judges out, and so on. President Karzai was never ea-ger to risk removing his political supporters from influential positions, but with a declining security situation and the government looking and feeling increasingly weak, he was doubly reluctant to accede to our pressure. Security was trumping everything else in his consideration.

In meetings in March and mid-May he repeatedly raised the ideas of rearming tribal forces to contest the Taliban and its allies operating in the east.[10] Many Afghans looked to the nineteenth and early twenti-eth centuries, when tribal forces were a major element in national de-fense, and pressed the same idea on us. We resisted this approach. On this General Eikenberry and I agreed, as did all the ambassadors of allied states and the UN and EU chiefs.

The great tribes of old had been fractured by the years of fighting. Militia commanders had displaced tribal leaders. While these leaders each had a tribal base, they were not the undisputed tribal leaders of old. The groups had many rivalries and were marked by changing sides, betrayals, and undermining rivals as well as being frequently rapacious and lawless. Their inability to unite had plunged the country into civil war among the commanders after the Communists were defeated. The resulting chaos helped lead to the growth of the Taliban and its initial popular appeal. Even if militia forces backed up by coalition troops and air strikes could win local victories, we would only be strengthening forces inimical to central government. We would be reversing all progress made since the Bonn agreement in developing a state. Local victory in this way would be meaningless in the longer term. General Eikenberry and I recommended jointly against funding tribal militias as President Karzai requested.

The problem was that the police who should have filled the gap could not. Initially Germany had been the lead nation charged with building the police and coordinating help from other states. The Germans built an officers academy and worked on a training syllabus but moved rather slowly and received no help from anyone else, including us. U.S. efforts at police training had begun only in early 2005 and were inadequate. The training began as short courses for individual policemen. This might have helped if we were working with a real national police force, but in fact this was not the case.

What we called the national police was largely a collection of local militia commands that had transformed themselves into "police" at the end of the war with the Taliban. They were heavily corrupt and loyal more to local leaders than any national command. Those we trained might well return to corrupt forces or simply be sent home while their commander collected their pay. We were training thousands but had no way of knowing how many were in the field since payrolls bore no relationship to real force levels. We hoped to get on top of this through a gradual program of reform from the top down that would replace local commanders with more qualified leaders. This would be a long process, although at the time we still did not understand how long.

In the meantime, the police were badly equipped with little ability to match the heavier weapons that confronted them. They had few vehicles and fewer radios. Early efforts to supply nonlethal equipment through military funds were halted in 2005, when it was pointed out that this use of the Commanders Emergency Relief Program (CERP) funds was prohibited by law.[11] An effort to transfer a measly $200 million from army to police equipment encountered six months of bureaucratic delay in the middle levels of the Pentagon and was finally broken loose only when I called the deputy secretary of defense, Gordon England, who resolved the internal problem within twenty-four hours. I mentally kicked myself for not having called him earlier.

Bureaucratic struggles between, on one hand, the military, which worried about the police surviving attacks, and, on the other hand, State civilians and German trainers, concerned that the civilian police force would become militarized, lasted months. There was some virtue on each side and none in their refusal to reach agreement. General

Eikenberry and I finally held a meeting with all our senior staff members to work out a reasonable practical compromise that sidestepped the arguments over principle. The police would get whatever defensive training was appropriate to the threats in their area but not be trained for offensive military actions. Some of our staff still grumbled, but at least they had all heard the same command direction and fell into line.

So gradually we were putting into place plans, programs, and schedules for improvement, but most of them were untested. And, in the meantime, what we didn't have was a functioning police force or any way to rapidly provide the increased security for which Afghan civilians were clamoring. It was no wonder that President Karzai was getting increasingly desperate in his search for answers.

In response to these concerns and the worsening situation, Maj. Gen. Bob Durbin, the commander in charge of the Combined Security Transition Command–Afghanistan (CSTC-A), and his Canadian deputy, Brig. Gen. Gary O'Brien, came up with new plans agreed to by our INL staff, which had policy responsibility for State Department police programs. The corrupt highway police, which had never been good for anything but extorting tolls, would be disbanded. The patrolmen would have a choice of losing their jobs or going as individual reinforcements to the provinces most threatened. If they quit we would have space in the authorized force levels to hire new police. There would also be a readjustment of province manning levels since, Durbin and O'Brien pointed out, the ratio of police to population was greatest in the provinces with the lowest threat. A new effort would be mounted to inventory the numbers of police actually present for duty. Police pay would also be raised to help with enlistments. Eikenberry and I liked the plan and agreed.

That was only a start. The Germans needed to agree. The plan needed to be briefed to the UN leadership. Fortunately all of the leaders agreed as did the Canadians and British, who were very interested parties. The new pay scales would put a strain on the Afghan budget, which was being pulled at from many angles. Finance Minister Ahadi was reluctant but eventually agreed after several high-level meetings, including a particularly important one with the German ambassador and myself. We still had to have the International Monetary Fund's agreement to the changes in the budget, but eventually it too agreed. We were into May before we had all the pieces in place. President Karzai, frustrated that we were so slow and happy that at least we had a direction, agreed to the plans. But while we had new direction, we were well into the fighting season of good weather and were little better off on the ground.

Could we have done better? With better foresight in 2002, certainly. By 2005 and 2006 we were dealing with entrenched plans, a variety of agencies and states, and no ready way to bring new funds or equipment rapidly to bear on the problems. We were realistic about what was not working but lacked models for solutions. The U.S. military had built armies in many countries. We knew how to do that. But to build a competent police force on the ruins of a destroyed country and in the middle of an escalating insurgency was new to all of us. The theories of police building that we had started with were inadequate. Trial and error had to guide us. The failure I saw in Iraq—training only low-level members of a corrupt force—helped me to understand similar problems faster in Afghanistan but provided no sure solutions, especially with far smaller resources than those in Iraq to work with. Reorganization is a slow process, and new lessons lay ahead of us. The full weakness of the police was about to hit like a thunderbolt.

Kabul Riots Destabilize the Capital

On the morning of May 29 a routine U.S. Army convoy of heavy trucks was on its way from Bagram to Kabul. As it traveled down an incline, one truck's brakes failed and it smashed into several civilian vehicles. A hostile crowd began demonstrating. Nervous gunners mistook the degree of threat and fired into the crowd. Unarmed civilians died. Massive rioting broke out throughout the city. Police units collapsed and deserted their posts. Some individual policemen joined the rioters.

By noon the conflict was heating up. I was finishing lunch on my patio and talking to the RSO who had come by to make sure I agreed to the use of lethal force if rioters entered the compound. As we were talking, firing began to increase not far away. We decided it was time to lock down the compound and concentrate our personnel. When the firing moved farther away we shifted two or three hundred of our people from exposed offices in containers to the lobby of the chancery.

I spent a couple of hours at the Marine post by the front door, where I could hear the radio reports from our lookouts and monitor the cameras mounted in various locations on our walls. I was able to see the traffic circle near the embassy. The crowd there seemed to ebb and flow in a rather aimless way but did not seem to grow beyond two to three hundred and made no concentrated effort to push past the defensive police positions and move on the embassy. I kept in touch with President Karzai throughout the afternoon by phone. Firing was breaking out all over town. I went out into the lobby periodically to tell our people what I knew and assure them that we would keep them safe. I sometimes roamed the halls to check on the staff and see how they were doing. Tactical control stayed with the RSO, but I wanted to be on hand in case the demonstration got ugly enough that we had to decide to kill in self-defense. Fortunately, it never reached that point.

The local police in our immediate area did well. Elsewhere their performance was poor, in part because they had neither the training nor equipment to deal with a riot. (The equipment was on order—not much help given the circumstances and another indication that our entrance into the police program came too late.) The police also lacked radios (those too were on order). The cell phone system broke down from being overloaded, and units were out of touch and unable to call for help or to assess the situation around them. The police units' isolation resulted in their breakdown.

One bright spot was the performance of the Afghan army. General Wardak put on his fatigues and showed up to take charge of the Afghan command center. His large command presence was stabilizing to the Afghans. He brought two brigades of Afghan troops into the city and set up forty checkpoints. The army gradually restored order. It is not correct, as some have alleged, that coalition and ISAF forces refused to leave their barracks.[12] They were on standby, ready to move, and rescued some EU diplomats, but General Wardak explicitly requested that they stay out of the fray. This was clearly a prudent decision. Foreign troops firing again on Afghan civilians would certainly have made the situation worse. As it was, things were bad enough.

Looting took place all over the city. Foreigners were attacked, and although none were badly hurt, there had been some close calls and some of their compounds were burned out. The international aid community wondered if they could continue operations. Numbers of Afghans were dead. Some of the mobs were reported to have chanted, "Down with Karzai!" Karzai himself was silent and off the air until he called for calm on television in the evening. The diplomatic community was deeply shaken. The public perception was of Afghan government weakness and chaos. In the afternoon when the situation had quieted, I drove to see President Karzai.

The government was in a flap. The advisers around Karzai were either enflaming a sense of conspiracy or not arguing against it. Rumors abounded that hostile forces had instigated the riots. Within a day many Pushtuns were blaming the trouble on Tajiks of the former National Alliance Party, claiming that either they had planned the riot or jumped in when it started to enflame it. I was skeptical of all this. Afghans frequently look to conspiracy as the cause of trouble. However, given the weaknesses in command and control of all the political groups and the speed with which the riot spread, I was more inclined to discount conspiracy theories in favor of an outpouring of pent-up anger over unemployment, accumulated grievances, and a sudden chance to loot. It seemed not too different in terms of causes from the Watts riots in 1965 in Los Angeles, which I had experienced as a teenager. Over succeeding days I continued to find evidence for conspiracy weak and unconvincing, but I probably never managed fully to convince President Karzai of this.

These were difficult days for President Karzai. He had no immediate resources of his own to throw at the problem. He was heavily dependent on foreign help and wondered increasingly if it would be adequate or fast enough to meet the need. He could have been more dynamic, but he had a weak hand to play. It took time, but his spirits revived and he regained control.

Our immediate task in the aftermath of the riots was to shore up President Karzai's morale, begin reorganizing the police, convince the rest of the world that the war wasn't lost, and proceed with the changeover of command to ISAF in the south. Drugs and money still bedeviled us. And if the major issues weren't enough, we had six members of Congress in town shortly after the riots and a second major congressional delegation a few days later. A joint State and military team arrived to start an inspection of the police. Yet in the midst of all this we went ahead with a long-planned festival of Afghan music and dance in the embassy compound that the staff had organized. We had a big crowd sitting on Afghan carpets in front of our main building. I joined it for some time before heading to an ISAF dinner. The diplomatic scene was still functioning despite riots and a 10:00 p.m. curfew.

Some might find these social events trivial or even inappropriate, as did our cohosts at another embassy, which had pulled out of our Valentine's Day dance after some of their personnel were killed in February. I sympathized, but after spending my adult life in an unstable world where I have lost friends and colleagues to violence, I have decided that life has to go on despite crises. Relaxation is important to cope with stress and to maintain clear judgment. So I enjoyed the singing and went off to dinner.

5

Afghan Institutions and Donor Cooperation

As we dealt with the aftermath of the riots, we were dealing also with funding challenges to U.S. development budgets, reorganization of the international donor strategy and the approach to rebuilding Afghanistan, the changeover of command to NATO/ISAF in the midst of the summer fighting, and a wide range of Afghan and bilateral U.S.-Afghan political developments. A major struggle over freedom of religion didn't make all this easier.

The International Development Dimension

The London conference established a new five-year strategy and a new structure for donor-Afghan coordination, but we still had to breathe life into the form. The first challenge was to agree on the composition of the Joint Coordination and Monitoring Board (JCMB). As conceived, this body had a key oversight role. It had not only to report on progress toward the many benchmarks of the London Compact but, far more importantly, to drive progress forward with some sixty donors and the Afghan government. The smaller the JCMB, the more agile and effective it was likely to be; the larger, the more it risked becoming a forum for endless discussion without action.

The task of winning agreement for the board's composition fell to Tom Koenig, the new UN secretary general's special representative in charge of UNAMA. A German civil servant who had seen relevant service in the Balkans, Tom had been fairly far left in his youth, reportedly giving a substantial part of his inheritance to the Viet Cong. I was not sure how he would hold up his end in fighting a war or how we would get on. At one point I joked with my wife, Elaine, that I might introduce myself by noting that I spent my younger years trying to kill the people he spent his youth funding. My wife didn't think this was either a good joke or an effective way to start our relationship. In the end, my fears were groundless. Tom turned out to be a good leader and an activist, sensitive to humanitarian issues but well prepared to countenance military means when needed. He pushed his headquarters in New York repeatedly for more resources to expand UNAMA's presence in the provinces as well as to effectively carry out its responsibilities in Kabul. He got only a portion of what he and I believed necessary. Tom also needed the patience of Job as he wrestled with the JCMB composition.

On two points all major nations had the same view: the board should be small and they should be on it. This was impossible. The key members were quickly agreed to: as major donors and troop contributors the United States, Japan, Germany, Britain, the EU, and NATO would have seats. CFC-A was going to continue being responsible for a significant share of the fighting after NATO took over, so it needed a representative in the group. But what about the Dutch, who were about to deploy? The Canadians made a strong case. The Italians thought they should be members, and while their case seemed weak, Washington backed it. The Russians were insistent that they be represented and prudence counseled accepting them. The Indians were a substantial donor, but if they had a representative, the Pakistanis would have a fit if they were not represented. In the end all the border states were given places, including Pakistan and Iran.

Capitals were sending démarches to Washington and New York as well as having their ambassadors rush to see Tom and me. Weeks were taken up with these consultations. President Karzai was deeply involved. It was important to him that we did not end up offending those who could make trouble for the country. In the end the board comprised twenty international members as well as six Afghan ministries.[1] The cochairs would be President Karzai's senior economic adviser, Ishaq Naderi, and Tom. I had expected more or less this result given the inevitable pressures and the reluctance of any major state to say "no" to essential allies.

Clearly the JCMB was going to be larger than we had hoped. It brought the Indians and Pakistanis with their bilateral tensions inside the group. The Afghans were suspicious of Pakistani and Russian intentions. All this was going to make frank discussion and cooperation difficult. Tom was concerned about how the JCMB could operate under these circumstances.

When we were originally negotiating the London Compact, then–UNAMA head Jean Arnault and I had considered creating a smaller informal group to manage business. The idea was to have a core group that would always be involved, essentially the same core we started with in the JCMB, but to rotate in other ambassadors and heads of international organizations depending on the issue. This would ensure that those with an interest stayed involved but would also keep the group manageable. I had talked about it as a group with no official status that would get together for coffee as needed to resolve issues. Tom liked the idea and christened the informal arrangement the "Tea Club," in view of his not being a coffee drinker. We were initially careful not to discuss the group too openly for fear that we would generate further international pressure to join and thus enlarge the group until it had all the debilities of the official body. The Tea Club became an essential feature of donor coordination, although not one much commented on and therefore largely unknown in the writing about the JCMB.

The organizational effort of creating the JCMB was larger than has been appreciated. Working groups were reformed to bring all the donors into a single organizing structure. There was a careful process of deciding which country would chair each group. The United States had an interest in every sector and money in most. We were careful to seek the chairmanship for only a few groups of critical importance so that we did not appear to be trying to run too much. USAID director Fulgham and I carefully selected our targets.

The London Compact had also set up a new UN–Afghan Secretariat to handle the extensive planning necessary to reach the benchmarks on time. The challenge was to keep the planning effort in balance. Some planning and monitoring were essential. But if the planning effort grew too large, it would become a black hole, sucking in all of the few qualified Afghan staffers. If we were not careful everyone would end up planning and no one would be doing anything. Tom found answers. Perhaps we should have made the planning group larger, but we were unwilling to pay the price in the loss of operational efficiency of the larger Afghan government. And many of the problems we encountered were more matters of political will than of planning as such.

Finally the JCMB was able to hold its first meeting on April 30, 2006. I doubt it could have been stood up faster than the three months spent. It is a useful lesson about how long it takes to get from an idea into the starting blocks when multiple nations' interests have to be considered.

Early on we began to utilize the new Tea Club mechanism. A major effort to bring electricity to Kabul involved the construction of a large transmission line from Uzbekistan, Turkmenistan, and Tajikistan to the city. The Americans, Germans, Indians, World Bank, and Asian Development Bank were all building parts of the transmission line. We were not working closely together, and even within my embassy the Afghan Reconstruction Group and USAID experts had differences of opinion, which were magnified by disputes over who should lead.

When I brought our experts and section chiefs together, I realized that there was actually a great deal of agreement on the technical points and what needed to be done. Out of this we were able to draw up a unified plan for new cooperation. One of its most important aspects was the need for the Afghan government to organize an interministerial committee to cut off the arguments and finger-pointing between ministries that were immobilizing Afghan decision making. Another was the need for donors and Afghans to start work jointly on power purchasing agreements with the Central Asian states so that there would be power to send through the line. As it was, each donor was working in a vacuum and no one was paying attention to the regional dimension; it was a bit like making an extension cord without looking to see if there was a socket to plug it into. My staff suggested that I approach President Karzai to push the Afghan aspect and talk to each of the donors. I decided to use our new mechanism.

We put all our recommendations into an analytical paper in early May 2006. UNAMA took ownership of the process and called all the relevant ambassadors together. We reached a consensus. We did not get every one of our recommendations, but most of them were agreed to.[2] The involved donor governments began a discussion with the Afghan government that pushed for acceptance of our agreed policy. Agreement took months. None of the ministries wanted to cede any power to a new group. Ismail Khan, the former warlord of Herat, seemed to believe that if he resisted our actions for long-term change, the donors would have to fund more short-term fuel and generator purchases to keep on the few lights in Kabul. I thought this was backward. The donors would not keep endlessly funding a process that built nothing. The United States alone had spent $70 million the previous winter on diesel fuel for Kabul and three provincial cities to power their generators. We were burning money without building anything. We could not sustain this. The arguments went on for months.

At one point I withdrew all our advisers from the Ministry of Power and Water. I wanted to avoid a public fight, which would make it hard for Ismail Khan to back down, but I also wanted him to feel pressured. Subsequently I withheld a $10 million payment for fuel to increase the pressure. The Afghan government was starting to feel pain, but Ismail Khan apparently mistook my actions for an effort to make him look bad politically. That was not my intention, since he was not doing badly with what he had. But what he had wasn't much. As one of my advisers said, "The ministry has four hundred people on the payroll, 180 come to work, ten have university degrees, and only four understand the issues." The numbers might have been a bit off, but the basic description was correct.

The donors hung together reasonably well in pushing our common position. Finally Mohammad Jalil Shams, the new minister of economy who had been Ismail Khan's deputy, brokered a peace deal between us. In true Afghan fashion we let Shams work between us until we had agreement, thus avoiding anyone losing face. Then we had a dinner at Ismail Khan's to cement our new relations (but not to discuss the deal). I released the money and sent back the advisers.

UNAMA had kept the donors together and avoided having the dispute become one of American bullying. Working together we also discovered problems in the connections between parts of the project constructed by different donors that would reduce the amount of electricity that would actually reach Kabul. We could not make up for time lost but were able to go forward more coherently. The Afghan government did use the new Inter-Ministerial Committee on Energy to resolve issues. The result was not speedy, but it was more efficient than having each donor nation deal individually with separate ministries that, in turn, would blame other Afghans more than they would resolve problems. The whole affair lasted two and a half months and stood out for me as an illustration of the differences between having a policy and implementing it.

Among the more pleasant diversions during this period was a reception I held for a group of young Afghans departing for yearlong Fulbright and Humphrey fellowships in the United States. Some would study and others would teach Dari, for which there was a growing demand in American colleges. It was not only the re-start of important educational exchanges after years of war but a link with my own past. More than one Afghan told me about meeting my parents in their regular receptions for departing and returning students. I felt as though I was picking up a family tradition. I continued to hold these affairs. Later, one of the returning students brought her mother with her to a party. She presented me with a framed photo of my mother making a call on her in Kunduz in 1968. I wished my parents had lived to know how their memory continued in this far-off land.

Parliament and a New Cabinet

Our struggles over electric power took place in the midst of shifting politics in Kabul and problems in the U.S.-Afghan political relationship, and in the middle of all that we had the riots. In Kabul, Parliament assembled in December 2005 after votes were counted and fraud claims investigated. Many of the wartime leaders had been elected, but none of them had the voting strength most observers had anticipated and each had difficulties in keeping his own block under full control.

Parliament's first business was to elect a speaker. Deputies trooped to the U.S. embassy in search of support. None believed that we would not intervene. I repeated endlessly to them and to the press that this was an Afghan decision. Only months later, after the selection, did some of the deputies acknowledge that, finally, they believed we had been neutral. All thought that this was a good thing, but the experience illustrated how strongly Afghans are prone to believe that foreigners maneuver endlessly to manipulate their country. And far too many are prepared to be manipulated for a price. Meanwhile they argued over the speakership.

President Karzai switched candidates, perhaps because he discovered that his influence was insufficient to elect former president Burhanuddin Rabbani to the job. The relationship between Karzai and Younis Qanooni from the National Alliance festered in suspicion. Karzai appeared to back Abdul Rasul Sayyaf, whose conservative Islamist views and background of alleged human rights violations alarmed many of the Western ambassadors. "What will we do if Sayyaf is elected?" was a repeated refrain in the diplomatic corps. We still remained neutral. The Afghans had to make their own decisions if their new institutions were to put down roots.

Politics made strange bedfellows. The Hazara leader Mohammad Mohaqqeq joined in support of Sayyaf despite the two having waged a bloody confrontation in Kabul's suburbs during the civil war. The move caused Mohaqqeq to lose much of his Hazara support for several years but failed to put Sayyaf over the top. Qanooni won by a narrow vote. Sayyaf made an excellent speech respecting the results, congratulating the winner, and promising full support in Parliament.

Now it was up to President Karzai to select his new cabinet and present it for parliamentary approval. This was a difficult process. The previous cabinet had been a power-sharing arrangement and was not really Karzai's government. The president felt keenly the need to maintain political support. This led him to consult broadly but perhaps to make a few too many promises, not all of which were kept.

He and I consulted frequently about potential candidates. I tried to concentrate on the qualities needed for positions but to avoid pressing for particular persons. Some ministers were weak; some candidates and incumbents strong. Karzai was under enormous pressure from every faction and ethnic group to reward their candidates with ministerial portfolios. The idea of a small, more efficient cabinet rapidly fell victim to the need for enough senior jobs to allow more balancing of competing interests. President Karzai was prone to put a premium on loyalty. I tended to put more weight on the need for effective administration. But in the end I felt that the decisions needed to be President Karzai's. If the Americans picked the ministers, we would be held responsible for all mistakes. Under such conditions it would be impossible to build any sense of Afghan responsibility.

I turned down every individual request for support, telling each requester that it was time for the Afghan government to make its own decisions. Nevertheless I knew it would be intensely difficult to convince Afghans that we weren't calling the shots. As one minister said to me, "Ambassador Khalilzad made me a minister. I want to be the 'American minister.'" I didn't want "American" ministers.

President Karzai procrastinated until the end of the constitutionally allowed period before reaching final decisions. Then he received a surprise from Parliament: the deputies actually chose to exercise their right to confirm or reject the proposed ministers. The palace had proposed that Parliament hold a single vote to confirm the cabinet since the Constitution is not specific about how confirmation votes will be taken. This would have been a rubber stamp since there could not have been a majority to reject the cabinet. I had met enough deputies and seen enough parliaments to suspect that the deputies would not easily cede their rights this way. But parliamentary politics were new for everyone, and it was something of a shock to the palace when Parliament refused and began to vote on the ministers one by one.

This exercise in democracy was marked by intense political lobbying, charges of payoffs, and many political declarations by deputies, some of whom might simply have wanted to drive up the price of their vote. The palace was nervous about suffering a major defeat. There was a danger that if the situation became too polarized, Parliament could deadlock in battle with the palace, and nothing else would be addressed in the midst of an insurgency and with a government that still didn't rule in much of the country. I was making a general point to politicians of all stripes: vote against a minister if you really feel he is unqualified, but think of the country and don't make the cabinet appointments a political bloodletting. Whether this message had any effect was difficult to say.

In the end, for all its rough edges Parliament behaved responsibly. Most of the proposed ministers were accepted. A very conservative chief justice of the Supreme Court was rejected. A new, reform-minded chief justice opened up the doors for judicial improvement. At least two ministers who would have been modern reformers were rejected, although one may have lost less for his being a reformer than because he failed to understand the need to lobby Parliament. On the day of the vote for minister of culture, Dr. Sayed Raheen, the incumbent who had done much to bring media reform into being and to encourage a vibrant free press, was out happily tending to an archeological dig when Parliament rejected his nomination. He had not spoken to a single deputy to seek backing—not because he was arrogant but because it did not occur to him. A great deal that we consider natural political behavior in a democracy is actually learned behavior. Americans get to learn young. Afghans were learning in a harder school.

I did intervene in one nomination, reluctantly crossing my own red line. The Northern Alliance, feeling that the ministerial power it had gained at the Bonn conference was continuing to slide with the proposed new cabinet, was particularly focused on demanding its own candidate for interior minister. Although the nominee, Ahmad Moqbel Zarar, came from a Northern Alliance background, he had thrown in his lot with Karzai. The NA wanted its own man and had several candidates in mind. Various deputies were making pronouncements that the nomination would be rejected.

Zarar was not a candidate I was wildly excited about. He seemed a decent man but was perhaps a bit weak. He had been acting minister since Ali Jalali had left for America months earlier. Karzai claimed to have looked at several potentially stronger candidates, but one lacked the university degree required by the Constitution, another was somewhat unwilling and went to a different ministry, and Karzai backed off from a third choice. Perhaps the president didn't want too strong a figure in this critical ministry. In any event, Zarar got the nod and seemed acceptable if not stellar, although he certainly could not be said to be "my candidate." However, the suggestion that he would be voted down as a partisan reprisal was alarming because it could lead to chaos in the critical Interior Ministry.

After some reflection I decided that the danger of not intervening was unacceptable to our larger interests. I quietly talked with some leaders and asked my staff to radiate a common message to others. We noted that the opposition could reject President Karzai's choice but did not have the political strength to force him to choose its own candidate. If the minister were not confirmed, there would be a weak ministry for months while the different parties squabbled about who would get the job. We explained that the United States had a lot invested in the ministry in money and police training. Fighting was going on and American deaths would be part of the price for chaos, so we were, in that sense, a party in the discussion and not just interfering in an Afghan decision. We urged an affirmative vote. I hoped our stance was nuanced enough not to be too damaging to our overall neutral position. I was aware also that this was the first time I was putting my influence to the test, and if Zarar lost, the American position would be somewhat weakened. In the end, he was confirmed. It was impossible to know how much we had influenced the outcome.

Dr. Rangeen Dadfar Spanta, the new minister of foreign affairs, also had a difficult confirmation battle. He was briefly very far left in his views as a youth. Some attacked him as anti-Islamic while others were just out for political blood. On a recent trip to Germany, where he had long lived, he had a lengthy debate with German leftists. They maintained that no democracy could grow from American interference. He replied, "Then what about Germany?" I liked him. He worked the deputies effectively to lobby for support and in the end was confirmed.

Strategic Partnership Rides Out Storms over Religious Freedom

We had signed a document establishing something called a strategic partnership during a trip President Karzai made to Washington before my arrival in Afghanistan.[3] It had provoked intense regional speculation about how Washington might be intending to use its position in Afghanistan to expand its influence into Central Asia. The Russians were particularly suspicious. The truth was too simple to be believed: the document had no purpose outside Afghanistan and was little more than symbolism inside. It was not even a U.S. initiative. President Karzai had strongly pressed the partnership agreement to provide a visible symbol of America's intention to remain in Afghanistan, a counterpoise to the recurring Afghan popular fears that they would be abandoned as they had been after the Soviet withdrawal. After some hesitation, Washington had agreed and the agreement was duly signed. It committed the parties to yearly meetings for "strategic dialogue."

Although many analysts and regional governments based lengthy hypotheses about new U.S. regional strategies on the partnership, the fact was that there was no strategic plan. In truth, despite the agreement, we at the embassy spent much time after my arrival trying to figure out with the Afghans what we were actually supposed to do. Continuing the strategic dialogue was important as a symbol of America's determination to stick with Afghanistan. We needed to have another meeting to maintain the validity of the dialogue, but neither purpose nor approach had been decided. Foreign Minister Dr. Abdullah and I spent many hours in discussion with periodic reference to President Karzai and Washington. We eventually resolved on a program for a day and a half of meetings in Washington hosted by Undersecretary Nicholas Burns and Abdullah.

This came off satisfactorily, with working group meetings on governance, economic cooperation, and defense, the latter chaired by Undersecretary of Defense Eric Edelman. The meetings were a bit longer on talk than on substance, but we had made a start that eventually ripened into a fairly useful forum. Burns and Abdullah held a press conference that stressed the U.S. determination to support Afghanistan as well as the need to work against narcotics and pursue economic development. Burns made sure to note our other themes that, while standard, needed to be mentioned lest their absence cause speculation.[4]

While the talks were going on, a political crisis was mounting in Kabul. An Afghan named Abdul Rahman had returned to Afghanistan after years in Pakistan and sought in an Afghan religious (Sharia) court to recover his children who had remained with his long-estranged wife. Normally in Islamic law, custody passes to the father after the children reach the age of six or seven. In this case the mother fought the decision. She alleged that Rahman had converted to Christianity, thus forfeiting his rights under Islamic law, and moreover she accused him of beating his daughters to compel them to convert. The lower court sentenced Abdul Rahman to death for apostasy. The case ignited a firestorm in the United States and Afghanistan that began just as our talks in Washington were getting under way.

Members of Congress, civil rights groups, and supporters of religious freedom expressed outrage that a Christian might be put to death for his faith. Western European governments also picked up the issue. The public outrage from the West provoked a strong reaction from the Afghan mullahs and a large number of Afghan citizens who declaimed and threatened to demonstrate against Western interference in their country and their religion. Afghanistan had experienced demonstrations the previous year over derogatory cartoon depictions of the Prophet Muhammad in a Dutch newspaper, so a repeat was an all too real and unpleasant prospect.

I had planned a short vacation after the strategic dialogue but found myself spending hours each day on the telephone with Secretary Rice and President Karzai. Karzai assured me that Abdul Rahman would not be executed but wanted time and quiet to cool off the political climate in Afghanistan. Secretary Rice understood the need for careful handling but also had a deep belief in religious freedom stemming from her own principles as well as her upbringing as the daughter of a Baptist minister. Apart from her personal convictions, there were domestic political considerations in play for the administration as well. The Abdul Rahman issue united the religious Right in the Republican Party with the human rights supporters among the Democrats. And the 2006 congressional elections were only eight months away.

I explained to President Karzai why these features of American politics made any hope for quiet out of the question. In his turn, President Karzai explained the political pressure rising in Afghanistan against "bowing to the Americans." Each statement of outrage from one country provoked fiery rejoinders from someone in the other nation, and all were picked up and rapidly circulated by the world's media. All of us understood that if we did not find a speedy resolution, the ascending public outcries were likely to take the problem beyond the governments' ability to control things.

Secretary Rice had appearances scheduled on several Sunday talk shows. The Abdul Rahman issue would be front and center, and without resolution it would be difficult for her to avoid statements that would inflame matters in Afghanistan.

At the last moment an upper court in Afghanistan, citing his mistreatment of his daughters, decided that Abdul Rahman was mentally unbalanced and therefore unfit for trial. He was released. It was officially an Afghan court decision and could be defended in Kabul as not a matter of the government backing down to foreign pressure. A friendly government and an international group courageously managed to spirit Abdul Rahman out of the country and out of danger.

As these developments were taking place, I was on the telephone to Kabul and back to Secretary Rice as she prepared for her first interview. News of the release came just minutes before she was due to go on the air. She stressed our devotion to principles of religious freedom but was able to avoid saying anything too contentious. The ending was not an elegant victory of principle; the cultural differences were too great for that. We were able to return to fighting a war without giving the insurgents a huge propaganda victory.

One sad footnote to the Washington talks was the departure of Foreign Minister Dr. Abdullah from the government. I had found Abdullah to have strategic insight and to react to crises quickly. He had been a major element in setting up the Bonn arrangements and had been foreign minister ever since. We had worked well together in confronting numerous problems, and he was widely respected abroad. Still, President Karzai had decided on the change for reasons of his own as he was entitled to do. I did not feel I could intervene, particularly as I also respected Dr. Spanta, who would move from Karzai's staff to the Foreign Ministry.

Abdullah knew the change was coming but had understood it would not be announced until after the strategic dialogue talks concluded. Technically this promise was kept, but the announcement of the new cabinet broke while Abdullah was still in Washington for bilateral meetings. He handled a deep sense of personal embarrassment with professional discipline and distinction, carrying on all his meetings with senior American officials most effectively. I never respected him more than at this difficult time.

Money

The denial of a supplemental budget in early February required us to reassess how we were using our existing USAID funds. Even as we dealt with the new government's issues and prepared for strategic dialogue talks, we were conducting a complete review of our fiscal year 2005 and 2006 budgets to see where money could be swung to higher priorities. Ongoing projects carried a total estimated cost of $3.2 billion. Legal and regulatory requirements to pay future bills—a mortgage in bureaucratic terms—amounted to $666.3 million. There were also congressional requirements, or earmarks, that had to be respected. The analysis had to carry forward for fourteen months, until the 2007 budget appeared, to make sure no project would suddenly run out of cash. It was a complicated undertaking of juggling numbers and assessing priorities that consumed our USAID mission for some time.

In the end we recommended reprogramming to allow the start of three high-priority roads and funding of part of the southern power project, but we lacked funding also to begin raising the dam, which would have increased arable land. Instead of the $125 million we had wanted for agriculture to begin alternative livelihood work in potential poppy-growing provinces, we would have $22.4 million, but only to reinforce essential work in provinces where we were already operating. We were able to add a small amount for the PRTs. To free up these funds, we slowed work in building health clinics, curtailed construction of courthouses, and slowed pieces of many other projects.

Our recommendations went forward on March 6 in an unclassified telegram. However, shifting money already appropriated for one purpose to something else requires sending notification to Congress and allowing for a waiting period during which Congress can object. All this took time, and it was June before approval was granted. The delays are part of our constitutional system, and there is no escaping them, although few outside of Washington are really aware of how much they impact the implementation of policy.

Even the meager $32 million in new money the administration had requested for the power sector was in danger. A House committee removed the money during consideration of the administration's overall supplemental.[5] On the margins of the strategic dialogue talks in Washington and when not dealing with the Abdul Rahman case, others from the administration and I talked with congressional members and staff.

A great deal of assistance came from Deputy Assistant Secretary for South and Central Asian Affairs John Gastright. His detailed understanding of Congress from his previous service there was invaluable in targeting my efforts. We were able to get the Senate to agree to restore the money when it considered the bill. Further conversations on the House side secured agreement that the representatives would not oppose the Senate action. My father once told me that our system of government was constructed to allow a free people to govern themselves and remain free, not to provide efficient government. I quoted him to my associates when they became frustrated with all these complications.

As security continued to deteriorate, General Eikenberry and I emphasized in public as well as in private the need for additional roads. Where we opened roads security increased, the economy expanded, and it became harder for the insurgents to conceal bombs. We endlessly quoted Eikenberry's statement, "Where the roads end, the insurgency begins." He and I conceived a plan to build roads that would link every district center in the south and east with its respective provincial capital. We estimated the price tag at $600 million for a three-year crash project using the combined resources of USAID and the U.S. Army Corps of Engineers. In early June 2006, I formally recommended this to Washington, couching the request in security rather than developmental terms.

On June 14, I followed up privately with Secretary Rice to complain about the slow pace of decisions. I pointed out that it had taken six months to get authority to move $200 million from buying army equipment to buying police equipment. It had taken five months to do the recent reprogramming of USAID funds. We had virtually no new supplemental. And the decision to withhold a brigade of the Tenth Mountain Division in December had lowered our military potential. In late June, I pushed the issue again in a meeting of the Deputies Committee, which I joined by secure video link. I pushed as hard as I knew how to but wrote my wife that evening that getting action was like trying to nail Jell-O to the wall.

Secretary Rice actually was getting the message, but without a supplemental she had no money to respond with, nor any further room for reprogramming. On June 28, 2006, Rice again visited Kabul. Even though she had no funds in hand, she made the decision to promise President Karzai $60 million for roads. She pushed in Washington for a recommendation on how to find the money to make good on her promise, but the bureaucracy had a difficult time identifying sources for the promised funds. Then Congress had to be notified and some staff objected to small cuts in programs in Africa from which some of the money was to come. Overall I felt no sense of urgency from Washington. Eventually the money—10 percent of what we had asked for—arrived, but it was 2007 before any construction could start. Worsened security made the construction harder and more expensive for the three road links in Kandahar and Zabul provinces that we and the military deemed most critical out of our long list of road projects.

Justice

Money was important but so too was how we carried out the projects we funded. One area that particularly needed attention was the justice sector. Police reform could achieve only so much without a functioning justice system. The problems were immense. According to the new head of the Supreme Court, Abdul Salam Azimi, over half of the Afghan judges had no university degrees and many had only an Islamic religious education that scarcely equipped them to deal with new legislation on commerce and banking. Responsibility for justice was divided among the Ministry of Justice, responsible for writing law and managing the courts; the Supreme Court, which controlled judicial appointments and training; and a prosecutor's office, similar to our Office of the Attorney General in some ways, but more like the French system in its operation.

The Italians had initially taken responsibility for judicial reform, but their effort was underfunded, was outside the control of their very capable ambassador, and had led to some friction with Afghan authorities and particularly the conservative former chief justice. Our own plunge into judicial assistance was chaotic. USAID ran some programs through contractors. State had its own contracts but was also paying for several experienced prosecutors on loan from the Department of Justice who often seemed to operate independently. The U.S. military was funding some work on its own, but neither we nor they knew what the other was doing. Coordination among our elements was weak and relations were strained.

After trying for some time to grapple with these issues, I realized that neither my deputy nor I could pull away from other issues and crises consistently enough to provide the required oversight. Washington agreed to my recommendation to set up a senior coordinator position, but it was not easy to find someone who had both the policy judgment to work harmoniously with the Afghans and the legal experience to earn the respect of our prosecutors and contractors with legal backgrounds. Richard Baltimore, our departing ambassador in Oman who had a law degree, agreed to delay his retirement for some months to help out. He made a very credible start at pulling things together, but when he left we had a lengthy gap before we were able to bring on board Gary Peters, a former Justice Department prosecutor who combined his legal background with experience in State. New Italian personnel were very cooperative. Chief Justice Azimi was interested in reform, and we began to move ahead slowly.

As ISAF joined the discussions there was a renewed enthusiasm from several parts of the international community. Sometimes I found myself pushing back against justice proposals from the international participants. The United States and other countries could fund and help design programs, but the Afghans had to take the lead in determining the scope of reform since foreign designs in such a culturally sensitive area would certainly backfire. At times my colleagues probably thought I had spent too much time in the east and lost a sense of urgency. I looked at some of the foreign proposals as culturally ignorant attempts to impose Western styles.

We were at least three years late in paying proper attention to the area of judicial reform. The process continued after my departure. In 2007 the international community and the various Afghan agencies agreed on comprehensive plans for reform and proper funding began to come on line. Only in 2008 would the European Union start to engage deeply in this area.

Judicial reform is slow in the best of times. It had taken USAID two years of hard work just to compile a full record of existing Afghan laws. Massive training programs for judges and prosecutors will take years to show results. Corruption and low salaries remain great obstacles. Striking the right balance between traditional tribal and Islamic legal structures and practices, on the one hand, with modern court systems and prosecutorial approaches, on the other, remains a formidable challenge, and one for the Afghan people primarily to resolve. Afghan political will to curtail the existing extrajudicial immunity of senior figures is still in doubt as these words are written. Many countries and people are now taking judicial reform more seriously, but success is far from certain.

Political Struggles and Police Reform

The political fissures along ethnic lines that were revealed in the cabinet confirmations became much more pronounced after the May 29 riots. Within a day the Pushtuns all seemed convinced that Tajiks had either instigated or stimulated the riots. The Tajiks reacted defensively. The weakness shown by the police collapse was making everyone nervous and causing ethnic groups to draw inward for security. I was seeing many political leaders with a single message: this is a time to pull together, keep reform moving, go back to work, and focus on the common enemy of the Taliban. In long private meetings it was clear that Karzai needed strong support as much as he needed advice about looking forward rather than backward. Washington made public its continued support for him.

On June 12, I held a large press conference to convey the same message. I told the press we continued our support for democracy, the elected president, and Parliament. This was an attempt at a subtle message that we supported both the president and a political process; we were not picking sides or being hostile to the opposition. As a symbol of our commitment, I announced the $103 million for the hydropower project at the Kajaki Dam in Helmand and our work on the northern electrical power transmission line as well as other projects. There was a lot of discussion about fighting in the south, and I repeatedly emphasized our continuing military commitment as well as the courageous performance of new NATO/ISAF troops in the south.

The press was very selective in what it chose to report. The Afghan press focused most of its coverage on the announcement of the Kajaki Dam and our efforts to stick to our guns in the south. Perhaps the line about support for democracy was too subtle or had been used too often, although two days after the press conference it began to show up in editorials. The international coverage focused almost entirely on my saying that part of the fighting in the south was with drug lords. This was a small comment in a longer discussion about the different forces engaged in fighting in the south. The Western press paid no attention to the effort to support the government, our ability to work in the south, or anything else. They just cherry-picked one sentence and ran with it. It was not a particular problem, but it's no wonder the U.S. public had little idea what we were doing.

In April Elaine and I began talking about my volunteering for a third year in Afghanistan. Our discussions lasted several weeks. Neither of us liked the idea of more separation, yet the job was fascinating and important. Elaine reminded me that I had often said I was most effective in a third year at a post. Finally, on May 10, 2006, I told Secretary Rice I was willing to stay until 2008. The decision was hers. She said she had not realized this was a possibility, wanted to talk to the president, and would get back to me. I heard nothing for several months.

I continued a heavy schedule of provincial travel. It was important to form my own idea of what was going on, and the travel made a continuing public statement about American involvement and concern for the country. In early June, I visited Nuristan.

We came up from the south, stopping in Konar in a barren bowl of low hills to pick up some passengers, and then flew into the mountains. As the helicopter skimmed north the hills gradually became steeper. Small bushes and then stunted trees appeared. The hills turned into steep mountains with black and brown rock formations, and trees with rounded tops became thicker and larger. Soon we were flying up a steep V-shaped valley at 7,200 feet elevation with the mountains soaring another thousand feet higher on either side. Higher still and the mountains were covered with pine trees with meadows dotting the sides of the steep hills, a rushing river down the center, and snow in the distance. We landed in a meadow with plumes of bright green smoke, used by the security forces to mark the landing zone, streaming away in the blast from the rotor blades. Walking up the single dirt road to the governor's house reminded me of Colorado, with mountains all around us and the scent of pines in the air.

The governor seemed a go-getter. He had sold a string of pizza shops in Sacramento to return to Afghanistan. His father had been mayor of Kabul before the war and had known my father. The governor's father and three uncles had all been executed by the Communists. I found many family tragedies like his when I scratched beneath the surface of seemingly cheerful Afghan stories. Talking to officials I found that the last U.S. ambassador to visit Nuristan was my father. The idea that I was, even if unknowingly, following in my father's footsteps in this remote corner of Afghanistan gave me a sense of my connection to the country.

I came back from these trips soaked with sweat from wearing body armor and with my eyes burning from sweat, sun, dust, and the wind in the helicopters. But I returned each time with a sense of exhilaration and new knowledge. We had doubted that security conditions would allow a USAID officer in a new PRT to function effectively and had traveled with General Freakley and USAID director Fulgham to make a unified judgment. We found conditions more suitable than we had expected. We reached agreement on all points and decided to establish a PRT in Nuristan with State and USAID participation. Stabilizing the province would be a long struggle after decades without authority. We would have to start with a temporary location in the western edge of the province until a road could be built to the capital in Parun, where we had visited. It all took longer than we had expected. As I write, fighting is still heavy in Nuristan. Yet I believe pushing into the province was the right decision.

A week later I visited Assadabad in Konar Province. Governor Asadullah Wafa seemed in firm control in the town, but the province was much contested. I visited with the parents of children who had been killed by an insurgent rocket that missed our base by a mile or more and landed on their school. The "school" was really just a large cement slab outside a small building. Each class sat in a group on the cement, and that was where the rocket hit. High winds delayed the helicopters for our return until 10:30 in the evening. I used some of the time to do an interview with an Afghan TV crew we had brought along.

Afterward I asked the reporter about his own impressions. With artillery banging away on a fire mission behind us and all the soldiers we had seen on the short drives we had taken, I was startled when he told me that in Kabul the press thought Konar was violent and he was surprised by how "quiet" it was; nothing was going on. I could only dimly imagine what impression he had of the province if he thought this was quiet.

I late June my wife Elaine made a short visit to Kabul. Having her visit had been my one condition for staying a second year. I had tried to get the privilege extended to other members of the mission, thinking that it would help morale and might encourage some officers to remain a second year. The idea made State Department security officials too nervous, however, and they rejected it, although they later agreed to let spouses who wanted to work come permanently to Kabul. Apparently this was somehow less risky than two-week visits.

While Elaine was there we flew to the remote central Afghan province of Ghor, which we had both driven through thirty-nine years earlier. In Ghor the tiny state of Lithuania managed to maintain a PRT with the help of Croatia and Iceland, and this presence allowed us to house a U.S. embassy and USAID officer there. It was a very successful partnership, and we would not have been able to stretch to field a presence in Ghor without the help of these small nations. As we visited a road project, one villager told us that without the income from the project he would have had to send his family to Iran because they wouldn't have had enough food for the coming winter. Gohr is snowed in for months, and survival decisions have to be made early.

The violence in the country made police reform more essential at the same time that ethnic-based political factionalism was increasing the strains. The first phase of police reform had gone reasonably smoothly with the replacement of thirty-one top police generals through a merit-based process jointly run by the Germans, Afghans, and ourselves. The next phase was tougher. It involved new appointments of all the province police chiefs. Again there would be a written exam followed by the same trilateral selection process to provide a merit-based list of three potential candidates for each position. President Karzai would make the final selection from the merit-based list.

In parallel with this we would go forward with opening five regional police centers. Each not only would handle training but would eventually have a strong reserve force of police that could be dispatched to deal with local threats. The process of sending reinforcements from a central force in Kabul had not worked well. The new regional centers would align the police with the army's regional commands, and we hoped that this too would improve police-army coordination.

On June 9, 2006, shortly after the riots, I was in Kandahar for the opening of the second regional police center. We turned over to the Afghans two hundred trucks, a thousand rifles, and millions of rounds of ammunition and had much of it on display, which made a good show for the press. I made a speech (what else do ambassadors do?) and noted to myself again how impassive Afghans are when they are listening. They just sit, bearded and turbaned, and stare back at the speaker. It doesn't mean that they aren't listening and they may even be pleased, but they don't show the body language Western audiences do. I wondered whether they had always been that way or whether it was a function of the years of war and seeing one government after another fall, to be replaced with another making speeches and promises.

President Karzai remained deeply troubled by police performance. His discontent was reinforced when a district center in Uruzgan fell to a Taliban attack. Some of our military tended to see this as only a distraction from other operations. "We took it back the next day," one officer said to me. I had to explain that for President Karzai his inability to respond to calls for help was a serious political matter. I finally got through by pointedly saying to the officer, "Look, if somebody holds the house next to yours for two days and the police then get it back and say nobody was killed, that isn't going to make your wife feel about better staying at home." He got it.

Shortly afterward we had a similar threat to another village. This time Karzai alerted us to the threat in advance, and our embassy officer in the PRT confirmed that the threat had been reported up the military chain of command. General Eikenberry instantly understood the political significance of the threat to a village full of government supporters. He ordered an immediate relief operation. It went well, and the Taliban was repulsed. It had been closely run, and nerves were a bit on edge. The episode only reinforced President Karzai's tendency to be on the cell phone with people all over the country. His well-known operating style made it difficult to maintain a disciplined Afghan chain of command. It was a deeply ingrained habit and very Afghan style of control from the top. And sometimes Karzai was clearly right.

These strains bubbled up in the replacement of police chiefs. The demand for literacy had the unintended effect of favoring Tajiks who had served under the Communists and thus had more access to education than those in the resistance. Hazaras and Uzbeks were particularly disadvantaged. On top of this, political pressures after the riots for ethnic balancing were more intense than ever, and a weakened president was looking carefully to maintain political backing.

I pressed strongly in private meetings to get the list of police chiefs signed and eventually agreed in a late-night phone call to letting Karzai make some last-minute alterations. We were about to undertake military operations in the south, and there were some bad police chiefs I was keen to see removed. I did make a rapid check with our own side on the names of some chiefs Karzai planned to leave in place, but I probably should have checked more closely with UNAMA, whose records were more extensive.

When the list came out it retained fourteen police chiefs with poor records mostly in the north of the country. Some of the fourteen had deplorable backgrounds of human rights violations. The Germans and the UN felt that President Karzai was not dealing honestly and that the reform process was being subverted, particularly as we were dealing with a return to the use of tribal militias in some areas. They were not wrong, but I felt that they were pushing for too much perfection all at once. If it had not been such a serious matter, I would have been amused at some of the outraged international reaction to the violation of "rules" when applied to the Afghan situation.

The foreign public savaged President Karzai. The International Crisis Group was particularly scathing. I felt somewhat responsible since I had supported the decision in my haste to get 80 percent of the problem solved. Now we needed both to support Karzai and to get the process back on track. We slowly reached agreement on a probation process for the fourteen. Over three months they would be evaluated by both

Afghans and the international police monitors. We established a probation board, chaired by the minister of interior, with Afghan police generals, the Americans, the Germans, and representatives of the EU and
UNAMA, all of whom could add information.

It was a tough process that lasted several months. Reports of our
meetings quickly leaked to the press, and some of the generals on the
board received threats of retaliation for their decisions. They displayed
considerable courage in voting to remove officers. Afghans made their
decisions on the basis of new information. Everyone could honestly say
that these were Afghan decisions made without regard to old information provided by foreigners. The international role was to stiffen Afghan
political will while staying in the background politically. In the end, almost all of the fourteen were moved by decisions made with full agreement of all on the board. President Karzai accepted the recommendations.
He was able say to supporters of the dismissed officers that they had been
given a second chance and failed to measure up. One of the dismissed
officers did receive an appointment as a deputy governor. That was dis-
appointing, but perfection was a dangerous goal in Afghanistan. Overall,
my judgment was that the process had strengthened Afghan institutions.

My main outlet from strain was the embassy's sandlot volleyball
game on Fridays, played with great enthusiasm if not always much regard for international rules. I played for my own enjoyment but felt that
it set a good example for the staff that it was OK to get out of the office
occasionally. If I was no champion player at least I held my own, and
when I managed an occasional good shot, the psychic boost of hearing a
Marine forty years younger admonished, "I told you to watch out for the
Ambo," was sheer balm to the ego. I did think my assistant, Bill Paton,
was getting reckless when he bet a case of beer that the embassy/USAID
team could beat our Blackwater security guards. They were generally
younger and certainly fitter. However, we played better as a team and
won to their distress and our amusement. With such events we kept up
morale in the midst of long workweeks and occasional danger.

Passing the Southern Command to ISAF

British and Canadian units were fighting under U.S. (technically CFC-
A) command in the south, but Regional Command South would soon

pass to ISAF control. British lieutenant general David Richards had already taken over ISAF command in the north, the west, and Kabul from the Italians on May 4, so the stage was set for all NATO and other foreign military forces in Afghanistan to come under formal NATO command within a few months. I attended the change of command ceremony. It was a warm day and the lazy breeze blew away most of the largely routine words that are spoken at such times, noting appreciation for the work of those departing and saying of the slain, "they will not be forgotten."

It is a routine phrase, but it occurred to me how empty it is. Of course the families will live with the pain, the pension checks will arrive, and a few friends will remember, as I remember those I knew who died violent deaths. In that sense they will not be forgotten. But the world moves on, and few remember the names of the dead after a short time. I suppose that is the way it must be or the accumulated memories would be too painful for us all.

General Richards's talk was not formulaic. There were many doubts that ISAF would be up to its task, and Richards was clear and crisp in saying that his forces would undertake active operations, including narcotics eradication, to support the mission. He pledged to seize the initiative, "including by military means," and concluded by saying that while ISAF would be a friend to the vast majority of Afghans it would "be an implacable foe" to those who opposed them. It was dynamic and just what was necessary. Now the words needed to be backed by action.

General Richards brought with him the headquarters of the Allied Rapid Reaction Corps (ARRC), NATO's first high-readiness force. That gave him a core staff with experience working together. It was a stronger management tool than ISAF had enjoyed previously but still considerably smaller than the CFC-A headquarters, which was managing the battles in the south. It also lacked some communications and intelligence assets. General Eikenberry shifted some forces and assets from east to south to help, and General Richards was generous and public in his expressions of thanks. The switch to full ISAF command would involve NATO in its first real land war (Kosovo having been entirely an air campaign), and there were a number of issues to be surmounted.

On the basic issue of whether ISAF would fight, I was not unduly concerned. Upon the transfer of authority for the south, phase III of NATO's assumption of command for the whole country, new rules of engagement for NATO/ISAF would come into force. These rules were quite robust, they gave Richards all the authority he needed for combat operations, and I had the impression that he was prepared to use them. However, the national caveats or limitations on what nations allowed their forces to do were another matter. Decreed from capitals, the limitations were outside Richards's control. There were several other issues of military concern (discussed later). However, if military operations failed, the political fallout would be serious. I agreed with General Eikenberry, and we felt strongly that certain problems had to be resolved before the United States agreed to the actual transfer of authority. We could not afford to be on autopilot for a fixed transfer date if essential conditions were not met.

I would have aroused some resentment in U.S. military channels if I had weighed in with official cables expressing skepticism about the transfer, but I kept State informed by less formal means. I wanted to make sure that my political colleagues did not press too much for agreements merely in the interest of NATO political harmony that would not be sustainable in actual combat. I may have worried too much. In the end there was no serious political pressure from Washington for unreasonable haste, and my colleagues in the U.S. mission to NATO in Brussels were strongly supportive of rigorous conditions for the changeover, thanks to our very effective ambassador to NATO, Victoria "Toria" Nuland.

One particular issue was whether Dutch forces to be deployed in the south of Uruzgan Province would come to the aid of U.S. Special Forces in the north of the province if the latter got into trouble. Under a unified coalition command this had not been an issue. The Dutch finally agreed that in extremis they would assist in the north. They kept their word.

Another issue of concern was the rather weak Romanian force assigned to Zabul Province. General Eikenberry reinforced it with a U.S. rifle company as well as the communications element noted earlier. However, he correctly insisted that the Romanians had to be fully operational before the transfer of authority. There were other issues. They were detailed and military, but it was essential that we got them right. Generally we did.

An issue of concern to me was ISAF support for poppy eradication in the south. General Richards would have preferred to defer eradication for a year to avoid stirring up additional resistance and give more time for building alternative livelihoods for farmers. He had a point, but I had to disagree. If we backed off it would encourage resistance to eradication elsewhere. The problems with Congress would have been uncontrollable and might well have hurt us on overall USAID funding levels. And the NATO consensus, reflected in the overall operations plan, that ISAF would support eradication had been very difficult to reach with the allied governments and the Afghans.

ISAF, however, had no responsibility to conduct eradication, only to support if eradication forces got into trouble. In the end, I put in writing a series of specific questions about ISAF's willingness to carry out support. General Richards's written reply was precise and satisfactory and enabled us to sidestep the broader disagreement over policy.

General Richards correctly understood that winning in Afghanistan required building the government and economic development as much as fighting. The problem was that he was an intellectual who liked expounding his views. The press would repeat them in highly simplified fashion, and this sometimes created the impression that he was really saying the Americans had never understood the need for development over what the military calls "kinetic" action and that now the war would be in better hands. General Richards specifically and publicly rejected the press interpretations, but there was still some resentment, especially among my military colleagues who were far ahead in managing a mixed strategy of fighting and development. Despite these rubs General Richards and I were essentially on the same page, and the occasional verbal volleys did not cause any great problems.

General Richards wanted to cultivate what he called Afghan development zones, a sort of "oil spot theory" in which development could proceed in secured areas and gradually radiate outward as security improved. The Afghans supported increasing development, and so did we Americans. However, the Afghans were concerned that we not talk too much about the ADZs, as they came to be known. Minister of Education Atmar explained that if we publicly defined some areas as outside the ADZs and therefore out of immediate development, the effect would be very negative. Rather than wanting to increase security and join the ADZs, Atmar told us, those Afghans outside the ADZs would consider themselves discriminated against on tribal grounds and hence move into opposition. President Karzai was quite concerned about this point and gave explicit orders that while the ADZ approach was acceptable, it was absolutely not to be discussed in public. Of course the zones were mentioned, but we survived, perhaps because not too much visibly changed on the ground.

One very useful invention of General Richards's was the Policy Action Group (PAG), a formal structure of the major Afghan ministries, ISAF, and the British, Canadian, Dutch, and U.S. ambassadors, whose forces were fighting in the south. Chaired by the national security adviser, Dr. Rasoul, the PAG replaced the less formal structure we had tried to use the previous winter. It permitted somewhat more structured decision making and had better staff support, mostly from ISAF since the Afghans had so little staff to throw at the problem. It did not solve all our problems, but it helped.

Overall General Richards and I got on well. I learned to respect his determination and keen mind and swung out economic resources to help whenever I could. He, in turn, was more than generous in allowing my staff great access to his headquarters so that I was kept fully informed of what was happening. We met at least weekly for a private conversation and kept in close touch by phone and e-mail. We each knew we needed the other.

On July 31 transfer of authority in the south took place in a formal ceremony at Kandahar Airport. ISAF was fully in the fight, and it was about to get tougher.

The end of July also marked the departure of my assistant, Bill Paton. He had done a remarkable job of taking a huge load off my shoulders without letting the authority go to his head. We had traveled and worked side by side, and I would miss him. He was replaced by the no-less-competent Suzanne Inzerillo, who had also served with me in Iraq and who curtailed her comfortable tour in Australia to take Bill's place. Much of the embassy was turning over in the summer, but we were getting good people as replacements. I was confident that I had an excellent team as we confronted the strains to come.

6

Where Is the Margin for Victory?

Fighting intensified throughout the summer and fall of 2006, somewhat as we had predicted but not entirely. NATO/ISAF held but lacked the means to consolidate victories in the field, while U.S. forces made slow but contested gains in the east. Slowly, ever so slowly, as summer turned to fall and then to winter, Washington woke up to the need for money.

The Koreans Come to Town

Diplomacy sometimes brings the strangest problems. In early August 2006, approximately fourteen hundred private South Korean citizens, including women and children, arrived in groups in Afghanistan to hold a demonstration. Some two hundred of the Koreans also held U.S. citizenship, so the embassy was responsible for looking after their welfare. The march was supposedly for peace and development, but rumors picked up from the Korean press suggested that they actually intended to demonstrate in favor of evangelical Christianity. The organizers denied this, so the issue did not become another crisis of religious freedom.

But because of the rumors the Afghan government was concerned that serious riots could break out as had happened previously over religious subjects. The Afghans confined all the Koreans to their hotels and then arranged transport out of the country. A gutsy young consular officer and an equally intrepid human rights officer from our embassy made sure everyone had food and water, but otherwise we stayed out of Korean-Afghan politics and found it almost a relief to get back to worrying about the war. There was plenty to worry about.

Heavy Fighting

However much NATO nations hoped they were deploying to Afghanistan for peacekeeping duties, the reality was battle. As August passed, the fighting grew heavier in the south. The Taliban was convinced that through major engagements it could break NATO/ISAF's will to fight. We had correctly predicted major fighting, but we had thought that the Taliban would stick to small ambushes and bombs after the losses it had suffered the previous year when it tried to engage with large forces. That judgment was wrong. Whether because of overconfidence, because it believed that politically NATO could not stand the strain of losses on public opinion, or because it was locked into the strategic thinking of the battles against the Soviets and during the Afghan civil war, the Taliban increasing threw large units into battle despite their repeated failure to overrun ISAF forces and the heavy losses the insurgents suffered. Although they brought no Taliban victories, the tactics surprised us, and when supplemented by suicide bombings and roadside improvised explosive devices (IEDs), the impact was serious.

I was concerned about whether NATO would have enough forces and the right mix of support to take over the full war when ISAF transitioned to so-called Phase IV command of regular U.S. forces in the east. General Eikenberry had the first-line responsibility for recommendations on timing of Phase IV, and he and I consulted frequently and closely.

In late August, I reported to Washington my judgment that neither the Americans nor NATO was winning in Afghanistan. My report recommended accelerating the supply of equipment for the Afghan army and police, pushing Pakistan harder to stop infiltration across the border, and pushing the Afghan government harder on issues of corruption and good governance. General Eikenberry and I had concluded that road construction also needed to be considered a security, and not just a developmental, issue. Where we built roads, IED bombings were reduced, security forces moved more easily, and government authority expanded along with the local economy. We devised a "southern strategy" for greatly expanded road construction. The price tag came to $400 million. In our view the south had been neglected, and a large road-building program, in addition to improving security, would provide jobs and clear proof that the previous promises of economic development were being fulfilled.

The worsening security was alarming the Afghans. Some parliamentarians talked to me about restoring the military draft Afghanistan once had. I liked the idea of an Afghan national response to the threat, but there were huge problems with the idea. Our military trainers pointed out that we lacked the training facilities, equipment, and funding for a sudden enlargement of Afghan forces. Some of the parliamentarians were clearly considering the difficulties of a slow startup as an excuse to call militia commanders with their retainers back to service; this was not something we wanted to encourage. I put the idea aside. However, we did decide to shift significant funding to a new effort to expand the police (discussed later).

One particular concern in late summer was how we could start construction of the hydroelectric project at the Kajaki Dam in Helmand Province. This project, for which we had reprogrammed major funds, was to be the centerpiece of development in the south, expanding low-cost electricity to enable new industries to start. Mortar and rocket attacks at the dam were frequent. Conversations with ISAF were frustrating. ISAF fully understood the importance of the project, but it became apparent that we had different appreciations of the security situation. ISAF felt that the situation was better than we thought it was and therefore could not understand why we were not starting work.

To find a common view I decided to visit the dam with a senior ISAF officer. U.S. major general Steve Layfield, the ISAF deputy commander for stability, willingly agreed to go along as did our new USAID director, Leon "Skip" Waskin. The day before we left, my crusty defense attaché, Col. Mike Norton, reported from the dam that they had received some small arms and rocket fire. He forwarded me a situation report with the typically laconic notation, "Sitrep from last night at the Dam. Game ON!!!"

On August 27 we flew first to Tarin Kowt, the capital of Uruzgan Province, to spend the night with the PRT on our way to the dam. The PRT had recently been turned over to the Dutch, although most of their fourteen-hundred-strong maneuver battalion was still arriving and would not be fully operational until November. Australia had sent two hundred engineers to help enlarge the base, and they would later be able to work on civilian projects. The area was violent: U.S. forces in the province had suffered nine dead and twenty wounded in the past nine months. They had a firm grip on the need to link fighting with development, and I was proud of their service.

The PRT sat in a barren bowl with the sun bouncing mercilessly off the "gravel," much of it fist-sized rocks. This gravel was the only means to keep down the talcum power–like "moondust" that was ankle deep on the camp/construction site. The Dutch base expansion would include a small hospital as well as shelter for the troops. In the end four thousand truckloads of gravel would be brought in. I was glad I had worn boots as I stumbled about on the stones, especially at night when the walk in the dark to the bathrooms seemed mysteriously longer than it was in daylight. We had good discussions with the Dutch. In the morning we started for Kajaki, or at least we tried to.

For an hour we sat baking in the sun on a helicopter with its rotor blades turning. ISAF headquarters insisted that we couldn't fly because the dam was under attack with a "hot LZ" (landing zone). The helicopter had no way of communicating with the forces at the dam. Eventually the assistant defense attaché got off the helicopter, made a satellite phone call to our advance party, and confirmed there was no attack and no fire had been received for thirty-two hours. We had not even started and already we had our first lesson in the coordination problems that were part of my concerns.

Although our schedule was somewhat constricted by the delay, we had good briefings at the dam and were able to tour the defensive positions. The dam had been a flagship project of USAID during its engineering heyday in the 1970s. On top of a steep and rocky mountain after we busted one radiator in our ascent, we found British paratroopers living hard lives under canvas strung between rocks and having small fights every few days in which they used accurate antitank missiles to engage mortars firing from the plains below. The paras attributed two days of calm to having killed all immediately available Taliban mortar crews but expected fighting to recommence as soon as Taliban replacements arrived. The paras had been told that the U.S. ambassador was coming to visit with a senior general but had considered the story so improbable that they were surprised to see us appear. However, they enjoyed the visit, as did we.

The strong points around the dam were sufficient to protect the site but were in no way satisfactory for the additional civilian contractors we needed to bring in to begin the project. Desertions among the contractor guard force and local Afghan militia were high, and the Afghan army presence numbered only ten soldiers with a capable British captain. The Taliban controlled the low ground around the dam. An old Afghan engineer who had worked at the site since USAID built the dam told us that he frequently talked to the Taliban fighters, who allowed him to go back and forth. All the actions confirmed that the Taliban had little interest in attacking or destroying the dam itself; it wanted to control it and the irrigation and power it provided as a symbol of political control in northern Helmand.

The small group of U.S. contractors at the site was prepared to accept some risk but not to work under rocket and machine-gun fire every few days. Our strategic problem was clear: we needed to control a belt of territory around the dam so that the Taliban could not shell it and impede the work. Additionally, a new road would have to be built to move supplies, especially a large turbine, to the dam, and a new transmission line constructed to handle the increase in power the dam would generate. The program elements were an interlinked package and all required a measure of territorial control.

The problem was complicated by the fact that British forces had initially been positioned to defend a number of district centers, and while they were strong enough to hold their positions against frequent attacks, they had essentially become fixed in place. Without more force they could not maneuver. Yet if they gave up the centers, the Taliban would quickly reoccupy them in a show of political strength.

As it was, the Taliban was able to range at will in the surrounding areas.

There were few Afghan soldiers or police to take over the static defense duties. The need to get more ISAF troops was clear. So too was the need to inject more local Afghans into the fight on the government's side, but without additional foreign forces to back them up, this was unlikely to happen. And in the aftermath of the reign of a corrupt former governor, there were all sorts of tribal rivalries and feuds, some going back years, that helped place many locals with the Taliban.

As we were leaving for our helicopters, a single mortar round dropped a kilometer away. It was not clear that it was even fired at us, but it made the loading and departure of the helicopters more exciting. A rocket poised on an adjoining ridge had no one around it, so whether it was on a timer or abandoned we didn't know. The Apache gun ship flying escort expended a quantity of taxpayer funds shooting it up as we left. My guards did an excellent job and I never felt in danger. The British paratroopers were the ones to admire. Colonel Norton seemed somewhat disappointed that he hadn't gotten into a real fight.

The trip was a success in giving ISAF and ourselves a common view of the situation. It would be a long time before we had the security in place to begin the project, but from then on ISAF headquarters, USAID, the embassy, and the British forces in Helmand were able to work cooperatively and closely in planning how to go forward. One cannot exaggerate the value of having senior people see a situation for themselves to gain a common understanding of what is needed.

Security was not an issue only at Kajaki. Three days after the trip I was awakened just after 1:00 a.m. with information that a rocket attack on the embassy was expected shortly. We alerted ISAF. In consultation with the RSO we decided that with very little time until the expected attack we would not try to move staff from the more vulnerable hooches to the chancery. Such a move would risk having people bunched in the open without time to get them to safer locations; it was better to leave them spread out in their beds. Three rockets were fired but all missed by a kilometer; thank goodness the Taliban fighters were bad shots. The next day we published a notice to all the staff explaining what had happened, what we had done, and why. It was important to distribute information quickly before distorted rumors could suggest that we weren't concerned about keeping our people safe.

Meanwhile, the real fighting of the summer was about to kick off in the south. In a major tactical error the Taliban apparently decided that it could repeat tactics used during the battles against the Soviets and dig in and fight near the important southern Afghan city of Kandahar.[1] Reporting from various sources made its intentions clear. General Richards was fully up to the challenge. Canadian, U.S., and Afghan forces with heavy air and artillery support and backup from UK, Danish, and Dutch forces fought a major battle, called Operation Medusa, from September 2 to 17, 2006.[2] (Preparations, called shaping operations, had begun a month earlier.) The action was carefully prepared, and civilians received advance notice to quit the area. Hundreds of Taliban fighters were killed, but there were also significant ISAF casualties, particularly among the Canadians.

The heavy fighting redoubled discussions in Washington and NATO capitals about whether the transfer of the rest of Afghanistan to NATO command should take place at the end of September as tentatively planned. Most of the formal discussion was in military channels, but I engaged informally with colleagues in NATO and Brussels. ISAF was clearly understrength. Only 80 percent of its force requirements had been met, and those plans were probably out of date, having been written at a calmer time. Helicopters and fixed-wing transport aircraft were in short supply.

There were arguments about whether keeping a split, a "seam" in military jargon, between ISAF and the U.S.-led CFC-A was dangerous. I recognized the problem, but cooperation between generals Eikenberry and Richards was good, particularly during Operation Medusa when U.S. Special Forces under CFC-A had cooperated closely with ISAF troops. The danger did not seem serious.

Some were worried that a delay in the transfer would alarm the Afghan government. I thought not. It was the United States they were concerned about, and if a delay was prompted by our insistence that NATO field adequate forces, the delay was more likely to please than worry the Afghans. But would a delay pressure NATO nations into committing more force or only lead to squabbling among the allies?

The issue was a major point of discussion when the North Atlantic

Council (NAC, as the ambassadors to NATO are called) visited Afghanistan in early September while fighting raged. The talks I had during the visit, particularly with our very able ambassador to NATO, Toria Nuland, finally convinced me that having the United States hold up the transfer would not successfully pressure our allies to put in more force. Such decisions, if they came at all, would have to be made by individual nations on the basis of their domestic politics and their belief in the importance of the mission. Neither factor was yet strong enough to produce the results we wanted. I reluctantly backed off and gave up the idea of a formal objection to the transfer.

The splits within NATO were clearly manifested in a dispute over whether Afghanistan would be allowed to participate in the Partnership for Peace, a program designed to provide some military training exercises to former eastern bloc satellite countries. France staunchly objected, saying that it was against expanding the program beyond former Soviet areas, but in reality French president Jacques Chirac was well known to be resistant to NATO becoming a tool of American policy. On our side one general noted sourly that if the Soviets had won in Afghanistan, the country would have been automatically entitled to participate in the program. In the end, a solution was reached based on delicate diplomatic maneuvering and drafting, but the incident showed how far NATO was from being a unified alliance of nations fully committed to fighting a war. Complaining wouldn't change that reality until nations saw it as in their interest to change. In the meantime we would have to deal with the situation.

On September 8 we received an ugly reminder that danger existed in Kabul as well as in the south. A suicide bomber drove his bomb-laden car into a convoy from one of the PRTs only a hundred yards from the embassy. The explosion shook the buildings. Bystanders were killed along with two U.S. soldiers, including a woman reservist in her late forties who had been manning the gun turret. Body parts laced the trees along the road where the explosion had occurred, and parts of one victim were blown onto the roof of the Health Ministry, adjoining the embassy.

One Humvee in the convoy was ripped open. The bodies of the two American soldiers were moved into our enclosed vehicle entrance, and one who was wounded was evacuated to our small infirmary. We locked down everything while we assessed the situation. Colonel Norton performed with great credit as he left a workout and, still in his gym shorts, took charge of the stunned survivors, helped collect bodies, and evacuated the wounded. The injured soldier seemed in good spirits when I visited him. Unwounded survivors seemed more in shock than the wounded soldier. The stunned PRT crew huddled in the marble lobby of our new chancery, numb with grief and silent since army protocol prevented them from contacting friends or relatives until the next of kin of the dead had been notified. My guards escorted me on a walk around, but there was no further threat. I stopped by our command post to congratulate them on doing a good job of reporting and taking control. We kept everyone locked down until we could clean up the trails of blood into our entrance. It was not a task most Foreign Service general services officers expected to perform in their careers.

The attack so close to the embassy was demoralizing to some of the staff members. One of our Afghan employees who had been on duty close to the blast site was killed. In the afternoon I was asked if we should go ahead with our weekly volleyball game. I said of course we should. The last thing we needed was to have people sitting at home moping. I didn't issue any instructions—it was just a passing conversation with my staff aide Suzanne—but apparently word spread because the game was well attended and one person thanked me for getting them out of the office and away from reflection on the attack.

In the fall of 2006, war in southern Afghanistan faced four strategic problems: a shortage of ISAF troops needed to win fights, insufficient Afghan forces to secure the population, a lack of competent governance to deliver a sense of hope and progress to Afghans, and an inability to deal with the opium poppy cultivation that was expanding with Taliban encouragement and compulsion. Farmers were already taking loans from drug traffickers in the fall based on opium harvesting in the next year. But the poppy would not ripen until the spring. Policy discussions would take time. The fighting was more immediate.

Operation Medusa illustrated the other three problems. It was a tactical victory of no strategic consequence because we could not follow it up. But it did teach us how to do better. The Taliban had been driven out of two important districts close to Kandahar, but now the civilian population needed to return and rebuild houses and police and government authority need to be established. None of it went well.

The need for rapid reconstruction was clear, but means to do so were lacking. Unlike U.S. forces with their CERP funding, NATO militaries had no money with which to begin reconstruction. Assistance agencies were designed for long-term development, not rapid tactical response. The Policy Action Group in Kabul understood the issue, but all of us in the group felt as though we were running in sand as we tried to move quickly. The Afghan government was bogged down because of the lack of competent people and the administrative machinery to respond promptly. One PAG decision was to supply six qualified Afghan staffers to each of the governors in four provinces, a tiny number for which the foreigners speedily came up with the funding. But actually finding twenty-four qualified individuals willing to go to the area took several months. That was a microcosm of the problem we faced as the insurgents gradually infiltrated back into the area.

The U.S. military put CERP funds at ISAF's disposal. USAID swung about $25 million in to cover both immediate relief and midterm costs, and General Richards was strong in his public praise for the aid and implicitly recognized other assistance organizations lacked the flexibility to help. General Richards and the Canadians under his command were particularly keen to build a road into the Argandab Valley and across the river of the same name. Much of the Canadian battle group was being used to secure the temporary dirt road it had bulldozed, but new roadside bombs were being placed on it regularly. To speed matters we agreed in mid-October that USAID would fund the short stretch of road. The active and competent German ambassador had been pushing his government for action as well. It began to appear that the Germans might also fund the road, but the final decision was unclear.

We were faced with a delicate diplomatic task: move the project quickly while avoiding any sense of America throwing its weight around and preventing others from acting. I agreed with General Richards that ISAF should take the lead in holding a meeting to set deadlines and delegate responsibility. I assured him we would happily step back if others could fund the project. ISAF should decide how fast it needed to make decisions. In the end, the German government did take on the road project, and we shifted our funding to a longer-term effort to bridge the river. It was a small incident, quickly over but still an interesting example of how one can promote allied cooperation—or not.

But while we solved some problems, we could not conjure up from thin air the necessary Afghan army and police units needed to secure the district. The Taliban continued to reemerge, as local villagers were voluble in telling us. Our own lack of force was no secret. General Richards repeatedly told the press and public as well as his superiors that he needed more forces;[3] at least the force levels that NATO planning itself had stated were required. Gen. Jim Jones, the NATO commander in Brussels, was equally public about the need.[4]

In several interviews during the fall I was simultaneously pushing three themes: the United States would stay the course, a tough situation did not equal disaster, and the response should be reinforcements, not despair. The turnover to NATO was still not well understood by Afghans, and their questions about whether we would draw down forces were frequent. I carefully avoided excessive optimism as I believed that painting too rosy a picture would lead only to later disillusionment. We needed to steel public opinion for the long haul. That required a balance between recognizing the reality of what the press was reporting— heavy fighting—and explaining what needed to be done.

My interview with the German publication *Spiegel* ran under a quote that *Spiegel* considered worth a headline: "We are not going to evacuate. We are not going anywhere." In the interview I talked about the length of modern insurgencies, the need to achieve security at the village level and speed development at the same time (a counterpoint to the frequent analysis in European publications that development alone would turn the tide if the Americans would just stop shooting), and the need for others to send forces, remove caveats on the use of those forces, and pay for the development of a police force. When asked about different European ideas, I was a bit tart in responding, "Yes, some of them obviously resist the idea that you have an army in order to fight." Overall I tried to focus on why Afghanistan was important and worth the NATO effort.[5] The article was quoted for some time but probably didn't shift many views.

In October, I said to National Public Radio that the "east has gotten better and the south has gotten much worse. Security doesn't reach down to the village level, it isn't broad-spread enough." The task is "to increase the size of the police, to upgrade the Afghan army." I noted that if we got all the money we wanted, it would "be a year before you'd get the money out, get contracts, receive equipment, train people—all these things take time. And the American people need to understand that we're going to be at this, and fighting an insurgency, and rebuilding a country for a good number of years."[6] A month later I said to the *Financial Times*, "Next year is likely to be just as bloody as this year but the fight is still winnable."[7] I urged donors and Afghans alike to use the usual seasonal winter slowdown in fighting to prepare for more effective action the following year.

Police

We were pushing for police reform, trying to respond to new threats, and moving in multiple directions at one time with too few resources. The complexities of police reform seemed endless. The May 29 riots had exposed the need for much faster efforts to stand up a disciplined riot control force. Our trainers accelerated those efforts but had to draw on a fixed pool of trainers in the short run. Police reserve forces were needed to bolster areas threatened by the Taliban, but creating them again caused slowdowns in other parts of the program.

Since the United States has no national police force from which to deploy police mentors and trainers, such personnel are recruited by contract. But the contract management was a nightmare. So-called cost-plus contracts, in which the contractor is paid a percentage of costs, can lead to waste, but at least they provide a rapid way to adjust to changing circumstances. However, the State Department was using a fixed-price contract for police trainers. This meant that when we wanted something new—for example, riot control trainers—the contract modification had to be negotiated and prices agreed on before any new trainers could be recruited. Worse, the contract was not even controlled from Kabul.

When I looked into the matter I discovered to my amazement and horror that there was a single contract that covered police training in Iraq, Afghanistan, and even Jordan. This unwieldy mechanism, festooned with countless contact amendments over time, was not even managed by INL, which manages police matters, but rather was handled by contracting officers in State's Bureau of Administration. It was no wonder the contractors were not very responsive to us in Afghanistan: they looked to the holders of the purse strings in Washington. Our contractual arrangements were distant, rigid, bureaucratic, and terribly ill suited to fighting a war.

On August 23, 2006, I recommended that when the current police contract expired it be rebid as an Afghanistan only, cost-plus contract. In the short run, I sought to move contract management to Kabul by stationing approved contracting officers at the embassy. In response we eventually got a single officer with some contracting power, but the system remained sluggish, ill adapted to war, and managed too heavily from Washington. Its debilities also contributed to strains with our military colleagues, who chaffed at our slow pace in responding to common problems.

The more I traveled, the more problems in our police program stood out. The responsibility for training was diffuse, in part because the lack of adequate numbers of trainers forced us to use whomever we could even if they were in different chains of command. Infantry battalions, PRTs, military trainers in Kabul, and civilians were all in the game. The State Department's program lead was managed through contractors, and aside from the problems noted previously, there was and is a more basic problem with the use of contractors for managing operations in a war. That is simply that a contractor, even the best, is hired to carry out a contract, not to tell the government that the contract's objectives may themselves be wrong, inadequate, or unresponsive to changed circumstances. The individual trainers in the field were generally highly motivated and often highly frustrated by problems they saw and reported but could not correct. But the criticisms passed slowly if at all into embassy and military channels. The result was that as we made our separate and joint trips, General Eikenberry and I repeatedly discovered new problems that came as complete surprises since they had not been reported to us.

In Kandahar, as we toured together for the opening of the new regional police training center, Karl and I discovered that the weapons looked pretty but the trainees were not getting to actually shoot them because of a shortage of ammunition. Without live-fire training, the new policemen were not likely to have confidence in their weapons. Ammunition was in short supply, but once we knew of the problem our military could and did tap sources to acquire ammunition to start training.

Weeks later we discovered that peacetime rules required the construction of proper shooting ranges before live-fire training could take place, and this in a country where most adult males owned at least an assault rifle if not a machine gun or grenade launcher. But the contractor had to worry about liability issues if he violated the rules. The amount of effort required to move forward on this issue was excessively time consuming. Our tempers were not improved by the fact that we discovered these issues piecemeal in our travels, often long after they had emerged. Problems in my own staff also delayed the necessary responses until new personnel with less bureaucratic attitudes arrived.

While we were fixing individual problems, we were not solving the basic problem of getting more guns in the field to secure Afghan civilians in their villages. Trying to stand up a working police force in the midst of an insurgency in a country split into hundreds of local power groups was intensely difficult. Our plans to rebalance the police (described in chapter 4) were not working. Police from the corrupt highway patrol preferred to quit rather than move to the regular police. Changes at the top were happening but too slowly. Recruitment was not adequate in the provinces that were the most in need of reinforcements, and much more time was required to fully implement the concept of police reserves in regional centers. We needed a new idea to fill the gap until longer-term efforts could come to fruition.

In the summer General Durbin proposed a new idea: auxiliary police that could be quickly stood up, receive limited training in matters such as vehicle searches and checkpoint security, and provide fixed security to supplement other better-trained but very slowly growing Afghan security forces. To avoid the problem of arming militias, the new auxiliary police would be recruited individually and placed under regular police command. I liked the idea, used my authority to direct civilian police program policy to switch considerable funding to the new program, and announced it as a unilateral initiative at a PAG meeting. However, the program could be only a short-term stopgap. We saw it as a two-year effort after which the best of the auxiliary police could be recruited for the regular force.

We proposed to pay the new salaries through the existing Ministry of Interior police pay structures, inadequate though they were, and to channel the funding through the existing Law and Order Trust Fund, run with German supervision. The Germans were supportive, and others came on board. In September 2006 the new Afghan National Auxiliary Police (ANAP) came into being under a decree signed by President Karzai.[8] Before we started I made sure we had the funding to carry the program through the first year by ourselves. However, more money would be needed, and I left the resource issue unclear to encourage other donors to participate. The Germans were helpful, and the Canadians, Dutch, and British, who all needed Afghan help for their forces in the south, responded well.

From the start I was under no illusion that it would be easy to get the ANAP to function the way it was designed to work. I had great respect for the Afghans' ability at the local level to transform Western ideas into Afghan practices, including particularly that of funding favored militia commanders. Militia commanders might help local security for a time but would be part of the resistance to real government authority in the future. We began the program in only six provinces because we knew a great deal of work would be needed to keep it on track.[9] I was determined to keep a close eye on how the program developed.

In early November, I was in Zabul Province. There were some good developments. The cooperation between Romanian forces (also in command of the former U.S. PRT), a U.S. infantry company, and other U.S. forces not under ISAF command was first-rate, and the embassy political and USAID officers were working well with them. An electricity project for the province capital of Qalat was moving forward. A hospital built by the United Arab Emirates that had been empty of staff when I first visited the province now had nineteen doctors and was a going concern.

I attended the graduation of the first class of ANAP officers. They had already proved they could fight, having broken off training to rescue some local police. But they were not getting paid. The lack of prompt pay was cutting into recruitment. I was able to rectify that when I returned to Kabul. I did not like interfering directly in Ministry of the Interior business and my doing so embarrassed some senior police generals (although the minister was happy to help), but the pay problems were a continuing drag on the police and were not going to be solved by the occasional application of ambassadorial weight.

On November 26, I visited Khost Province. The province has a long border with Pakistan and great problems of infiltration across the border, but there were positive developments. Although the province had the largest number of roadside bombs in Afghanistan, it also had by far the largest number reported by Afghan civilians before they went off, a measure of civilian opposition to the insurgents. The new governor appeared to be a competent administrator. He claimed to be making substantial progress in recruiting local police on a balanced tribal basis. It sounded impressive, but I realized we had no way of verifying the report. The visit helped to crystallize an idea of how to dig deeper into the ANAP program.

The idea nurtured in Khost grew into a new reporting scheme. We formed a team of officers from the embassy's Political-Military Section, the police oversight group in INL, the contractor (DynCorp), and CSTC-A. Province by province the team traveled to evaluate the program and to fix problems on the spot. Where UNAMA or the EU had local representatives with political insight, we involved them. We expected to find problems, and we did—everywhere.

In Ghazni only Hazaras were being recruited, but the problems the province faced were primarily in Pushtun areas. In Helmand the recruits were all coming from outside the province. In Kandahar there were too many recruits from only a few tribes, and the suspicion that we were paying for a local commander's militia force was strong.

Each province had problems, and each was different. Our team was able to solve many of the issues, particularly as I had full support from General Durbin. None of the problems were being reported to Kabul, where the briefing slides continued to report progress untrammeled by messy facts from the field until after each provincial visit. It was clear that repeated visits would be necessary to keep the program on our intended track, not because there was deliberate misreporting from any of the U.S. elements involved but because Afghanistan required us to learn new ways to operate.

Reflection showed that the problem we confronted was deeper than the individual issues. Neither our military nor our civilian police trainers had the experience to find out who they were actually training. They would seek information from their official contacts, for example, the governor or police chief, but those might be the very individuals who were manipulating the program. Left alone, the trainers would train whoever showed up.

The embassy officers in the PRTs had no experience in managing a police-training program. Left alone they would eventually report that there were problems in the program but would do nothing to fix them. Only by bringing together experienced political reporters and trainers were we able both to identify problems and to repair them. The effort was labor intensive and generated repeated frictions at lower levels where it crossed institutional borders.

Detailed oversight became harder to manage as the program expanded into more provinces in the east in 2007 and pressures increased to grow the ANAP faster. Even by my departure in April 2007, it was becoming intensely difficult to keep up the level of supervision necessary as the number of provinces multiplied. Later the field trips ceased. By 2008 the program had run as long as we expected it to, was experiencing many difficulties for reasons that are outside this memoir, and was consigned to the scrap heap. But in 2006 it did provide a limited additional force when it was badly needed and taught us valuable lessons about how to manage civil-military oversight, which were essential if PowerPoint briefings in Kabul and Washington were to be tied to reality in rural Afghanistan.

Back to the Budget

The declining security situation in the second half of 2006 made clearer than ever the need for increased funding. General Eikenberry and his staff gradually developed recommendations for very sizable increases in the equipping of the Afghan security forces. The original design of the army was for a force of seventy thousand men but with no armored transport, little air or artillery support, and virtually no way to rapidly evacuate the wounded or resupply those in battle, except when operating with coalition forces. We had made only a limited commitment to the equipment that a reorganized police would need. All this clearly needed to change. That would take time and the convincing of Washington, but at least there had been additional funding for the security forces for 2006. My attention remained on the economic side.

To us in Afghanistan it was clear that force and development were the two major tools at our disposal. Both needed attention, but only the military side seemed to have much resonance in Washington.

In May the new administrator of USAID, Randall Tobias, had visited. He explained that in his new dual role as head of USAID and director of U.S. foreign assistance with the rank of deputy secretary of state, he would make a new effort to coordinate assistance worldwide. Big decisions would be made in Washington, but the field would have considerably enhanced authority to allocate funds within the broad levels. We showed Tobias everything we could to make our case, and he left us with a sense that we would have some support if we could answer very detailed questions about what we would use the money for and how it fit into long-term planning. Before the month was out the USAID staff had compiled and sent to him a briefing comprising thirty slides of details.

I had raised economic issues in various discussions in early and mid-August but found the budget climate sour. I was not optimistic that we could increase funding beyond the base budget projections but believed we had to keep trying. We were again scrubbing the USAID budget to see where we could shift money to more roads. We found a little—"little," that is, in terms of what we needed, since several million dollars would have been a sizable sum in other countries. I consoled myself that wars had been won with less, and we drove on.

In late August the USAID director told me that despite his constant efforts, USAID Washington had slipped badly and had still not finalized a major contract for road construction. With his help I drafted a stinging cable and then sent it by e-mail to selected offices to let them know what would be sent formally if the contract was not finished. Much scurrying produced a promise that the contract would be done in a week and a request not to send the cable. I agreed to hold off a week but wrote that if the contract was not finished, the cable would go out with an additional line that it would have been sent a week earlier except for a specific office's unfulfilled promise that action would be completed. The promise was kept, the contract finished, and I did not send the draft. It was a small success and satisfying to our egos in Kabul, but it didn't make up for the time lost or solve our larger problem.

At the end of August we put forth a new proposal for major funding for roads. The new proposal built on but expanded our previous proposal. Army Corps of Engineers officers under General Eikenberry's command worked closely with USAID to put forth a plan for "Strategic Provincial Roads in Southern and Eastern Afghanistan." Our joint recommendation was for a major program to link all provincial capitals in the south and east to all their respective district capitals at a new cost of nearly $600 million, involving 1,700 kilometers of unpaved road and a further 385 kilometers to rehabilitate all-weather provincial roads.[10] No one could say we were thinking small.

Our continued expansion in what we recommended for roads seemed to cause confusion in Washington, which asked us for a total for the road-building program. In response I explained that views on road construction in Afghanistan had gone through various phases. Initially (immediately following the war in 2002) the United States had been reluctant to work on large-scale infrastructure. This was followed by a recognition among many donors of the need to rebuild the so-called ring road around Afghanistan. That vision on roads guided funding from FY 2003 through FY 2005.

The second vision laid out a program in the supplemental request for FY 2006 for additional critical roads. OMB rejected that request, although the three highest-priority roads were funded through reprogramming of existing funds. This was followed by our plan for critical provincial roads along with a restated need for roads requested in the earlier supplemental. A potential fourth phase would be necessary to expand the road program to the rest of Afghanistan. However, that would include areas of the country where security was not as large a problem, so it was possible that other donors working in those areas might bear part of the cost.[11]

We took advantage of every visitor to make our case for more money. Congressional visitors, U.S. governors, and administration officials all heard why economic funds were part of a war-fighting strategy. General Eikenberry's briefings made the same point. President Karzai continued to put roads and power high on his list of priorities with visitors. The $60 million promised by Secretary Rice in the summer and eventually delivered was a small milestone in this effort.

In late September and early October, I was in Washington for President Karzai's visit and for consultations. I saw Rice, National Security Adviser Hadley, the president, and many of Washington's senior-level officials. My message was stark: We were not winning. We were not yet losing, but if we didn't get the resources we needed, my successor might well be saying a year hence that we are losing. My interlocutors needed to break away from compartmented thinking in which military funding was considered part of a war and economic resources were seen as strictly developmental.

The administration seemed to me to have drifted into thinking about Afghanistan as a postconflict economic development operation, in which what is not done one year can be attended to the next and one balances budget pressures by doing only what one must in any one area. Under normal circumstances that would be a logical way to handle the conflicting budget pressures that Iraq was steadily imposing. My task was to get people to recognize that working with a small margin was a lousy way to fight a war. We needed a wartime mentality in our approach to funding.

By the end of the visit I felt that the combined efforts of all of us in Kabul, strongly supported by the Bureau of South and Central Asian Affairs in State, were beginning to gain traction. How much was the fighting and how much the steady banging away we were doing in reporting from Afghanistan was unclear, but thinking seemed to be shifting. We were being heard in a way we had not been the previous year. But what I had so far was a feeling, not a decision.

The USAID staff did a fantastic job of documenting our funding proposals. Reams of e-mail streamed back and forth. The thirty-slide PowerPoint created for Randall Tobias detailed the rationale for programs, priorities, and projected costs. This presentation became a sort of bible to which our supporters in Washington referred again and again to answer detailed, frequently repetitious questions from OMB and the USAID and State budget "bean counters." I might grumble that if they didn't trust us to know what we were doing, we ought to be replaced. I might wonder how knowing the exact priority order of $600 million of roads and their estimated per-kilometer cost would really help someone in Washington decide whether we had the priorities right or not. But if getting money needed details more than passion, we were determined to supply the details. We received strong support from Assistant Secretary Boucher and his deputy, John Gastright. For all our paper and push I doubt we could have made headway without their detailed backstopping and endless help.

By October 27, I was informed that Secretary Rice was pushing strongly for a supplemental. At last the big guns were starting to fire in our support. At the same time I agreed to restore funding for additional diesel fuel for Kabul's generators. I disliked using the money in such a nonproductive way, but the government was being heavily criticized and we could not let the few lights flickering in Kabul go out.

ISAF and Security

Security remained difficult as we moved into the fall. In September the Tenth Mountain Division kicked off the last of its major offensive campaigns in Ghazni Province. Conditions had deteriorated steadily since my first visit in the summer of 2005. The governor was an incompetent former commander with important political contacts in Kabul. The local police had fallen apart. Our embassy officer in the PRT was reporting that in some districts there were only ten or twenty policemen with a single vehicle, no radios, and no heavy weapons. Militia forces brought in by the governor were said to be closely linked to crime. The province was an open door for insurgent infiltration. I regularly reported these details to President Karzai. Just before President Karzai left for a September visit to Washington, he changed the governor. With a new offensive, economic resources the embassy and military were putting in, a new governor, and the ANAP program, we seemed to have at least a chance to stabilize conditions.

In the south we had also a long-running political controversy with the British. In October an agreement was signed allowing local control of the area around the Helmand district center of Musa Qala. Under the agreement local sheikhs were to keep the peace, ISAF and Afghan government forces were to stay out, and the Taliban was supposed to cease attacks. Under the agreement British forces pulled out of Musa Qala. This development in one tiny district of 360 districts in Afghanistan touched off a political controversy that convulsed Afghanistan and radiated back to London and Washington.

The actual tactical problem of Musa Qala was not very great. The district was small, and even if the Taliban used it as a rest area, the threat was not enormous. The problems were political. There was a fierce discussion in Afghanistan as to whether the local leaders were really in control or were only a front for the Taliban. The agreement was all too reminiscent of agreements during the fighting with the Soviets, when the mujahideen used temporary truces to consolidate power until they were ready to fight again. Time after time Afghans told me of how the late Ahmad Shah Massoud had deceived the Soviets in this way. Now, they insisted, the same thing was happening to ISAF.

In Parliament deputies from all over Afghanistan were discussing rumors of other truces that would turn over additional areas to the Taliban. More exaggerated rumors accused the British of conspiracy to turn over larger parts of Afghanistan to the Taliban, although the question of why they would want to do such a thing had no rational answer.

General Richards protested in repeated public interviews that the deal was an Afghan arrangement made by the local governor and agreed to in Kabul, not a British deal at all.[12] I thought there was something to this view. Mohammad Daoud, the governor of Helmand, had mentioned to me some time earlier that he was looking at a possible arrangement with local tribes. I was not comfortable with the arrangement but thought we could work our way through the problem and hoped we could keep the discussion quiet. Then on October 25, 2006, the *Telegraph* printed an article under the headline "US Envoy Attacks British Truce with Taliban."[13]

The headline was seriously misleading. I had said nothing of the kind as the journalist acknowledged in an e-mail pointing out that he had no control over the headline writers, which was perfectly true, and that the accurate quotes in the article itself had quite a different slant. What I had said was, "There is concern about who the truce was made with . . . and whether it will hold." The agreement needed to be "rigorously tested" to ensure that Musa Qala had not simply morphed into "a sanctuary for an area governed by the Taliban." In the press guidance I acknowledge that if the truce "moved people from support of the Taliban to support the government that would be good. The point is not to argue about the arrangement but to test it."

Even Brigadier Ed Butler, the outgoing commander of British forces in Helmand, was quoted in the same piece as saying, "I fully acknowledge that we could be being duped; that the Taliban may be buying time to reconstitute and regenerate. But every day that there is no fighting the power moves to the hands of the tribal elders who are turning to the government of Afghanistan for security and development."[14]

Charges that there was a major rift between General Richards and me were exaggerated.[15] We did not always agree, but we worked together more and better than the press understood and frequently helped each other. On Musa Qala, I had two objectives. The first was to ensure that the agreement was not replicated elsewhere. That was agreed to, with President Karzai's strong backing. Once that was done, the major political problem was solved, although it continued to agitate the press.

My second objective was to implement a portion of the agreement that allowed Afghan forces to operate in the district. If the Afghan army or police could go in and operate, fine. That would show that "local control" was not a cover for Taliban dominance as several reports were alleging and as I suspected was the case. On the other hand, if the Afghan forces were attacked, that would violate the agreement, allow ISAF to reoccupy the area, and end the discussion. ISAF was willing to make the test but did not want to be drawn into a major fight until it had forces in place to handle the operation. Agreement was eventually reached but not immediately implemented. Eventually the truce broke down, it became clear that the Taliban and not local elders were in firm and repressive control, and ISAF eventually took back Musa Qala, although not until December 2007.

Although I would have preferred to have seen the operation mounted earlier, I was fairly relaxed about the matter once we reached agreement that the Musa Qala deal would not be replicated elsewhere. By itself it was strategically insignificant. The major issue was political, and we managed eventually to quiet the storm, although perhaps not all the various Afghan suspicions.

The same day the *Telegraph* story had kicked Musa Qala onto the front pages, I had a long meeting with President Karzai. A thunderous rainstorm was pouring down outside. As I left the palace there was a moment when the rain was still coming down, bits of hail were dropping on the doormat, and I could see the sun shining in the west and glinting off the roses—all at the same time. It could have been a metaphor for working in Afghanistan.

7

Progress, Not Victory

November brought rain and then snow, relieving fears of a drought and eventually slowing fighting in the east but not much in the south. We were learning useful lessons. Washington decided to expand funding but not my stay. The north and east also had their issues, but everywhere the situation was different. And the counterdrug operation was full of problems.

Strategy and Travel

In mid-November two-thirds of the ambassadors to the UN Security Council visited Kabul. They and others in foreign capitals reacted to the security problems with a search for new strategies. I thought most of the ideas were poor. They underrated the need for lots of work, time, money, and troops and overrated the idea that some tinkering with the coordination mechanism or finding a bright policy idea would make things suddenly better—an unlikely expectation. There were several dangers in the discussion that preoccupied the multiple chanceries of the troop and economic donors.

One danger was that any suggestion that the major powers were rethinking the basic political structures of the Afghan state would touch off deeply destabilizing political rumors inside Afghanistan. Afghans live in a world of rumors and suspicion of abandonment. The wounds of years of war and betrayal between ethnic and tribal communities that had taken different sides during the years of struggle were not fully healed as the riots had starkly illustrated. There were crazy rumors that parts of the country would be turned over to the Taliban in secret negotiations. The north was afraid of the Pushtuns' power and vise versa. Thus any suggestion that the basic political arrangements of Bonn were being rethought would energize these divisive forces. In the end, these fears would fade before the reality that they were unjustified, but we could do without the intervening period of instability.

A greater problem in my judgment was that new arrangements or the grand strategic conference that some were considering would have to be negotiated with the Afghan government. There were only a few competent ministers and no fully competent ministries. Diverting time into lengthy negotiations would directly detract from the hard business of pushing forward the real work already agreed to.

These views were broadly shared in the diplomatic community in Kabul. In conversations with the UN representatives passing through, the ambassadors in Kabul were able to get across many of these doubts. In the meantime there was a NATO heads of state summit coming up in Riga, Latvia, in November. Afghanistan would be at the center of discussion. The United States would be pressing for more NATO troops, but only a few of the nations were prepared to do more than they were already doing.

In the late summer I was circulating among Afghan leaders to calm the mood by making clear that there were no secret negotiations and that no part of the country would be turned over to the Taliban. I consulted closely and repeatedly with President Karzai, so we were working in concert to calm things down. I wanted him to make a big speech to the nation to address many of these issues frontally. However, that was not his style.

Underlying the rumors was the basic tension between the old Afghanistan of tribal and ethnic balancing and the idea of a new state that drew everyone together and promoted merit over connections.

Accomplishing transition from one to the other would be a long task, and Afghans would have to shape it in ways we could not imagine. But insecurity strained faith in the possibility of change. Karzai was not at all alone in looking to old practices to face immediate threats.

There were some beneficial changes. Very gradually the quality of governors in the south and east was improving. They were not all good, but increasingly they were servants of the state rather than of their tribe or themselves. They could be changed at will; none were strong enough to dispute a presidential order to give up their positions. The bigger problem was the lack of qualified replacements for the poor performers.

A negative indirect result of the fighting in the south and east was that it sucked up too much attention and too many resources. There was a reluctance to challenge corrupt local leaders in other areas if things were quiet. And the ISAF troops in the north and west were predominately from nations that were inclined to approach their work as peace-keeping. They were content to leave things as they were if they were quiet, rather than supporting actions to overcome local resistance to legitimate central government control. The result in these provinces was that crime and drugs were deepening their roots in the local government and police. These were not the forces that would build a stable state, even if there were no outright challenges for the moment.

My concerns about the north were sharpened by a trip I made to Mazar-i-Sharif at the beginning of November to help open the last of five regional police centers. Briefings from the German general commanding forces in the region helped me realize how stretched his resources were. Out of nearly three thousand troops, only some seven hundred were infantry—fighting forces. Even if there were no caveats, we could scarcely have pulled any of these troops to the south. The general told me he had done a comparison of force to population between Kosovo and Afghanistan. If the forces were to be equalized, NATO would either need to go to 400,000 troops in Afghanistan or decline to 187 in Kosovo. Of course, neither was going to happen, but the analogy did illustrate the problem a dedicated German officer had to deal with in trying to control a broad swath of territory across the north.

One illustration of the multiple tensions blew up in late November over the ISAF arrest in the north of a Pushtun tribal figure. He had a despicable human rights record and may have been implicated in preparation of a suicide bomb attack. He also had strong local political backing that aroused a political clamor to release him, claiming that the government and the foreigners were picking on the Pushtuns. Supporters argued strongly that the arrest was politically motivated and showed discrimination against the Pushtuns. Why, they said, were we not going after murderers and major drug smugglers of other ethnic groups? This seemed to them to prove that the issue was political.

It seemed to me that the government would look weak if the man was released. President Karzai agreed to ask the attorney general to review the case and give us all an opinion as to whether conviction was likely on the basis of the evidence. There was also a question as to whether excessive force was used in the arrest, in which one Afghan was killed, and the military was reviewing the matter.

At President Karzai's request and in order to reduce the political pressure, ISAF commander General Richards and I met with the family and several tribal leaders from the north. Interestingly, the family did not repeat the political arguments of anti-Pushtun discrimination. The father explicitly rejected that approach, saying the problem was not ethnic but a result of the governor's criminal corruption. The translator elided much of the criticism of the governor, but we had a Pushtu speaker with us who filled us in. We had considerable evidence that we were able to muster to show that there were solid reasons for the arrest, and we promised to pay attention to the attorney general's conclusions. So, while the meeting did not resolve anything, it lowered the political temperature.

However, the general complaints about ISAF pressing only on Pushtuns had some merit. The problem was another illustration of the complexities of working in Afghanistan. ISAF's mandate was to suppress insurgents. In the north such insurgents came from minority Pushtun communities in largely Tajik and Uzbek areas. ISAF had no mandate to arrest criminals, and the Afghan government was too weak, and in some cases too corrupt, to enforce the law. When arrests were made, corrupt judges frequently released the accused. The only real pressure was from ISAF arrests, and to the local Pushtuns the technical details of the ISAF mandate were neither comprehensible nor credible.

ISAF had power and used it against only one group, so it must be acting politically. That is the way the locals reasoned. Yet while the problem was evident, an easy solution was not.

ISAF troops could not become local policemen on the beat. Quite apart from inadequate numbers, foreigners would never have the expertise to unravel the complexities of local politics, crime, and feuds. The effort to build a credible Afghan police was correct but far too long-range to eliminate the growing tensions in a timely way. There was a risk that the perception of discrimination would lead more Pushtuns to side with the Taliban. Could ISAF find more immediate ways to bolster Afghan government authority? The issue needed to be taken up by NATO headquarters in Brussels but was not even understood as a problem.

I did not see clearly how to change this situation in the north but thought that if I began discussing the problem with colleagues, we might make some progress. The business of moving from ideas to shaping government action is fascinating. It is a far more incremental matter than it is one of laying out a grand idea and having everyone jump up and salute. Real policymaking isn't like that. Rather, one has to start talking and writing, use conversations to build alliances, shift the specifics of ideas to incorporate the thoughts of others, and take advantage of opportunities to move forward. In this way, what starts as a limited conception of one or a few persons gradually becomes the accepted common wisdom, lacking specific authorship (which some would resist) and more a matter that everyone sees as obvious and needing action. It is absorbing work and an endless study of human nature. Sometimes we made progress, but on the particular northern issue I never found a way to energize the debate.

We did have some moments of progress to encourage us. On November 20, I visited both Ghazni and Assadabad in Konar Province. We were making some progress in both. Although the PRTs and our political officers in them had doubts and questions about both new governors, each was more active than his predecessor. One valley in Konar has always been a problem for central authorities. In response to recent security incidents, a former schoolteacher who was now a district governor was particularly active. He and the province governor were threatening to raise a tribal *lashkar*, essentially a tribal army, to move in and live on the land of the offending local population if it didn't behave. It was very Afghan, not a modern state concept, but they were not asking us to pay for weapons and we would leave it to them.

In the end, the *lashkar* idea was not followed up. The two officials fell out. Eventually both were removed. Such challenges illustrate the two-steps-forward, one-step-back situation that characterizes much of the work in Afghanistan and makes it so difficult to provide a clear public bottom line.

A day before visiting Ghazni, I had flown with General Freakley to officially open the PRT in Nuristan that we had decided on earlier. We were not in the beautiful green valley we had visited; putting the PRT there would have to wait until the completion of a road. But we were moving forward with a temporary location on the southern edge of the province, and from there we would be able to mount more development activities as well as project force. The PRT sat in a bowl surrounded by jagged, barren mountains. In the stark clarity of the light that is so apparent in Afghanistan and so difficult to put into words, the mountains seemed to have an infinite variety of brown tones. In the distance, snow-clad peaks filled the horizon.

Each trip brought new ideas as well as new information. On the visit to Khost, Deputy USAID Director Carl Abdu Rahman and I began thinking about ways to improve the effectiveness of our USAID officers in the PRTs. Quick impact projects were important, but the military could do many of them faster than USAID could and had more funding available through CERP than we had been able to get for the PRTs without a supplemental budget appropriation. What the military couldn't do well were the long-term projects: linking road construction to setting up long-term road maintenance to repair winter washouts, linking a school to the ministry budget to ensure there were teachers and materials in the out years, and all the kinds of long-term training that Afghans desperately needed to staff a government and build a country. These longer-term and national-level efforts were where USAID had its greatest strength. We needed to do more, as Carl put it, to link the single USAID officer in the PRT with a larger toolbox of national-level help that could be connected to the PRT's military resources.

The NATO summit came and went without any visible change for us. Everyone appeared to have pledged continued solidarity to the Afghan mission. A number of countries also pledged additional assets, including fighters, helicopters, and infantry companies as well as training teams that would mentor the Afghan National Army. NATO's secretary general said that this meant 90 percent of NATO's force requirements had been met.[1] Our analysis was that we had gained a few useful bits and pieces but not the battalions or the combat power that were really needed.

Without much additional combat power, the search in capitals for "new" ideas and strategies returned. At the NATO summit in Riga and for a time afterward, the French were pushing the idea of a contact group. In the Balkans this had meant a small number of nations that had directed the political efforts and pressure fairly successfully. The idea was not suitable for Afghanistan. I may have been the most outspoken, but I was not at all alone in the Kabul diplomatic group in saying so at a meeting of NATO ambassadors.

There were numerous problems with the contact group idea. In comparison to the Balkans, Afghanistan had a far larger and less cohesive group of donors, many of whom would insist on being involved as they had in the JCMB. The Afghans would not accept orders the way the government in Bosnia had. (This judgment was proved right much later.)[2] Many of our problems lay at deeper levels of detail than a contact group would focus on. And the effort to negotiate a new effort with the Afghans would detract from what the limited number of competent Afghans needed to be doing in country. Privately, I also wondered why the French, who at the time were doing little within the NATO context to help and provided only small amounts of economic assistance, should suddenly have a large seat at the political table. In the end, the idea died away before anything had been achieved, although it continued to have some political echoes.

As we discussed ideas among the ambassadors from NATO nations, I joked that what we needed was PMT: patience, money, and time. My Italian colleague perceptively added "simple" (as in, "keep it simple") to our list of essentials. PMTS became our in-house joke, but we continued to tell our governments they needed to focus on this concept.

Improving Justice

Democracy may be a new concept, but justice is fundamental to Islamic understanding of proper government. Injustice is one of the few reasons for overthrowing a ruler sanctioned by the Koran. And everyone agreed that the Afghan justice system was rotten. It had not always been so. There had always been a measure of impunity for very senior figures, but in general Afghan courts, before the years of fighting, had been respected and judges had held high social standing. That was all gone. Judges needed training and motivation. Salaries needed to be raised to a living wage. Courthouses needed to be built. Above all, Afghans needed to see that offenders were arrested instead of protected.

Early efforts at judicial reform stalled amid squabbling among the allies and Afghan perceptions that they were being dictated to. Even the reform-minded Afghans resented the way early efforts at justice reform were carried out. The appointment of a new chief justice to the Supreme Court and changes in the international approach opened new possibilities. But large-scale reform would be extremely slow. There was an increasing public clamor for arrests. A key figure was the attorney general, who in Afghan practice has many of the investigative functions that belong to the police in the American system.

In early August 2006 President Karzai was considering whom to appoint to this highly charged position. He discussed the issue with many people. He and I had several discussions on the subject. Overall I tried to press for the appointment of someone who would crack down, carry out arrests, and raise the prestige of the government. President Karzai said he agreed with me on the qualities needed, but the list of candidates was not extensive and he was trying to balance political, ethnic, and regional factors in his senior officials.

The discussion came down to Dr. Abdul Jabbar Sabit and one other candidate. Sabit was controversial. Looking like a figure from the Old Testament, Sabit was erect and lean, had piercing eyes and a long gray beard, yet he wore Western suits. Sabit was deeply religious. He had been close to the extremist Gulbuddin Hekmatyar (now with the Taliban) in the mujahideen but also had a Western degree from Canada, where he had settled his family. His children were in school in the United States. He was prone to outbursts of anger and famous for making rapid, sometimes snap decisions. Sure of his convictions, he had a reputation for being difficult to control.

Sabit had also been extremely helpful and hardworking as legal adviser in the Ministry of Interior in drafting and putting through critical antidrug legislation. Veteran prosecutors from the U.S. Department of Justice held him in high regard. He was bitterly opposed to corruption. There was no question that if appointed Sabit would arrest people, but he might also provoke major political tensions. In short, he was the ultimate wild card.

In discussions at the palace I emphasized that if there were someone else who could be depended upon to go after criminals and corruption, I had no special brief for Sabit. The problem, as President Karzai agreed, was that none of the other candidates seemed to fit the bill. Whether my distinction between the man and the qualifications was believed or was taken to be polite language surrounding an American message to appoint Sabit, I cannot be sure. Afghan conversation is often indirect, the search for hidden meanings is constant, and sometimes it is difficult to have a simple message believed as meaning no more than is stated, even when one is aware of the communication problem and making every effort to seem truthful.

Some of my European colleagues were pushing for a different candidate and were disappointed when Sabit was appointed. One argued that a particular person would be "adequate" if supported, but political support was exactly what was not likely to be available if the going got tough. I joked that we had a choice between "an unguided missile and one that won't launch." I preferred the unguided one. At least it might hit something.

I wondered whether I had made the right call. I had pushed harder than I preferred but felt that movement was essential. Sabit went to work quickly, making numerous arrests for corruption. He became famous for traveling around the country making rapid investigations and throwing officials in jail. Long lines jammed the waiting room at his small office, as desperate villagers from all over the country brought their individual complaints of corruption and wrongdoing to his door. When some officials were too high-ranking for him to reach, he protested loudly and publicly. Complaints to President Karzai were numerous. We provided him with an armored SUV for protection.

Unfortunately, Sabit and the chief justice, unquestionably the two most reform-minded senior justice officials, did not get along well and clashed over several issues. Working with others in the international community, we tried several times to make peace between them. More than once we fielded urgent cell phone calls from Sabit threatening resignation. Neither official had a monopoly on virtue. The courts needed to show in public and open trials that they could produce just sentences. The attorney general needed to show in court that he had the evidence to back up his arrests. Most of these issues were irrelevant to the mass of Afghans among whom Sabit, often wildly acclaimed on the street, became popular.

Uzbeks and Turkmen were unhappy with Sabit's appointment. They believed President Karzai had promised the job to an Uzbek, and the Uzbek and Turkman parliamentary delegates walked out of Parliament in protest. They felt the appointment was a capstone to growing ethnic discrimination. Although the pressure was heavy, I urged President Karzai to hold firm on the appointment because there was no other qualified candidate. The Uzbeks complained to the president in a long meeting. Based on that conversation they concluded that I was responsible.

I met with a delegation of Uzbek parliamentarians on August 12 to try to calm matters. We had a long but polite meeting. I was as frank as I felt I could be in telling them what I had done and what I had not done. If necessary I felt I should take a bit of extra responsibility rather than enflame the already tense relations between the Uzbeks and the president. I urged them to return to Parliament and settle their differences there. Eventually matters calmed down.

Another aspect of our efforts to improve the justice system focused on the province of Wardak. USAID had a provincial justice project there, and we had decided to build a prison. A prison may sound like an unlikely aid project, but Afghan prisons were terrible. A modern prison was also to be a training center for Afghan correctional personnel and would provide spin-offs for the local economy.

In September, I drove the short distance to Wardak to see how the project was going and to keep a long-standing promise to provincial Governor Abdul Jabar Naimi to pay a visit.

Most of the two-hour drive was spent negotiating Kabul's traffic. We wove through crowds of men in their long shirts and floppy trousers; past piled-up pushcarts and stands overflowing with delicious melons stacked in rows; past butcher shop after butcher shop with meat hanging outside in the bone-dry air; past lumber yards with hundreds of thin, pale bark-stripped poplar trunks, which the Afghans use for construction, standing on end and pointing toward the blue sky. Finally we crossed the bridge above the river and the flat where hundreds of cows, sheep, and goats waited to be sold and came out into the open country. Despite grinding poverty and the huge challenge of building a modern infrastructure, there was no question Kabul was becoming a bustling center of economic activity. Outside the city, hills rolled away to more distant peaks standing out in the clear Afghan air.

In Maidan Shahr, the small capital of Wardak, the Turkish government had started construction of a PRT. They were already building three schools and had a number of other projects in the works. The Turkish ambassador met me there, and together we took part in several meetings. The Turks were approaching their mission seriously and planned to bring in an experienced civilian administrator as well as about a hundred soldiers. Wardak was basically quiet, but I was struck by how few police were in the province. There were no ISAF troops aside from the small Turkish garrison whose protection mission for the PRT was the maximum they could do. There was definitely progress, but I left the town aware of how fragile the situation was and how easily it could be disrupted.

Several other events in September provided cause for optimism. For months Mike Metrinko had pressed me to visit a private Hazara school in Kabul, and I was finally able to make time for the visit. The Hazaras are of Central Asian extraction, and there is a dispute about whether they came to Afghanistan with Genghis Khan or in a separate migration. While some may have roots in Buddhism, most Hazaras are Shia Muslims. We trundled through a section of town lined with shops selling new and used clothes. The area could have been in many parts of Central Asia with all the almond-shaped eyes and flat cheekbones of the passersby.

The school is funded by donations from the Hazara community and very small tuitions—about ten dollars a month. Some of the families are too poor to afford even the low tuition, though, and receive help from the Hazara community and private donations. Over three thousand students, both boys and girls, attend the school. I found it an impressive and all-too-rare example of self-help, but when I said so to others they hinted that it was all done through secret Iranian funding. I doubted that.

When I arrived, the boys, each in a blue shirt and dark pants, were all turned out in rows in the courtyard. I had to make a speech, so I talked about the value of education and told them about how my father would not have met my mother or come to America if his family had not scrimped to send him to a summer education program in Geneva, where the poor student from Austria met a young American girl. The education offered these Hazaras was impressive and so were the achievements of the students.

Later in the month I hosted a reception for Afghan high school students who had just returned from a year in America. They had lived with American families, many in small towns and one on a ranch. They had many stories of life with their American families. Most importantly, they brought back with them an understanding of America and Americans totally different from that conveyed by Hollywood films and heavily armed troops. Such events stood in happy contrast to the deadly attack on the convoy outside the embassy a few days later. Trying to keep all these images in a single focus can tax any imagination.

In mid-September, I drove to the Panjshir Valley for the annual commemoration of the assassination of Ahmad Shah Massoud. The drive from Kabul to Bagram Air Base covers dramatic but largely barren plains where land mines have retarded resettlement. Occasionally the charred remains of a Soviet armored personnel carrier, the steel bones picked as if by vultures, still mar the landscape. After Bagram the country changes into fertile plains: miles and miles of fields and trees, small villages, and watercourses.

The ceremony was smaller than the previous year but still well attended. I sat on a long veranda with the other dignitaries. No matter how many chairs are set up, people whose status has to be accommodated always arrive without warning resulting in a frantic carrying of chairs. Armchairs and plastic garden chairs were passed over people and crowded onto the porch four feet above the bordering flower bed. Just below our feet, crammed in among the flowers, were interspersed chairs for bodyguards, facing out toward the crowd so that each of these heavily armed and dangerous-looking men was sitting in the midst of roses and sunflowers nodding about his shoulders. The valley was peaceful and the increase in prosperity since my previous visit was clear.

ISAF Fights Better and Politics Get Harder

As we passed into November the security situation continued to cause serious problems. A roadside bomb in the south killed a respected senior Canadian diplomat serving at the PRT in Kandahar. Canada restricted all civilians to base until they could decide on improved security arrangements. Ashley Abbott, my dedicated USAID officer in Kandahar, continued to sortie out, getting rides from U.S. Special Forces to projects and discussions with local elders and officials. Her dedication was exceeded only by her extensive knowledge of local politics, having served two years in the field. She survived one convoy bombing and then a second in which a military friend died as she sat beside him. We brought her back to Kabul for a rest, but she was soon back in the field. Too little credit has been given to the risks our dedicated civilian volunteers run to carry on with their missions.

In the east, U.S. forces working closely with an effective Afghan governor cleared out the Taqab Valley in Kapisa Province near Kabul. The location had been a base for mounting attacks into Kabul. The operation was meticulously planned with the active input of the governor, who moved into the valley with the U.S. forces and reinforced the mutually designed military operations and aid projects with his personal efforts and communication outreach. It was a great example of what could be done—and for a time it worked, but only for a time.[3] None of our smaller successes were compensating for problems in the south.

I made several trips to Kandahar and met the new Dutch general, Ton van Loon, who took over command of the southern region in the fall. We developed a solid, cooperative relationship. His challenge was that our collective inability to build on the success of Operation Medusa had allowed the Taliban to gradually reoccupy positions in Panjwai and Zahre districts near Kandahar.

The Budget Gets Better

Meanwhile we were making progress with getting more funding from Washington. On the military side we were putting forth a large plan designed by Generals Eikenberry and Durbin and their staff for much larger funding to equip the Afghan army and police. The Afghans themselves had mounted a major program to reduce desertions and coax absent soldiers to return to the ranks. We proposed to increase army pay and to fund significant reenlistment bonuses. We planned to propose an increase in the police force from 62,000 to 82,000, if we could secure the funding. Afghan soldiers were fighting well, and in general we felt that there was a solid basis for building a better-equipped force. Washington support for the large military increases was not certain but seemed to be encountering smaller obstacles than the economic funding. (The economic funding too was slowly gaining agreement, particularly after Secretary Rice lent her support.)

In early November National Security Adviser Hadley visited. We were able to review our proposals in some depth. He had good meetings with President Karzai and senior leaders and made a trip to Kandahar for an update on the situation in the south. These meetings strengthened his support for our proposed budget supplemental. A few days later the resignation of Secretary of Defense Rumsfeld was suddenly announced. We shed no tears in Kabul.

A meeting of the Deputies Committee in the first week of November was followed by an important National Security Council meeting on November 9.[4] I participated in both by secure video links. In the second meeting, the NSC finally made the important decision to go forward with a major supplemental for fiscal year 2007. It still remained to get OMB agreement to the numbers, and I feared they would again make cuts.

My one intervention in the NSC meeting was to remind everyone that it takes a long time for funding decisions to have an actual effect. If the funding was strung out over time, I said, we might pay heavily in the war. Assistant Secretary Boucher was also in Kabul for another of his many visits and gave strong backing to the need to move forward with the supplemental.

On November 28 it was cold in Kabul with the temperature in the teens, but I was warmed by the OMB decision (known as a "pass-back").

We would have over $1 billion in the supplemental proposal. OMB cut the sum into two pieces. Initially only $558 million was approved for the 2007 supplemental. After some pushing back from us, this was raised to $732 million for the 2007 supplemental and another $300 million technically in a 2008 supplemental. The two bills would be sent to Congress at the same time, but the 2008 bill would be voted on later. The division was something I had warned against.

We argued that "all funds requested in the supplemental are needed in the very short term and not 18–20 months from now when FY08 resources would be available. . . . We cannot win in Afghanistan on the cheap."[5] OMB had also reduced the FY 2008 regular budget submission by $184.6 million. The budget remained substantial, but the cuts, we said, "further undermine our counter-insurgency strategy."[6]

Still, this was a major victory. We had gone from virtually no supplemental the previous year to a major increase. OMB was still trying to make surgical cuts in a war budget, but the basic principle of the need for a major increase had been accepted. My account has focused on our efforts in Kabul, but the decision reflected the hard work and pushing of innumerable people in State, USAID, and the NSC who spent long hours working toward the final success. Our USAID staff in Kabul provided extensive data. Later, when the proposal went to the Congress, we were told that ours was one of the best laid-out and documented budget submissions sent up in a long time.

Of course, having a decision didn't end the discussions or requests for information. An additional NSC meeting on November 29 lasted over an hour, although the decision was clear in the first fifteen minutes. One of my staff perceptively said it reminded him of the movie *Groundhog Day*, in which the main character lives through the same day over and over.

More strategy discussions followed in early December with SCA presenting a comprehensive strategic briefing for Secretary Rice. There was discussion of trying to reach strategic agreements with the Afghan government on administrative reform. Whatever strategy they agreed on, the Afghan government would continue making decisions incrementally and tactically; a negotiation on "strategic" issues would expend much time for little result.

Other ideas surfaced on how to micromanage PRTs and assumed a degree of control we were unlikely to get, particularly over ISAF PRTs led by other nations. There were recurrent proposals to get NATO or economic donors to do more. I sympathized with the motivation. I too believed they should do more. But President Bush had just been to the NATO summit and had gotten little extra help, despite NATO's claim that success in Afghanistan was an existential issue for the organization's future relevance. Efforts to chase possible new contributions as an alternative to the United States itself doing more were akin to chasing a mirage instead of digging a well. I received strong backing from SCA in trying to keep Washington focused on the decisions it needed to make— more troops and more money—rather than trying to micromanage field operations or chase strategic diversions.

Underlying the individual discussions was a recurring tendency at senior levels to think that if they could only find the right policy, then issues on which we were painstakingly pushing forward would suddenly bound forward into a better world. I understood that there was a risk that some might think me too much the "gray bureaucrat," too often saying no to ideas from headquarters. For my part, I came to believe that the problem is that most civilian leaders have spent their professional lives working on issues where what counts are the big policy decisions made in Washington. They have little in their backgrounds to really understand the problems of implementing complex, long-term programs with thousands of individual pieces. It is not a matter of intelligence but of life and professional experience. In any event, I felt my professional duty was to give my best judgment on what would or would not work. I could try not to be brusque or offensive, but I could not shape my judgments to please others. All too often those judgments were that things were not going well.

Drugs Again and President Karzai Visits Washington

In August we were getting reports on the levels of poppy production from the UN and our own sources. The numbers were not good. In some ways we had not done badly. Eradication had taken place to some degree in most of the poppy-producing provinces. Altogether some 37,000 acres of poppy were destroyed, which would have been good had production not ballooned at the same time. The previous year's eradication failure had helped to convince many farmers that they could safely plant poppy. The resulting inclination to plant poppy was reinforced by pervasive complaints that promised economic development had not been carried out. Some of the expectations were unrealistic as were some of the promises. But overall the perception that poppy production was going up was correct.

There were all sorts of problems involved in creating a new bureaucracy, training people, and distributing money to the provinces to pay for eradication. We made some progress. New information units to carry out an integrated public information campaign in the provinces were coming along, but only a few were fully formed and most of them started work too late to have much impact on 2006 planting decisions. And, of course, we had not moved forward with agricultural development at anything like our desired rate because of funding limitations.

Some of these problems we could fix. My staff developed an improved program to have eradication validated by the UN and to pay governors a flat rate based on acreage destroyed. This would get us out of the endless hassles of seeking little understood receipts. The Afghan Eradication Force had improved and would do even better the following year. A new program to reward poppy-free provinces with cash grants to be managed by the provincial government was on the drawing boards and was to be well received.

But these were all seen as marginal improvements. The year 2006 was an election one in the United States, and Washington was feeling congressional pressure to show big gains. I understood this but saw no way of achieving the desired miracle. There were many discussions of chemical spraying. It was certain that the Afghan government would not accept aerial spraying. Ground spraying—that is, having workers administer the chemical spray on the ground by tractor or backpack sprayers—seemed a more controllable scheme and one we might convince the Afghan government to try. It would not produce a huge breakthrough in eradication,[7] but it would cross a major psychological barrier and show Afghan farmers and foreign audiences that the Afghan government was serious about reducing poppy production.

After considerable internal discussion, the idea of ground spraying was put forward during President Karzai's September 2006 visit to Washington. Karzai heard our arguments about the safety of ground spraying and thought Afghans might be convinced that the process was sound. Later some charged him with duplicity, but this was unfair in my judgment.

The decision came to a head in a meeting in Kabul on January 21. Much of the Afghan cabinet as well as the major international players, including ISAF, myself, and the British and UN representatives, were present. To the surprise of many of us, the ministers were overwhelming and vocally against the ground-spraying proposal. A highly educated deputy minister with a Western PhD in toxicology argued strongly that while we used thousands of pounds of the same spray safely in California, we protected our water sources; Afghans drink from open watercourses. He cited studies of the health risks. The security ministries were opposed, believing that Taliban propaganda would profit greatly from any spraying. I had never seen the cabinet so eloquent, outspoken, and firm in their views. The British (who were the so-called lead nation on counternarcotics) and I made our arguments as strongly as we could. However, the international community was divided with some nations hesitant to push eradication. The UN could not take a strong position because of differences within the UN agencies.[8] The international divisions certainly weakened our position vis-à-vis the united views of the Afghan cabinet.

In the end, President Karzai accepted the strong views of his cabinet. Perhaps he could have overruled them as Washington expected. But as I listened to the long debate I wondered how we could persuade illiterate farmers that what we proposed was safe if we could not persuade these highly educated, Western-trained ministers of our view? Perhaps President Karzai was right in his judgment of what would not work with his own people and the danger of bowing to foreign pressure. In any event, we would not have ground spraying in our toolkit for the next eradication season.

Washington was not happy but accepted President Karzai's decision. During their visits later in the year, Assistant Secretary of State for INL Anne Patterson and White House drug "czar" John Walters (officially titled the Director of National Drug Control Policy) worked with us to improve the programs we had to the maximum extent. Walters was realistic about what was achievable, and his hardheaded approach based on years of experience gave us hope that Washington would understand the need to allow time for the existing strategy to work.

In December we were deep in the discussion of eradication in Helmand. Working there would require ISAF support. This raised touchy issues about where to conduct eradication without making the insurgent problem worse. The military was not comfortable, but we were slowly working our way to practical decisions even if we could not fully agree on the underlying policy.

Back to War

Casualties continued. In December governors from several U.S. states visited National Guard troops from their states. In their meetings with President Karzai, one mentioned the death of a soldier from his state. That evening we were surprised to receive a written condolence letter from Karzai to the widow of the fallen soldier along with a box made of Afghan lapis lazuli. It was the completely spontaneous gesture of a fundamentally decent man. He lamented the deaths of foreign soldiers on behalf of his fledgling nation and was particularly moved that American women soldiers would place themselves at risk in order to defeat the Taliban—and that American society would permit this.

Fighting was slowing a bit in the east with winter's snow impeding insurgent movement, but I reported that the slowdown meant nothing; it was purely seasonal. The south had no snow. Fighting there continued. The gains of Operation Medusa were fading away. In mid-December ISAF attacked again into the same districts in Kandahar they had gone into before. The operation, this time with the Afghan name of Operation Baaz Tsuka, was carefully prepared and profited from lessons we had learned.

Civilians again received notice and evacuated the area. The Taliban did not put up the same resistance, and the area was reoccupied. A great deal of work in the Policy Action Group had gone into preparing for humanitarian and reconstruction assistance. Afghan ministers were deeply involved in the preparations. Several ministers made repeated visits to the area after the battle to implement Afghan reconstruction projects.

Certainly we were far from completely successful. Projects still took far too long to implement. Afghan forces were less numerous than needed. The area is not fully under control even as this is written in 2009. But lessons were learned and applied, and performance improved. And when one compares the level of security in the districts of Panjwai and Zahre brought about by the ISAF and Afghan forces with the inability of much larger Soviet forces to ever exert similar control, one has some measure of the weakness of the Taliban as compared to the Afghan mujahideen's resistance to the Soviets. That comparison provides no promise of success, but it is important to keep in mind when one hears simplistic arguments that Afghans always throw out the foreigners.

On December 10, I visited Lashkar-Gah in Helmand. I spent much of the day with the British task force and finished up with a helicopter trip to the training center for auxiliary police. There was some reporting about a possible suicide attack on the training center that justifiably agitated my security guards. I cancelled the participation of those who were going to travel by car and made sure no extra personnel would be posted outside the perimeter, but I decided I would helicopter in as planned. Gen. Nabi Jan was the commander of police in Helmand and had an excellent reputation from his previous work in Zabul, where I had known him. I wanted to show my support for what he was doing with the auxiliary police training. Further, he was expecting me, and Afghans set great store on personal courage. If I had not shown up because of a threat much smaller than what he lived with every day, he would have taken it badly. As it was, he greeted me with a big hug, and we had a brief ceremony in which I presented a certificate of appreciation. He gave me a very good briefing about security. Nothing at all happened, and I departed with new knowledge of some of the weaknesses in the ANAP program.

As planned, the trainees were getting only two weeks of training. Of this time, one day was devoted to explaining the Afghan constitution and police legal duties. I asked some of the trainees if they would prefer to spend more time on practical subjects like vehicle searches rather than the day of constitutional and legal training. Interestingly, they were firm in saying no; they were Afghan police, and they wanted to understand their country's governmental system. It was a more sophisticated response than I expected from young men, many of whom were illiterate, and something for those who ask if Afghans have a sense of nationalism to reflect on.

I was on the ground for only a short time, the danger was minimal, and I don't think I was reckless. It was important to show our people in the field and the Afghans that I would come to visit them. It wasn't normal diplomacy, but neither was fighting an insurgency.

Two days later I was back in the south when President Karzai held a PAG meeting in Kandahar on December 12. The meeting was symbolic, an opportunity for President Karzai to show political strength by visiting the field in the aftermath of a successful battle. Ambassadors, generals, and tribal elders all assembled. Governors from all the southern provinces were present except for Governor Daoud of Helmand, whose convoy was hit by a suicide bomb just before his departure, killing a number of his bodyguards. Daoud was unhurt but decided to stay in the province to deal with the aftermath of the attack.

As he always did, President Karzai engaged in direct, back-and-forth discussions with tribal leaders who pulled no punches in voicing their frustrations. He heard demands from many and was able to provide some guidance and answers. He threw most of the blame for the security problems on Pakistan, saying specifically that the bombs come from Pakistan. These statements were popular with Afghans, but I wondered whether ignoring the problems of corruption and governance didn't weaken the overall sense of Karzai's leadership. I announced the Kajaki Dam project for a second time, but the approbation made it seem original.

The logistics of bringing so many senior officials together in a somewhat dangerous city were formidable, but ISAF managed the burden well. Most of the foreigners returned to Kabul that night, while President Karzai remained for meetings with more tribal elders and provincial leaders. He enjoyed such encounters and always seemed to draw strength from meetings out of Kabul with his own people.

Despite the success of one battle, we clearly needed help. In a report on December 4, fully coordinated with my military colleagues, I had recommended three additional U.S. battalions, expanded resources to improve implementation, and a ten-year commitment to paying Afghan army and police salaries to make clear our determination to stay for the long haul and permit better planning. The message also recommended renewed pressure on the government of Pakistan to cut off cross-border incursions. On December 20, shortly after the meeting in Kandahar, I sent a further message restating that the forces deployed were not sufficient.

The December 20 message argued that ISAF needed to get additional forces in 2007 to position itself for offensive operations in 2008. With great help from General Eikenberry in shaping the recommendations, we specified that of the three battalions recommended previously we needed a battalion with full support (so-called combat enablers, such as helicopters) as a theater reserve and two more battalions for the south. We also needed two quick-reaction forces and thirty NATO training teams to work with the Afghan army. We recommended that there be a ten-year commitment in principle to fund Afghan army and police salaries to offset an anticipated shortfall. This would have provided needed predictability, for rational long-term planning instilled confidence among the Afghans and international donors who were concerned about the impact on the development program of increasing the security forces' pay. The recommendations were targeted for discussion as Secretary Robert Gates took over from Secretary Rumsfeld in Washington. Both messages underscored our disquiet with what was happening in Pakistan.

There was new leadership in Helmand Province. The corrupt former police chief was gone. However, he had been a tribal ally of the former governor, and to avoid alienating the tribe to which both belonged, Governor Daoud was also removed and replaced by Asadullah Wafa, who had been deputy minister of tribal affairs and previously governor of Konar. Wafa was a long-serving administrator who, it was hoped, would be able to handle tribal issues in Helmand. I met with him before his departure for Helmand and assured him of my support.[9]

The problem of finding governors who could be effective in the south was intensely difficult. Helmand had multiple tribes, some of which were internally divided by feuds reaching back many years. In Sangin District alone there were four major tribes with differences among them and three tending to ally against the fourth, which, in turn, had developed close ties to the Taliban and was implicated in the drug problem. Settling Sangin would require negotiation of a tribal settlement as well as force to suppress the insurgents and back up state authority. And this was only one district of fifteen in one province. Resolving these problems had to be melded sufficiently with the concept of state government to keep the Western donors on board yet not bend so much to Western concepts of governance that it offended local ideas of fairness. Sangin was a microcosm of the difficulty of trying to prescribe strategy from the eminence of distant capitals.

A governor in Helmand had to be Pushtu to have any chance of being accepted but could not be closely tied to one of the tribes or clans in the province. He needed to be of a certain age and seniority to command respect and yet be a capable administrator and not have too bloody a record from the civil war years. He needed to be able to maintain confident and productive relations with ISAF military leaders and aid donors on whom the governor would have to depend for force and economic projects. And a governor had to be able to keep President Karzai's confidence since any number of local leaders would regularly be making their way to Kabul to complain of wrongs, real or invented, to serve their parochial interests. To note that finding such a person willing to work under constant personal threat was not easy is a massive understatement.

The Problem of Pakistan

Pakistan was a recurring issue throughout my time as ambassador as it remains today. Training camps, recruitment centers, command and control of the insurgency, and fanatical instruction in some religious schools that helped bring new recruits to the insurgent cause were all to be found inside Pakistan. Whether this situation represented Pakistani policy or an inability to exert control was the subject of heated debate, but absolutely firm evidence did not come to my attention during my tour.

At times we seemed to be making progress in getting Pakistani president Musharraf to do more against the Taliban. When he and President Karzai met, they often seemed to make some progress, only to have matters degenerate within a week or two. Musharraf had moved from denying there was a problem to admitting the Taliban was present in Pakistan. Yet Pakistani actions were few. When pressure reached a certain intensity, there would be an arrest or a military action in Pakistan that was just enough to reduce Western, particularly American, insistence, but then there would be no follow-up when pressure declined. Whether this was because of a secret Pakistani policy to preserve ties with the Taliban or because Pakistani authorities were fearful of touching off battles they might not win was endlessly debated without conclusion. Opinions were strong, but clear evidence was lacking.

In early September General Eikenberry and I visited Islamabad with key members of our staffs for another discussion with Ambassador Crocker and his team on how to move the Pakistani government toward more action. We were particularly disturbed by the signing of a peace agreement between the government of Pakistan and tribal groups in the North West Frontier Province (NWFP) of Pakistan on September 5, 2006.[10]

In theory the agreement would stop cross-border infiltration into Afghanistan as well as attacks within Pakistan in return for turning over control of North Waziristan to tribal leaders. For three months while the agreement was being negotiated, we had watched the number of cross-border attacks rise steadily. There was no evidence that cross-border attacks were stopping or even slowing after the agreement was signed. The prospect that a similar agreement might be negotiated in South Waziristan was deeply alarming. Over time it became apparent that no part of the arrangement was being kept, but it was many months before the government of Pakistan would face that fact. By that time the government had lost even more authority and control in the tribal areas.

In September 2006 there was some hope that a trilateral meeting between Presidents Bush, Musharraf, and Karzai to be held in Washington later in the month might make a difference. Like so many meetings, it produced promises but no action on the border. It did set in motion a new diplomatic idea, that of a major cross-border Afghan-Pakistani tribal meeting, or *loya jirga*.

The idea was President Karzai's. It arose in conversations he had with senators the day before the trilateral dinner, and President Bush's first notice of it was from me in the briefing in the Oval Office just before Presidents Karzai and Musharraf arrived for dinner; it was neither an American idea nor an American plot as some speculated. President Bush seemed interested in the idea but wanted to see how Musharraf would react. We were somewhat surprised that President Musharraf accepted the idea, but he did.

Some have claimed that President Bush was a passive participant in the trilateral dinner. Neither Crocker nor I were present. However, the detailed descriptions of the meeting we received from the American side, largely corroborated by what President Karzai told me, made it clear that Bush had played his part in strongly seeking commitments from Musharraf to close down the infiltration while trying to keep the tone between the two neighboring presidents productive.

The problem was not the meeting but follow-up. The *jirga* idea caused a great deal of diplomatic action, mostly but not entirely between the two sides. There seemed to be a genuine disposition to make it work, but the slowness of the Afghan political and bureaucratic process, combined with ongoing infiltration from Pakistan, did not make for rapid progress. The Pakistanis were concerned that the Afghans would use the assembly to attack the legitimacy of the national border, the so-called Durand line that Afghanistan had never recognized.[11] The two sides eventually worked their way through a great many differences and suspicions and held a meeting eleven months after their 2006 meeting. It, in turn, created subcommittees. Nothing much actually changed for the better.

As the government of Pakistan touted the success of its tribal agreement in North Waziristan, we were seeing a very different picture on the ground. A detailed briefing developed by General Eikenberry's staff tracked the continued increase in cross-border infiltration throughout the months of negotiations. The briefing showed clearly that the new, higher levels of attacks were continuing uninterrupted.[12] The briefing was presented to National Security Adviser Hadley during his November 1, 2006, visit to Kabul. Hadley urged Eikenberry to bring the briefing to Washington and show it to senior officials. The briefing and related reporting eventually got some attention, but it was slow.

Infiltration continued. There was some slowdown in the winter in areas where snow closed the passes. At the end of November there was one of the periodic explosions that characterized Pakistani-Afghan relations. On November 29, I was meeting President Karzai when he handed me a newspaper article quoting Pakistan's then–foreign minister, Khurshid Kasuri, as having told NATO ambassadors in Islamabad that NATO was losing the war, should recognize that the insurgency was an ethnic conflict with the Pushtuns, and should accept the Taliban and work toward a coalition government that might exclude President Karzai.[13] The statements were outrageous, but were they true?

Tempers boiled over. The Afghans were incensed not only by the purported advice to NATO but much more by the assertion in the same article that the insurgency was an ethnic civil war, a charge that would call into question the multiethnic nature of the Afghan state and that totally ignored the many Pushtuns fighting and serving with the Afghan government. Harsh words were circulating. Since angry statements from one side almost always produced equally angry rebuttals and further reductions in what little cooperation existed, it was important to try to bottle up press commentary from the Afghan government until we could get to the bottom of the matter. President Karzai did agree to hold his fire in the press until we could check out the facts. Our embassy in Islamabad moved quickly to check with other NATO embassies that had been at the relevant meeting; none had heard anything remotely like what was quoted. Pakistan's foreign minister vehemently denied the claims.

The governor of Pakistan's NWFP, Gen. Ali Muhammad Jan Orakzai, who had a good deal of responsibility for the North Waziristan Agreement, may have been the real author of at least the sentiments if not the quotes.[14] However, he claimed that he was misquoted. In the end, yet one more crisis between the two neighbors passed with small effect and with even less improvement in the situation on the ground.

At least it was beginning to snow heavily. Afghan agriculture depends heavily on a deep snow pack for spring waters. The prospects for agriculture looked bright for the next year. Of course, everything has a price. On December 4 the snow closed Kabul International Airport for several days. Staff members waiting to go on Christmas leave were stuck and frustrated—the three-times-a-week UN flight and the daily Kam Air Boeing 737 flights were cancelled. Those returning from leave were stuck in the comforts of Dubai and minded less.

No Extension

While politics, war, counternarcotics, and economic reconstruction claimed most of my attention, there was also a minor distraction in not knowing my own future. In offering to stay for a third year, I was thinking that continuity in directing the embassy, along with what I knew about the country and the war, would be useful. Content to accept whatever Secretary Rice decided, I did not lobby. Months passed without any word. In early August there were rumors that Ambassador Zalmay Khalilzad might return, but I was told that at a very high level it had been decided that would not happen. On September 7, I received a call from Rice. She had decided against my staying. She told me that the administration had decided to make three changes—Baghdad, Kabul, and Islamabad—and "set the team" for the end of the administration.

The reasoning seemed thin to me, but it was her decision to make. Rice nicely asked if I would return to a Washington job or, if not, whether I wanted something else overseas. I declined both, not with any bitterness but simply because I felt that Kabul had been a high point whose professional satisfaction I was unlikely to exceed. It would be time to move on after thirty-seven years of diplomacy. I had found and continued to find Secretary Rice supportive in our many policy deliberations.

Washington is a town of rumors. In October, when I returned to Washington for the Karzai visit, a blog reported that my tour was being cut short. Unnamed sources alleged that I would be replaced early for having "failed to push Afghan President Hamid Karzai into making tough decisions." Others, equally unnamed, said of me, "He was too open about all the problems. That kind of talk doesn't fly these days." The article concluded, "Neumann appears to be a victim of the ongoing power struggle between the Pentagon and the State Department."[15] Whatever the truth of the rumors, the decision was made. The president and the secretary were entitled to make it. What did concern me was the timing.

In October Rice spoke of a winter transfer. I thought that a mistake. There was a lot going on. U.S. Army general Dan McNeil would take over the combined NATO command in February. I argued that it made more sense to have the new commander get his feet on the ground before switching out the ambassador.

On October 24, I heard that the nomination of my successor, Ambassador William Wood, might go to the Senate for confirmation in a lame duck session that was expected to bring the Senate back for about three weeks after the November 2006 election. An early nomination would be understood by the Afghan government as Washington repudiating me, eroding my influence while leaving me in place but unable to function effectively. As Napoleon's chief of police once famously remarked about something said to be a crime, "It is worse than a crime; it is a mistake."[16]

Of particular concern was the possibility that the nomination might not be confirmed right away. There was no reason the Senate would object to Ambassador Wood, then serving in Colombia, but the time was short, the Senate calendar full, and even one senator putting a "hold" on the nomination could delay its being heard in the narrow time available.[17] That would then leave the worst of worlds from a policy perspective: a weakened ambassador unable to advance policy goals remaining in place for an extended period since the nomination could not be heard before February at the earliest, when the new Congress convened. The last week of October was filled with calls back and forth as I made my points by telephone to selected senior officials. On October 30, I was told that the nomination would be held over for the next Congress.

On December 21, I presented to President Karzai the request for acceptance of my successor, what in diplomatic terms (still using French) is called *agrément*. Karzai refused to accept the document and said he wanted to call Washington to ask that I remain. I didn't want Washington to think I had asked him to make such a call. I have known ambassadors to request such calls from their host nation's head of state but always thought it extremely unprofessional as well as a pitiful way to act. He promised to make clear that the call was at his own initiative. It was a very kindly gesture, although he and I both knew it would change nothing. It did not.

Whether Secretary Rice or others felt that someone else could produce much better results, I was never told and I never asked. With the decision made, there seemed no point in pursuing the issue. I had long accepted the truth of Harry Truman's tart comment, "If you want a friend in Washington, get a dog."

We had prevailed on the economic assistance budget. The police force would be enlarged and billions would go toward the army. The need for more U.S. troops was beginning to be understood if not yet acted on. I had a great team to work with. The suspense was over; at least I knew I would be returning to Kabul after a Christmas break, and there was work still to do.

8
Force, Money, and Decisions

It was good to come home for Christmas, the first in three years. It was a quiet week with time for family. Then there was the usual round of calls on senior officials, a chance to speak privately and at more length than one could over a telephone. Over and over again my theme was the need for troops. The budget decision was excellent but would not show any real impact for a year or more. We had seven times more troops in Iraq than in Afghanistan, but Afghanistan is a bigger country, with a bigger population and more difficult terrain. The fighting would be tough in 2007. The field commanders were right in asking for two to three more battalions. No one disagreed with the facts, but there were no decisions yet. I picked up the papers I would need to fill out in preparation for retirement, a stack of forms larger than those needed to become ambassador.

Then it was back to Kabul through Dubai. The contrast between Dubai's wealth and glitter (it is a Las Vegas of the Middle East) and Kabul's noble struggling poverty was always startling. The military kindly loaned me a plane so that I could get back a day early to prepare for a stream of visitors. As usual, my first stop was the palace for a long discussion with President Karzai of events while I was away and a review of what I had heard and learned in Washington.

An ambassador actually has to report in two directions. Well understood is the responsibility to explain to Washington what is happening in his country of assignment. But also important is the need to explain to his hosts the mysteries of how Washington sees the world. Our diffuse system of government with its multiple power centers and cacophony of public voices is frequently confusing to foreigners. Explaining what is behind the noise, what senior American leaders are thinking, helps the foreign leader to correctly gauge how his actions will be seen and helps build a relationship of trust, and therefore of influence, between the ambassador and host country leaders. I found President Karzai relaxed, concentrating on things that needed to be done, and we were able to review key messages that we needed to get across to the visitors who would shortly be arriving. On the same day the press announced the removal of all but one of the police chiefs who had been on probation—a good start for the New Year.

First up, on January 14 were Senators Hillary Clinton (D-NY) and Evan Bayh (D-IN) with Representative John McHugh (R-NY), all on their respective armed services committees. In a six-hour visit shortened by a delayed plane arrival, we packed in an embassy briefing, lunch with President Karzai, a military briefing, and meetings with troops and a women's group. As we sped around Kabul from meeting to meeting, I found the delegation agreeing that we were on the right track. The snow had melted to frozen dirty lumps, but the cold was piercing.

The next morning brought Robert Gates, the new secretary of defense, for his first visit. We had an extensive discussion of the situation at General Eikenberry's headquarters. Secretary Rumsfeld had not seemed to encourage open debate. He had managed the war in Afghanistan for five years. Perhaps he was less sensitive to changes in the security environment since 2001. In any event, I had felt that he often seemed to be searching for facts to validate conclusions to which he had already come rather than reexamining those conclusions. Gates and the chairman of the Joint Chiefs of Staff, Gen. Peter Pace, now seemed much more open-minded than Rumsfeld as they listened to the case for two additional battalions and a third to replace one due to depart from eastern Afghanistan. General Pace pressed the question, "Are you self-limiting because of what you think are force availabilities?" It was very refreshing to get such a question. There were no decisions yet, but we were encouraged. We stressed also the need for 3,500 more military and police trainers. Without them the new military and police equipment to be purchased by the supplemental budget would have far less impact on the battlefield.

I have wondered in retrospect if we should have asked for more. Certainly, as I write in 2009, the need for more troops is clear and has been recognized by President Obama. We did not consciously lower our requests. General Eikenberry and his staff had made their judgments after very careful review, and I fully agreed. We did not foresee the later weakening in Pakistan that led to a sharp increase in cross-border attacks. Police reform went more slowly than we anticipated, partly for Afghan reasons but also because few of the necessary trainers arrived in 2007. But perhaps, after years of unsuccessfully pushing up-hill for additional resources, we did not think as expansively as we should have. In any event, it is unlikely that we could have gotten more than we asked for.

Secretary Gates had good meetings with President Karzai and visited a forward operating base. The discussion of Pakistan went off calmly. In the joint press conference with President Karzai, Gates said that Pakistan was a major ally against terrorism but said also that significant al Qaeda and Taliban command and control operated from Pakistan. Gates asked good questions and seemed determined that early success in Afghanistan not be lost through inattention. I wished he had arrived on the scene a year or two earlier.

The *Wall Street Journal* picked up the new tone, reporting that we were seeking large amounts of additional economic assistance, particularly for roads that the article called "the center of Gen. Eikenberry's plan." It noted also that General Eikenberry was requesting that a battalion of the Tenth Mountain Division, which had arrived on a four-month tour, be extended.[1] A few days later I underscored the need for troops by telling reporters that I expected heavy fighting in the spring but that I was also optimistic about the future.[2]

On January 21 General Eikenberry departed. President Karzai

presented him with a medal the day before in a touching ceremony for which CENTCOM commander Gen. John Abizaid flew in. A day later there was the military farewell. I regretted Eikenberry's departure. After two tours in Afghanistan he had a solid grip of the manifold political, military, and economic issues. Mostly, we had agreed. When we didn't, we had argued the issues professionally and generally found solutions. Out of it all we had formed a solid friendship and partnership. Three days later he called me from Europe to let me know that the next day the Pentagon would announce the decision to extend a full brigade combat team of the Tenth Mountain Division for an additional six months even as a brigade of the Eighty-second Airborne arrived.[3] We finally had the forces we had been seeking for so long. ISAF could launch its own offensive in the spring instead of waiting for the Taliban attack that the insurgents were boasting of.

The decision to extend the troops only weeks before they were scheduled to depart was hard on the soldiers and their families, but they took it magnificently. I had worried that there would be bitterness and a drop in morale. There must have been some unhappiness, but as I traveled I found only a solid professional acceptance of duty and the need for the mission.

Months later I was visiting Walter Reed Hospital and spoke with a young sergeant who had been extended along with the rest. Shortly after he would have been home with his family, he had lost part of his hand in a bomb blast. Sitting with his wife in the hospital, he told me that the decision to extend his unit was absolutely right; they knew the terrain and the situation, they were needed, and the decision was correct. I felt humbled by his dedication.

On January 22, I drove across the Shomali Plain to Bagram. It was a pretty drive with the flat plain all snow covered, the white mountain ridges beyond reaching up without foothills, and the blue sky arching above. We went on to Parwan Province's small capital of Charikar for meetings with the governor and assembled dignitaries. The town lies on the main road north with a busy bazaar lining the road and muddy lanes radiating away into the rest of the town. Like most places in the Afghan winter, it had few rooms that were heated, meetings took place with overcoats on, and the room in which I held a press conference with some Western and Afghan journalists who accompanied me was only a bit above freezing. I was able to get in strong statements of increased U.S. aid, so it was time well spent.

As always I learned things I hadn't expected. We had political and aid officers assigned as headquarters liaison staff at nearby Bagram Air Base and had thought that they were sufficient to also cover the Parwan PRT, which was physically housed at Bagram. The discussion made clear to the USAID director and me that our assumptions were not correct. We needed to find additional officers because those there already had full-time liaison duties and could not adequately cover both Bagram headquarters and the PRT. It was also clear that we had different views in Kabul and Bagram about the quality of a particular local official. Differences are natural, but the viewpoints weren't being exchanged. We clearly needed to improve how we shared perspectives. These perceptions, of a person needed here or there, of a need for better connectivity of information, are small in and of themselves, but collectively they make a difference in efficiency and in linking civil and military operations together. Commanders and ambassadors must travel endlessly to build such understanding because the amount of detail required is too large to emerge just through briefings in the home office.

Improving and expanding the Afghan army ran into one of those strange intersections of different policies, each valid standing alone but in conflict when taken together. In this case, security and economic policies collided. Originally our training program focused on a steady increase of new Afghan army battalions. Combat, desertions, and expiring enlistments had shrunk the battalions just as had happened to the Union Army in the American Civil War. To redress this problem, our military increased training so that replacements would flow into existing battalions even as we kept building new battalions.

The problem was that the unplanned increase in the immediate force would put new pressure on the Afghan budget to pay the additional salaries. The Afghan Ministry of Finance did not have the funds. The IMF wanted to safeguard a budget process that was linked to debt reduction negotiations for the large overhang of debt incurred over many years by many Afghan governments, a valid objective by itself. Some members of the international developmental community were opposed to transferring development funds to the military and wanted the military program reduced.

I refused to accept either that the army had to slow down or that the United States automatically had to cover the gap. In discussions with the IMF, I said that it was unacceptable that more U.S. and allied troops must die simply to keep the budget balanced while the growth of the Afghan army was retarded. The IMF understood but was not in a position to consider factors outside its mandate.

The problem did present an opportunity to press the Afghan government to raise taxes very slightly to come up with its own contribution toward the needed funds—a politically painful course but one that could leverage other donors to come up with more money. The amount involved was trivial, about $25 million, but the principles involved were large and the debate went on for some time. I worked closely with UNAMA to keep the issue from becoming a civilian-military tussle. UNAMA supported the idea that the Afghans had to find money to share the responsibility for national defense. Our willingness to let the matter become a crisis strengthened our negotiating position. I informed Washington of the position I was taking since the matter would be discussed among capitals as well as in Kabul. I was supported. Again it was easier to take a position than to ask for guidance. Eventually, after many conversations, meetings, and much time, the Ministry of Finance, with President Karzai's backing, found a way to increase funding. Donors helped, and the issue was resolved.

Police and Justice

The police program was making progress but slowly. The success of the probation process in removing poor senior officers gave us some confidence. So too did very gradual progress on implementing a program to pay police and army salaries through direct bank deposits in order to ensure corrupt senior officers could not siphon off part of the money. However, the bank system was primitive, and in many parts of the country no branch banks existed. The program began to work well for the army, but getting the police force paid remained a serious problem that seemed to defy solution.

Part of our police program involved training Afghan prison guards so that they would not resort to brutality and instead would use more appropriate methods to handle prisoners. In February when snow canceled another provincial trip, I took the opportunity to drive to the large national prison at Pol-i-Charki on the edge of Kabul. On the way I noticed children playing cricket on a muddy flat. The game was previously little played in Afghanistan but has been popularized by refugees from Pakistan and is becoming a national sport.

The prison at Pol-i-Charki is a cold pile of bleak stone with muddy puddles outside. Yet the U.S. trainers working on prisoner handling, human rights, and antiriot techniques were enthusiastic about the desire of Afghan guards to learn; I was told some Afghans were even paying from their own pockets to take public buses to the training site. Some of the trainers had also worked in Iraq. They told me the Iraqis were better educated but the Afghans were much more eager to learn and to apply what they learned.

Accompanied by the deputy minister of justice we toured the women's wing of the prison. To Western eyes it is bad, with six or eight women sharing a cell with their children. By local standards it was not so bad: the women all seemed to be well fed, the quarters were warm, beds and clothes were adequate, and there were rugs on the floor. The real problems were procedural. There was no method for following up cases and squabbling between the courts, and the prosecutor's office kept some women in jail after they should have been released. The deputy minister himself brought out the problems when he questioned the women. He was keen to solve them but was absolutely hamstrung by the total breakdown in the justice system after years of warfare. We could and did provide some help, but real solutions, like so much else in Afghanistan, would take years.

One block of the prison had been completely refurbished by the U.S. Defense Department in order to house prisoners to be released from Guantanamo. We were prepared, even eager, to turn over all Afghan detainees but wanted the Afghans to put in place a system to hold dangerous prisoners whose cases did not fit into criminal trials while allowing others to be reintegrated into Afghan society. The Afghans would be free to decide who to keep or release, but we insisted that they avoid a situation where dangerous insurgents would be free to return to the war if the strict standards of criminal proof could not be met. Not all those captured on the battlefield can be processed as criminals because soldiers in the middle of a fight are not collecting evidence the way policemen do. In some cases the evidence was too sensitive to release in an Afghan court, particularly in cases where it might put the lives of sources at risk. At the same time, we had to proceed gradually. While we did not want dangerous terrorists released, so palpable was the sense that Washington wanted to close Guantanamo and move out the prisoners, without turning them loose, that we also had to be sure the Afghans did not interpret this as an invitation simply to lock prisoners up and throw away the key in order to "solve" our political problem.

The Afghan government had agreed to one approach, only to have the minister of justice decide that it was illegal without a constitutional amendment. By the time I left Afghanistan we had managed to start an experimental program with the less dangerous prisoners to test newly developed Afghan procedures. Months of work were required to get even that far.

On the broader issues of justice reform we were slowly moving (everything moved slowly) to a new unity of Afghan and international views. The embassy's justice sector coordinator, Gary Peters, who had already begun to synchronize U.S. civilian and military rule-of-law programs, was also working well with the Italians, UNAMA, and other international groups involved in judicial reform. UNAMA head Tom Koenig and I consulted closely and intimately with the Italian ambassador. An informal dinner at my residence had helped bring the relevant ambassadors and most reform-minded Afghans closer together by providing a forum for a freewheeling brainstorming session, albeit one in which some of the ideas had been somewhat pre-scripted with a few of the participants.

The international justice sector working group was cooperating well with the Afghans. The three major Afghan players—the Justice Ministry, Public Prosecutor's Office, and Supreme Court—each were developing separate training and reform plans, but these were not in conflict. The Italian government was keen to hold a major judicial reform conference in Rome. My hope was that this conference would be a major occasion to endorse Afghan-designed reform plans and encourage additional international funding for them. The Italian ambassador was adroit at keeping us all on this track and the European Union was adding its weight to the need for judicial reform. The conference was held after my departure from Afghanistan but did meet its major objectives. However, this was no more than a start in what promises to be a very long process.

In the short term, policing remained a persistent challenge. The initial, if limited, success of the auxiliary police program produced new problems of its own. Our original agreement was to start the program in just six provinces. I had agreed to the funding for this. However, Afghan officials in other provinces had recruited additional tribesmen without any vetting and blithely wanted the United States to make good on their unpaid back salaries. With the security problems worsening, ISAF supported the Afghan position.

However, I felt that the Policy Action Group's decision to hold the program to six provinces had to be respected. To have us maneuvered into a totally different decision because of unauthorized actions would be a dangerous precedent. Further, I had doubts about who was being recruited, how they were being vetted, and whether we were seeing a surreptitious funding of tribal militias. For all these reasons I refused to authorize the additional funding and insisted that we needed to solve the many problems with policing in the besieged southern provinces before we enlarged the program. When we had done that and had a better idea of who had been recruited in the other provinces, I would be prepared to make a further decision. It was one of the very few times when I disagreed with my military colleagues. The discussion was professional; we all argued hard, but there was no challenge to my statutory authority regarding policy on U.S. support for civilian policing.

Some potentially good news was in the European Union's decision to take on a larger role with the police and share the load that had originally been placed on the Germans alone. We recognized the need for an additional thousand police trainers and mentors and welcomed the idea of help. The United States wanted to cooperate fully. The problem was that we were trying to move ahead quickly, and the EU had trouble keeping up given their bureaucratic structures. I explained to visiting EU missions that they could take over or reinforce any aspect of the program they chose. We were prepared to open up and share decision making. But we could not agree to a delay in critical decisions while EU structures struggled to agree on what they wanted to do as they designed their program. We urged the EU to assign liaison officers to our training mission in Kabul to keep the EU fully informed about what was happening and to allow for a dynamic decision-making process. Later I was able to follow up these discussions in Berlin.

Taking the JCMB to Germany: Strategy versus Implementation

Washington had agreed to a German proposal to hold one of the periodic meetings of the Joint Coordination and Monitoring Board in Berlin with senior foreign ministry officials, the so-called political directors, in the chair of their respective delegations.[4] As the fighting had worsened in 2006, several European governments began calling for new coordinating mechanisms and the need for a new "comprehensive" plan for Afghanistan. Searching for a new strategy seems to be policymakers' recurring default reaction to problems. Instead of asking whether the problem lies in some mix of funding, procedures, and troops—all of which would require additional money and people—to implement the strategy already decided, the search is launched for a new idea. Certainly ideas are more easily come by than money and soldiers. Sometimes the strategy may be faulty. In the Afghan case I believed that without fixing numerous problems of implementation, the search for new strategy would do little beyond absorb time and create overlapping organizations that would drag more of the Afghans' limited numbers of qualified staff members into bureaucratic exercises.

From my vantage point in Kabul, Washington seemed to sway between the two: tempted by looking for a "new" strategy at very senior levels and pulled back to reality by my efforts and those of Assistant Secretary Boucher; his deputy, John Gastright; and Tony Harriman on the NSC staff. Perhaps my perception is simplistic as I was not in all the Washington discussions.

In any event, the compromise was the meeting in Berlin. As Tom Koenig and I worked on preparations for the Berlin meeting, our intent was to reaffirm the London Compact as the core of the comprehensive strategy. We wanted to bring policy leaders away from trying to do our job in Kabul and back to solving the issues that only capitals could resolve: money, force, and personnel—along with a liberal underpinning of patience. Each of us worked on this approach with our own bureaucracies and with our fellow ambassadors in Kabul, who were generally in agreement, particularly those who had been longest involved in Afghan matters. Boucher had visited in early January and was sympathetic to our views.

The first day of the JCMB meeting, January 30, 2007, was largely devoted to speeches, frequently long statements of general policy. We spotlighted the new U.S. commitment of funding and forces and made some progress in using those decisions to leverage new aid from others. The second day featured a more normal JCMB atmosphere, with ambassadors heading the delegations, and was more of a working session. General Eikenberry was with us as his headquarters would continue to exist for another month and was a strong supporter in the security discussions.

Our delegation presented a planning paper on elections. Its thrust was that the donors needed to start thinking about how to cover the enormous costs of setting up the electoral machinery for the 2009 Afghan elections. The Afghan government was encouraged to think of simplifying the procedures and combining the presidential and parliamentary elections to reduce costs. The idea to energize this discussion at the JCMB meeting was one we developed in Kabul and illustrated the difference between our focus on solving individual issues and the search for strategy and general principles coming from capitals. Without the JCMB process it would have taken even longer to acquire this practical focus.

We were able also to secure agreement to enlarge the police force from 62,000 to 82,000. This decision was controversial because U.S. procedures created the impression that we were pressuring our allies. The enlargement was originally a U.S. proposal that was part of our internal budget discussions. Until we had U.S. policy agreement on the funding, we were not in a position to promote the idea with allies. Once we had the funding, we had essentially made a unilateral decision to revise the old force numbers that had been agreed to in London. It was the unilateral appearance of the decision that aggravated some other parties. I had done what I could in Kabul to explain to allies the debility we had in trying to reach multilateral decisions before we had agreement within our own policy process. At the JCMB meeting General Eikenberry and the Afghan ministers were articulate in explaining the need to enlarge the force. In the end, happiness was restored.

All of us in the U.S. delegation had numerous side meetings. Boucher, Eikenberry, and I held a joint press conference and attended a dinner at a think tank with a mix of German opinion leaders and parliamentarians. In general I found people badly informed about the reality of the situation; the public personalities were shockingly so. The overwhelming view seemed to be that the Americans wanted only to fight; ISAF personnel were the nation builders. I thought this wrong on both counts.

There was nearly no understanding of what was actually happening in economic development. In addition to providing the bulk of the troops, the United States was the single largest national contributor to Afghan reconstruction. At the same time, there was still a requirement for NATO military capabilities to protect Afghan villagers from marauding Taliban insurgents and al Qaeda suicide bombers. Our German audience seemed unaware of all this. I became much more conscious than I had been of how limited the European press coverage of the war was. The German press reported very little. The British and Dutch press focused mostly on the two provinces where their troops were based as though that was the totality of the story in Afghanistan. The American press was negative enough with its heavy focus on bombs and blood, but the European press was worse. Much of the impulse for a new strategy may have originated in this lack of understanding.

Our press and public discussion were useful, but official U.S. government credibility was low. We needed to get more opinion leaders to Afghanistan, and once there they needed to see the situation beyond Kabul and their own troops. We also needed to enhance Afghanistan's and ISAF's own strategic communications capabilities, to try to stay one step ahead of the nimble Taliban propaganda machine with its mobile phone speed dials set to eager Western media outlets. Ultimately European governments and ISAF needed to shoulder a greater burden of educating their publics and building support for the mission to which they had committed their soldiers' lives.

ISAF and the War

Fighting had slowed a bit during the cold weather but overall remained at higher levels than during past years. The British were fighting hard in Helmand but did not always explain in detail to President Karzai what they were doing. Karzai received reports constantly from local officials and tribal leaders, many conveying exaggerated views or rumors. There were persistent and wild rumors that the British were somehow conspiring to turn parts of the south over to the Taliban. While these rumors were ridiculous, Afghans have lived so long on rumors in the absence of reliable news that almost any rumor could gain some credibility for a while. Thus it was important to frequently brief President Karzai in far greater detail than most Western militaries would normally transmit to their own political leadership. From my discussions with General Richards, I believed that the British had a better story to tell than was sometimes appreciated by the Afghans.

From time to time the war moved to Kabul. On January 25 we received word late at night that there might be a rocket attack on the embassy the next morning. At 6:30 in the morning DCM Dick Norland and I decided to move people out of the flimsy trailer-like hooches into safer buildings. I didn't like waking people up on our one-day weekend, but I was living in one of the reinforced concrete apartments and had to be sensitive to the difference. We were able to get everyone up and moved well before the time when we were told to expect an attack. I took a cup of coffee and wandered over to spend time with our people in the chancery. No rocket came, and we eventually sounded the all clear. It did ruin a morning's sleep. There was shooting later in the afternoon in town, but it turned out to be celebratory fire for the birth of President Karzai's son.

On February 3 word began to reach Kabul that the Taliban had definitely violated the Musa Qala agreement by taking over the town. I wasn't sure it was true, but there was no reason to react quickly. U.S. general Dan McNeil was due to assume command of ISAF from General Richards the next day. If the report was false we did not want the United States to be accused later of provoking a crisis by violating the agreement as soon as we took over and without testing it. If it were true, ISAF would have time to react deliberately. General McNeil didn't really need my advice as he saw it the same way, but there was consternation in capitals. My advice to all was to move cautiously, keep ISAF in the lead while it coordinated closely with President Karzai and Helmand Province governor Wafa, and let the reaction be decided in Kabul. After some probably unnecessarily caustic e-mails on my part, the advice was taken.

It gradually became clear that the Taliban had moved into the town at least for a time and pushed the local leaders to the sidelines. What was less clear was why. It was possible that it was an angry reaction of temper by the local Taliban leader because ISAF had recently killed his brother.

Part of ISAF's preparation for its own offensive was a concentrated effort to kill Taliban leaders to disrupt the group's leadership and planning. In general the decapitation strategy was effective in the short run. The spring offensive never developed, and General McNeil made good on his commitment that the spring offensive would be ISAF's, not the Taliban's. The Taliban showed a considerable ability to regenerate its mid-level leadership. We understood this, but for the moment the strategy was effective.

What ISAF could not do was stretch to the north to impose greater respect for government authority. There were neither sufficient forces nor a willingness in NATO capitals to look seriously at the problem. In mid-February, I recommended in a telegram that NATO begin to address the problem. It did not happen.

One awkward side effect of General McNeil's taking over ISAF was that coordination between the commanding general and the American ambassador became more difficult. This had nothing to do with General McNeil himself, with whom I had an excellent relationship. The problem was one of appearances. General Richards could and did decree that ISAF would extend special cooperation to keep me informed because of the preeminent position of the United States in Afghanistan. Coming from a British general this was a statement of allied unity. Had McNeil, a U.S. Army general, made the same statement it would have been seen as the big United States bossing everyone else around. So we had to be a bit more circumspect in how we coordinated.

We managed well but were not helped by NATO's switch to a classified communications system that did not mesh with either embassy or U.S. military classified computer systems. McNeil and I could communicate electronically on U.S.-only classified systems. However, to keep the embassy in close touch with ISAF, we had to install several new computers in the embassy and find $40,000 in our budget to replace an unreliable satellite with fiber-optic cable strung down the street between ISAF headquarters and the embassy on the existing telephone polls. Such strange trivia has more to do with effective coordination in a multinational operation than is often reflected in high-level policy deliberations.

The economic centerpiece of McNeil's southern strategy was to get moving on the Kajaki Dam generator project to bring electricity to the area. The project itself would bring significant employment, particularly for the road construction to the dam.

There seemed to be a flow of recriminations between various military elements and USAID. One problem involved the difference between civilian and military organization. The military can organize people and then hold off for a time if necessary. But to mobilize a large contingent of civilian contractors and then not use them or, worse, have to demobilize would be horrendously expensive and might throw the whole project off budget. We wanted to get going but did not want to find we were trying to build a work camp in the middle of a firefight. Synchronization was key.

The military understood the problem when it was explained, but it was not intuitively obvious to it that civilian concerns should prevail. Too many lower-level communications found civilian technicians and military officers talking past each other. It was not clear if anyone had a full picture. I organized a senior team from the embassy and USAID to go to Kandahar and Helmand with senior officers from ISAF to resolve the problems. Snowstorms in Kabul delayed the trip for two weeks, but eventually it took place.

The project did not go smoothly, but at least we were working from a common understanding.[5] ISAF did launch an offensive into northern Helmand using the newly available U.S. forces as well as Afghan army and some British units. The offensive took a major district capital at Sangin, midway on the dirt track to Kajaki, but securing the area enough to begin construction was much more difficult given the small number of forces available for the task.

As spring came on in 2007 the situation in Helmand was unstable.

ISAF could take any objective. They effectively blunted the promised Taliban offensive with their own attacks. But what they could hold and secure was much more limited. The Taliban still exercised effective control over much of the rural population, although less than at the beginning of the year. It was clear that stronger political leadership was necessary in Helmand.

There were major tribal differences in Helmand. There were splits within the former governor's tribe. Other tribes and subtribes had differences and feuds, some going back years and others exacerbated by more recent misgovernment. Disaffected tribesmen were joining the Taliban and the drug dealers. Only Afghan political leadership could take charge of a process of tribal reconciliation that needed to be closely coordinated with military operations. Governor Wafa was exhausted and irascible. As one Afghan charmingly put it in somewhat fractured English, "Wafa is expired." He had few if any trusted and effective subordinates. He wanted out, but President Karzai had no immediately available replacement for his old friend. There were few officials who would have the mixture of prestige, tribal sense, and administrative competence to do well. The foreigners could not fill the requirement.

In Kabul the Policy Action Group met frequently and debated approaches. However, I began to recognize that while the PAG mechanism could develop policy options, they were not always getting to President Karzai in orderly form. He, in turn, was receiving a great deal of information directly from tribal visitors and telephone calls from Helmand. This information often shaped a perspective different from that in the PAG, which was driven by more Western approaches to formulating options and utilizing formal intelligence. It was not so much that one side was wrong, but rather that east was not meeting west.

At the end of March, President Karzai himself traveled to Helmand. It took a massive operation to get him there and keep him safe. Much extra security had to be sent down, particularly since the dirt airstrip was unsecured and the British ambassador's plane had hit a land mine on landing some months earlier. We added several State Department helicopters from our growing drug control air fleet to help move personnel. Having had to impose so often on my military colleagues for transport, I was delighted to be able to return a small part of the many favors.

The visit went well. President Karzai was beginning to engage, and visits out of Kabul always energized him. But a great deal more would be necessary to take control of Helmand. I would not be there to see future progress as my tour was then within two weeks of its end.

Messy Politics and Multiple Visitors

Problems never came singly in Afghanistan. Just as the JCMB meeting was ending, Afghan jihadi leaders—former factional leaders who were now prominent parliamentarians—were focusing on a Human Rights Watch report that repeated a previous call for war crimes trials for various commanders (sometimes called "warlords," although this is a loaded term). This caused little stir in the diplomatic community, which understood that Human Rights Watch was a nongovernmental organization following its normal standards and representing only itself. Its call had some moral force but was unlikely to lead to any concerted Western action given all the other problems in Afghanistan. But the jihadi leaders didn't see it that way.

They have lived their lives in a world of conspiracy and maneuver where statements are routinely scrutinized for what may lie behind them and there is no clear distinction between public and private realms. If Human Rights Watch issued a statement, something must be up; someone or some government must be behind it. They began to fret. The anxieties of one spurred on the worries of another. They were already nursing doubts about a long-range plan for Afghan accountability called the transitional justice plan. Endorsed by the Afghan government under strong international pressure, the plan was more a statement of principle than a call to any immediate action. But the jihadi leaders put the transitional justice plan together with the Human Rights Watch statement and decided that they were in danger. Human Rights Watch is an American organization, so perhaps, they reasoned, the American government was about to go after them. Their worries grew. And as the jihadi leaders collectively still controlled many armed men, their getting worried was dangerous.

President Karzai was talking to many of the leaders individually and in groups to calm the situation. He asked me to do the same. I saw several of the most prominent leaders. I explained the private nature of

Human Rights Watch. We did support the transitional justice plan—that was U.S. policy—but that plan left the initiative to the Afghan government; there was nothing new happening from our end and nothing to which the jihadi leaders had any need to react. I counseled calm: relax and get on with all Afghanistan's more urgent problems. In Afghan politics the calls themselves—the American ambassador asking for meetings and going to see them—were the message. The actual conversations were rather general.

In mid-February, I lunched with a group of former fighters including a Tajik, a Pushtu, and an Uzbek mullah and commander. They went on at length about the difference between those who really fought against the Soviets and the Taliban—the "real fighters" in their terms—and those with bloody records of human rights violations. They wanted me to understand the difference between them. I was not sure just how clear the difference was, but it was something to think about.

Just when the situation seemed to be calming, the issue erupted in Parliament, where many jihadi leaders had seats. After a heated discussion the lower house passed a law giving blanket amnesty for actions during the war years. That caused an immediate international reaction. Human rights organizations in several countries protested loudly that there must be accountability for war crimes. Governments began to pressure President Karzai to refuse to sign the law, an action that would have put him on a collision course with Parliament that might have the votes to override a veto. Afghan voices denounced foreign intervention in Afghan affairs. The jihadi leaders called for a massive demonstration in support of the amnesty law to be held February 23 in Kabul's stadium. Plans to bus in supporters from outside Kabul were reported. Estimates and rumors suggested that as many as 100,000 demonstrators might show up. The demonstration was supposed to be peaceful, but memories of the May 29, 2006, riots were still fresh. The alarming possibility of mobs marching from the stadium and outbreaks of spontaneous violence turning into a general riot was on everyone's mind.

President Karzai was on the phone and in meetings constantly trying to persuade prominent individuals to stay home and keep their supporters home. On February 23 the army and police were on high alert. All foreign missions, including ours, were locked down. Our guard force was readied, and our people were told to be ready to concentrate in the chancery if the demonstration got out of hand.

In the end, the day passed peacefully. About twenty thousand people came to the stadium for several hours of speeches but dispersed quietly afterward. No one tried to challenge the police or force their way through the coils of razor wire blocking all streets from the stadium into town. By 3:00 p.m. we called off the alert. The demonstrators had shown their political strength, although some observers noted that it appeared far less than they had claimed.

Ultimately, President Karzai found a way of defusing the crisis. He asked the justice minister for a review of the amnesty law's constitutionality. The review pointed out that Islamic law gives individuals a right to claim redress for crimes. Parliament could not override Islamic law, so the measure was returned to Parliament. The resulting discussions gave time for tempers to cool and the press hullabaloo to die down. Finally a modified amnesty law that offered some protection from government action but left individuals free to bring cases for human rights violations was passed. The law was weakly drafted and left much room for interpretation. No one was completely happy, but as there was no intention by the Afghan or any other government to actually do anything right away, there was no follow-up. The crisis passed.

In the same week as the demonstration, the Kajaki Dam issue was bubbling, the issue with the auxiliary police came to a head, snow closed the airport for two days, a congressional delegation spent a day with us, there was a crisis with Pakistan, a delegation arrived for the next round of strategic dialogue talks, and serious issues of poppy eradication in Helmand preoccupied us. And on top of everything else, Afghan health authorities started to report cases of bird flu in the country.

For a brief period we were afraid that a serious epidemic of bird flu might cause a partial quarantine of the country and grave economic damage. State Department health experts, blithely unconcerned that we had a war on, were talking about how the embassy might have to close and we might have to keep everyone in their quarters. Fortunately, the incidents of avian flu were few, the overstretched Afghan health authorities somehow managed to take appropriate containment measures, and my staff handled the required reporting and kept it off my desk beyond occasional updates. That crisis too passed into a footnote of an incredibly busy week.

Visitors were as thick as snowflakes in the winter of 2007. Speaker Nancy Pelosi (D-CA) led a large delegation of congressional committee chairpersons to Kabul in late January. We had good meetings and managed to introduce them to a number of parliamentarians. They left supportive of the budget requests. Bipartisan support for the Afghanistan war remained strong. Pelosi kindly gave me a seat on her plane to a refueling stop in Germany so that I was able to stay in Kabul for her visit and still make the opening of the JCMB meeting in Berlin a day later.

One question that came up with the members of Congress was about the many problems with USAID contracts. I pointed out that administrations of both parties had cut the size of USAID for years. The agency was a tenth of the size it had been when I had first visited Afghanistan forty years earlier. There had been more USAID officers during the war in Vietnam than we had had worldwide since the permanent staff was reduced over successive administrations to 2,200 officers. The result was that USAID no longer had the capacity to actually do things; it could only contract, and sometimes the contracts were so big and the USAID contract managers so few that there was a risk of the tail wagging the dog. To address the problem, the government would have to enlarge the agency, not tinker with the contracting complaints.

American state governors arrived in groups. Almost all of them had constituents serving in the National Guard units in Afghanistan. Several additional congressional delegations came for one-day visits. They took time, but it was an invaluable opportunity to give them a frank and detailed look at what was happening. I was always glad to see them.[6]

In the week of the demonstration we had sizable delegations from State, USAID, and Defense for working group meetings as part of the strategic dialogue that had been established between the United States and Afghanistan. We had experienced major problems scheduling the large meeting that had been promised the previous year. The State Department's undersecretary for political affairs, Nicholas Burns, was supposed to come to Kabul for a return visit to cochair the meeting.

However, the State Department was without a deputy secretary for an extended period, and Burns, temporarily filling that role, found that every attempt to stick to a schedule was derailed by requirements to undertake other missions or take over direction of the State Department when the secretary traveled.

The Afghans were understanding for a while but were beginning to wonder how to show their own people that America hadn't lost interest in a structured, high-level dialogue. To keep the process alive we decided to hold a series of working group meetings that would shape discussion for an eventual plenary. Designed as a stopgap, the idea actually improved the process. The working group meetings were longer and more substantive than had been possible the previous year, when they had to fit into a tight schedule of opening and closing plenary meetings. Sometimes misfortune brings improvement. We decided to maintain separate working groups for the future. A few weeks later, on March 13, we were able to hold the long postponed plenary. It went off well, although again Burns couldn't attend and Assistant Secretary Boucher and Undersecretary of Defense for Policy Eric Edelman took the U.S. lead.

Three days after the big stadium demonstration, Vice President Cheney arrived. The plan was for General McNeil, General Durbin, and me to helicopter to Bagram Air Base to meet Cheney. He would have military briefings and a visit with the troops. Then we would all fly into Kabul on his plane for a meeting with President Karzai, and Cheney would fly out. The weather had different ideas.

In the morning the cloud cover was too low for helicopter operations, so the generals and I drove to Bagram. By the time the briefings were over, we were getting mixed snow and rain, the plane couldn't land in Kabul, and the Secret Service was adamantly against the vice president driving a road they didn't know in the dark in a snowstorm. Cheney overruled some of the staff who wanted him to apologize on the telephone to President Karzai and fly out. Instead Cheney decided that it was important to show our support for Afghanistan. Cheney would overnight at Bagram and see Karzai the next day. It was the right decision. All the arrangements had to be shifted, but in Kabul my deputy, Dick Norland, handled everything smoothly with the Afghan government.

Our administrative staff, which had sprung into action to prepare for the possibility of the vice president and his large advance team having to bed down in Kabul for the night owing to the weather, stood down. I drove back to Kabul that night through a snowstorm as did three other generals in separate convoys.

The visit itself went well but was given an extra bit of excitement by a suicide bomber blowing himself up at the Bagram gate, through which I had twice driven the previous day. The vice president's party heard the bomb go off but was a mile or more away from the blast.

The Taliban claimed it was an attack on Cheney. I doubted that. His decision to remain at Bagram was not made until 8:30 in the evening, there was a press blackout and none of the correspondents were reporting where he was, and I had never seen evidence that the insurgents could react so quickly to developments. To me it was just an unfortunate coincidence, deeply tragic for the American and Korean soldiers and Afghan merchants and shoppers near the gate who were killed but without real political impact.

There was less than a month and a half left in my tour. I needed to focus on counternarcotics, electric power in Kabul, Pakistan, budget issues, and filling out my retirement papers.

9
Final Days

My father once remarked that diplomacy is a profession where you neither start what you finish nor finish what you start. One picks up the tasks begun by others and, in turn, leaves projects begun for one's successor to deal with. There are neither neat beginnings nor neat endings to the story except in one's own mind. My time in Afghanistan might have been drawing to a close, but events kept rushing along.

In January 2007 Ambassador Wood's nomination was announced. After some discussion we fixed my departure for April 10. I made plans for my wife to join me for the last two weeks. I was offered the opportunity to stay in State to offer advice or help on Afghanistan in some undefined way. The offer was sincere, but I didn't want either to be a marginal player or to interfere with my successor. This was exactly the sort of Washington oversight I had resisted throughout my own tour, and so it made sense to decline. I continued to wade through the mountain of forms one must complete to retire.

For some time I couldn't finish because the forms required a definite retirement date and I didn't have one. The department and I were interested in my staying on for a month of final consultations with

Congress to support the budget and a trip to Central Asia to discuss Afghanistan. But under State regulations I would be living on borrowed time after my appointment ended. Special permission was required from the director general of the Foreign Service to stay in service longer than five days after I left post. All of this was eventually arranged, but the discussions and papers filled what little time I had to spare from Afghan matters. I was so busy I forgot my wedding anniversary—the first time in forty years I had lost track. I tried to make amends with flowers and a telephone call. Elaine understood. I was content not to think about what I would do next. There would be time enough for that after the work on Afghanistan ended.

USAID Issues

In early February we continued to grapple with the new USAID budget system put in place by USAID Administrator and Director of U.S. Foreign Assistance Tobias. He was supporting our work, and I was grateful for that but skeptical about his redesign of foreign assistance. His ideas sounded reasonable when he explained them, but the system wasn't working.

It seemed to us in the field that the Washington staff had multiplied procedures, metrics, tables, and instructions. The work at post had gone up by hundreds of hours. We followed instructions because we had to in order to keep the budget process on track. At one point, however, we were asked to assign all funds to program categories. We knew that this exercise would have to be repeated when the supplemental and a continuing resolution (at lower levels than the requested budget) passed Congress since we would have to distribute the programs among the different fiscal years. I ordered our USAID mission to stop work on a complicated operational plan, to the great satisfaction of my USAID staff. I informed Washington of the order. A few days later I received a cable saying my "request" to stop was approved. We all enjoyed that message.

Assistant USAID Administrator Jim Kunder visited in mid-February. He had been the first USAID director in Kabul after the war and had a realistic perspective. Over dinner with Afghan friends, Jim reminisced about his first trip to the Education Ministry. He had found all the windows in the building broken. They had to grope their way down lightless halls to find the minister working with a single lamp and no computer. The finance minister added his recollection about taking over as director of the central bank at much the same time. They had only three computers, and no one was trained to operate them. For all our troubles these recollections reminded us of how far we had come in six years.

Even the winter weather provided moments of beauty. One day in February, I helicoptered to Bagram. At a little after seven in the morning, the countryside was still the drab gray of morning before the sun is over the horizon. But the sky above was blue, the air washed clear of dust, and the snowy ridgelines that fringed the valley glistened in white and rose with the rays of the rising sun.

For months Afghan ministers had asked us for help with expanding electric generator power in Kabul. We had rejected these approaches, believing that the electric needs would be supplied when the northern transmission lines eventually brought electricity from Central Asia. Short-term expenditures on generators appeared to us to be a long-term waste of money driven by political expediency. After the new cabinet was formed, the minister of economy, Shams, had returned to the discussion with facts and figures. He had a solid technocratic education and seemed to know his business. At my request USAID commissioned the firm of Black & Veatch to do a technical review of the whole issue.

We reviewed the firm's findings on January 15, 2007. The report was alarming. The northern transmission system was going to provide less power than we had expected, for various technical reasons. Power demands in Kabul were growing faster than originally forecast. Under the current plans, the lights in Kabul were not going to come on before the 2009 elections, a major political black eye. However, there was good news as well. New and more efficient generators could meet the need better and with less waste than those then in service. Most would still be needed after the transmission line was in service, and excess generator capacity could be shifted to other parts of the country later.

The plan we came up with was ambitious. It would require shifting about $100 million dollars within our budget. To succeed, the Afghan government would have to accept new commitments to long-term maintenance, take on a $20 million expenditure of its own, and move forward on a restructuring of the distribution and bill collection system in Kabul so that receipts would fund continued fuel purchases in the out years. Our own bureaucracy would have to move quickly, as would multiple Afghan ministries, to put the plan in place soon enough to have the first twenty megawatts' worth of generators in place before the 2008–2009 winter.

The USAID staff worked overtime to finalize the details. Washington agreed to support us. This was an essential step, since shifting budgetary funds would require congressional notification. During Speaker Pelosi's visit I was able to explain to her delegation and key congressional staff members what we were proposing. They agreed to support the plan. This was important in getting USAID Washington's help because there is often nervousness about asking Congress to change the use of appropriated funds.

Accompanied by key technical staffers from our mission, I visited individual ministers to explain what we would offer and what they would need to do. The reception was enthusiastic—we were proposing to meet a major request of theirs and to avoid a future political problem—but they realized that we were seeking unusual speed in Afghan decision making.

The next step was to put the plan formally to the Afghan government. I presented our plan at a meeting with the Afghan ministers who were on the Interministerial Energy Council (which we had pushed so hard to create) and President Karzai's senior economic adviser, Dr. Naderi. I told them that they had until April 9, the day before my departure, to agree. This was not a threat; I simply needed them to recognize that I could not bind my successor to support all facets of my plan if formal agreements were not signed. I briefed President Karzai separately and in detail. He gave the plan his full support.

There were still technical details to negotiate. The Afghans had ideas of their own about sources for generators that might speed delivery. There were negotiations about the types of generators to be purchased. We tried to leave the Afghans as much space as possible to make technical decisions. After all, they would have to live with the results. The discussions were intense. I stayed out of the technical talks because they were well beyond my competence but stressed repeatedly to my own team the principles on which it had to operate: speed and technical soundness. We would not insist on our views if the Afghan preferences were technically sound. The final agreement was signed on April 9; it was one of my last acts in Kabul. Moving from a $100 million idea to a signed agreement in less than two and a half months was as fast as I had ever seen the bureaucratic wheels of two governments spin. I was happy with my own role but fully aware that it could never have happened without the immense drive and technical competence of USAID and the superb contribution of American private sector experts in our Afghan Reconstruction Group. It was a moment to be proud of the whole team.

Pakistan Again

In February 2007 we had another of the periodic political explosions between Afghanistan and Pakistan. The governor of Pakistan's North West Frontier Province, General Orakzai, was quoted in the press as saying that the Taliban was acquiring the status of a national resistance against the foreign occupation of Afghanistan. The Afghan government was furious.

Senior U.S. officials had been working for some time on a dual policy of increasing private pressure on Pakistan to act against insurgents while trying to calm the verbal outbreaks between the two governments. The public recriminations never seemed to push real cooperation usefully and usually detracted from the private efforts. Fortunately, Foreign Minister Spanta called me to confer. I was able to get him and then President Karzai to agree to a twenty-four-hour delay in a public response, but I understood that having a Pakistani statement that called the Taliban a national liberation movement instead of a terrorist group was a position that could not go unanswered from Kabul if it were not retracted.

We worked with our embassy in Islamabad. I called my former boss John Negroponte, who was now installed as deputy secretary of state. With his backing, State pressed through the Pakistani ambassador in Washington. That produced a statement that the Afghans viewed as inadequate.

President Karzai said to me that if the Pakistani government believed that the Taliban was a terrorist organization, as it had told U.S.

and Afghan officials, why wouldn't it say so publicly? Pakistani handling of the incident appeared to the Afghans as a deliberate effort to portray the Taliban as an authentic ethnic rebellion. This was deeply insulting to Pushtuns like President Karzai himself. He felt that his government had to speak out.

I argued for keeping the Afghan statement moderate in tone: it could be written to attack the argument but leave the government of Pakistan room to clarify its views. Throughout I kept senior Afghan officials aware of actions we Americans were taking in Washington and Islamabad. The Afghans' moderation in public depended heavily on knowing that they were being supported.

The final statement was a bit more strident than I would have liked but did leave room for the Pakistani government to respond without rancor. More heavy pressure over the weekend in Islamabad and Washington followed. The Pakistani government finally issued a second and more reasonable statement on Monday, and we were able to close out the issue. I was pleased that the Afghans had shown themselves as reasonable to both the public and senior Washington officials; they had gained stature from their measured handling of the incident. I think they too were pleased with their own performance.

While the Afghan government had done well, the exchange was for them simply one more proof of what they had long believed, that Pakistan had a secret policy of supporting the Taliban. In the Afghan view only American pressure could change Pakistan's course. The result was that when they felt that U.S. pressure on Pakistan was mounting, the Afghans were more likely to heed our requests for public caution. When we seemed to be losing focus, the Afghans would become more strident.

A series of senior U.S.-Pakistani meetings were privately raising the pressure on Pakistan. The Afghans were generally aware of this situation. This helped my effort. I felt I had been reasonably skillful, but diplomatic efforts are much like guns: they are effective only when they have ammunition.

Poppy Again

The problems of opium poppy were constantly nagging even as other problems came and went. A few aspects of the program were working.

We had better organization with the Afghan authorities to circulate information against poppy growing. The antidrug forces were expanding, and some of the aircraft purchased to help in the effort were finally being delivered. For reasons of time, cost, and simplicity of operation, the American government had purchased Russian planes and was retrofitting Russian helicopters with American avionics. U.S. drug enforcement agents would soon be accompanying Afghan counterparts on the same type of helicopters that had supported the Soviet army. Afghanistan was always a place for strange contrasts.

We had also purchased a number of American-made Huey helicopters. They were small and did not have enough lift for the higher altitudes. Exactly why the decision to use Hueys had been made was never clear to me. Some alleged U.S. and congressional politics, but the order was signed before my time. Anyway we had them and used them extensively. It was the first time I had flown in this type aircraft since Vietnam—more memories of my past.

Six provinces were declared poppy free in 2006, and we had hopes of doubling that number in 2007. But the fact remained that poppy cultivation in the south, particularly in Helmand, was soaring and far outweighing the gains we were making elsewhere. We were neither going to get more agricultural assistance to work with immediately nor would we have ground spraying to add to eradication efforts. There was no question that if success were possible, it would require years. But in the meantime poppy was helping fund the insurgents, and the political pressures in Washington were rapidly mounting. The reasons were understandable even if some of the ideas they gave rise to were not. Our constant refusal to work with ideas we considered impractical in Afghanistan added to strains with parts of the State Department.

We did agree that legalizing poppy production in Afghanistan was a bad idea, but this concept arose again and again. It was put forward by a nongovernmental organization called the Senlis Council and adopted by others.[1] On the surface the idea had an attractive simplicity: Follow the example of Turkey, where opium was licensed for production of morphine, codeine, and other legal opiates. Build legal local factories. Cut off the power of the drug barons. Let the money flow to the legal economy instead of to the insurgents and criminals. The problem with the idea was that it wouldn't work in Afghanistan.

Turkey was a strong state able to administer its country and its program. Afghanistan was absolutely the opposite. A legal program without the ability to enforce strong sanctions against illegal cultivation would simply be a competing market more likely to drive up production than channel it into legal lanes. Further, the economic margin was immense between what the farmers received for raw opium and what major drug lords received later on. They could easily outprice the government if, in the absence of enforcement, the matter were one of simple economic competition. Good economics will generally beat bad policy, and clearly in this case the economics were all on the side of the criminals.

Finally, Afghanistan was struggling to reform one of the most corrupt governments in the world. Estimates suggested that the farmers received $600–700 million for their crops. The idea of funneling that kind of money through the hands of hundreds and thousands of miserably paid government officials to get it to millions of farmers without massive leakage was a fantasy. Whenever I thought of the concept, I thought of a man trying to carry water in a bucket shot through with holes.

Knocking down bad ideas, however, wasn't solving our problem. The poppy plants were pushing through the soil early in the new year. There were only a few months in which anything could be done before they were harvested. Whatever the mistakes of policy and resources, we had to do what we could, not just to eradicate but to keep Washington politically centered in support of the larger Afghan efforts. And we had to do it without making the insurgency worse, if that were possible.

Essentially the effectiveness of eradication came down to two policy lines. One was in Helmand, where we would have to use the national Afghan Eradication Force and have military support. The other was all the rest of Afghanistan, where governor-led eradication efforts had to be supported, prodded, and pushed. There might be a few places that had a bit of both strategies, but this was the essence of the matter. The tools for the two strategies were different.

For most provinces the process was simple in conception but infinitely difficult in execution. The essence of the policy was to press a public message against growing, encourage governors to take action against poppy, support them effectively when they did, and keep the national level strongly supporting the action of provincial officials. Getting this to work was a difficult job.

The Afghan government did make many statements, some by President Karzai himself, but whether they had any effect was difficult to say. Karzai had made a strong effort at public persuasion in 2004, but many Afghans felt his promises of development hadn't been kept by the foreigners. In large part they were right. President Karzai never said so directly, but I suspected and could understand that he might feel unwilling to make additional promises that he would have to rely on foreigners to keep. But his leadership was essential, and I joined with other ambassadors and UN officials in seeking his strong commitment to the policy.

The Afghan Ministry of Counternarcotics was definitely cooperating, but its function was to make policy and not to enforce policy. Enforcement fell to the Interior Ministry. We were getting cooperation from the antidrug unit but much more spotty results from other parts of the ministry. Some governors were strong in the eradication effort, and others were not. The interior minister was threatening to fire those who did not perform, but whether he was serious or they believed him were questions difficult to answer.

In February, I traveled to Mazar-i-Sharif with Interior Minister Zarar at his suggestion to meet with five of the regional governors for a pep talk. Zarar made good statements in public as well as in private about how poppy production threatened Afghanistan. He was particularly effective in replying to the governors' litany of how poor farmers needed to survive, saying that where there is poppy there is no law, no justice, and no state. Afghans had to choose which they wanted. He repeated these statements in a press conference we did together. In talking to the governors I noted that while growing poppy might help an individual, stopping production would be rewarded by release of "good performer" funds for the province as a whole.

All of the governors naturally wanted more economic development, but each ended by pledging that they would bring their province to zero poppy production. I thought three of them were probably believable, particularly Mohammad Atta, the governor of Balk, whose capital was Mazar. Atta was the one major commander or warlord who was still in power as a governor. There were questions about his honesty, but he was a strong supporter of President Karzai, had done a great deal to improve the city, and was moving out strongly on economic development. He was also feared, and if he decided to shut down poppy production, I reckoned he could probably do so. In fact, he did just that. In 2006 I had worried about an explosion of poppy production in Balk. By 2008 it was a poppy-free province.

Each province was different. In general where there was a modicum of government authority, there was progress. I had a strong team with Doug Wankel in the drug office and Elizabeth Richard, who had taken over the INL office in the embassy. They worked well together and had greatly improved the mechanism of repaying governors for eradication expenses. Their efforts and those of their staffs were far more complex and difficult than I can properly describe. I delegated a great deal to them and never felt let down. Their nights were often spent answering floods of e-mails from anxious offices in Washington. If our poppy-eradication program preserved some shred of credibility at home, it was largely owing to them.

The problem was that poppy production in Helmand was around 80 percent of Afghan production overall and was making nonsense of progress anywhere else. In Helmand the insurgency and the drug problem were closely related, and the problems were complex. Long meetings at the presidential palace in February focused extensively on Helmand, particularly after the decision to reject ground spraying.

Afghans had engaged with the U.S. and British embassies, ISAF, and CSTC-A in extensive planning for manual eradication in the central Helmand districts, which were under the most government control and were also some of the largest producing areas. These plans were nearly derailed in mid-February when Helmand's then-governor, Wafa, insisted that we do heavy eradication in other areas under Taliban control so that we would not be punishing only "friends" of the government.

The argument was logical, but moving into northern Helmand would have required a major military operation that could not be organized quickly. Stopping eradication until a whole new plan could be developed would have meant that the national Afghan Eradication Force would have been stopped in the middle of its deployment to Helmand.

Nothing would have been done, and the ripening poppy would be harvested before we got into action. This would be a disaster, not least in Congress, just as we were seeking funds, and Congress's criticism of President Karzai would have been intense.

The meeting was rapidly deteriorating with statements becoming more and more strident. President Karzai was called out to take an important telephone call. I used the unplanned recess for frantic lobbying with individual ministers. One of them talked privately to Governor Wafa. We worked out a few small compromises that allowed us to keep eradication on track in the central districts and were able successfully to present this modification of the plan to President Karzai when he rejoined the meeting.

I thought I had accomplished a rather nice bit of diplomatic footwork but was very aware of how much I had learned. A year or less earlier I might have fought out the issue at the table. While I might have gotten my way, I would have left many sore feelings behind if I had pressed the president in front of his ministers to reverse them. I had learned much about how to succeed in getting agreement on a core issue: pocket it and refrain from scoring debating points or discussing peripheral issues. I had gotten to know the ministers and knew how to use an opportunity to convince some of them to help and avoid a public confrontation. And I had been lucky that the interruption came when it did. With all the skill one can muster, luck still plays a hand.

Not all the problems were with the Afghans. We needed space at the airport for our State Department–funded counterdrug aircraft, both for INL and for DEA operations. ISAF needed more space as well, and the airport expansion plan agreed to previously with ISAF was coming apart amid mutual recriminations about bad faith, turf struggles, and potential leaks to Congress. It took a good deal of effort locally and with the relevant agencies in Washington as well as in Kabul. It was complicated to work out a solution without becoming only a State Department partisan, but the ambassador has to represent a broader constituency. Many helped, and we eventually sorted out the issue. I didn't mind the effort so much as I begrudged the time involved in bureaucratic wrangling.

Getting agreement for Helmand was only the start of our problems.

On February 2 the AEF operation in Helmand started to come apart. There had been some small-scale shooting at the force at night, and a panic set in among some of the U.S. contractors who were supporting the AEF. They began insisting that they were in danger of being overrun by a massive ground attack. I thought it likely it was no more than a small group that lacked the force for a major attack trying to run them off, but the contractors began to pull out without orders. Others then panicked as well. The subcontractor who handled logistics pulled back, taking the food and supplies with him. It was a disgrace and made us look very bad to the Afghans. The Afghans of the AEF and Gurkhas were solid but could not maintain themselves without the American support.

Both DCM Norland and I were out of the office and unreachable when the final meltdown occurred. Elizabeth Richard and Doug Wankel made the decision to pull the entire five-hundred-man AEF back to a British firebase until they could stabilize the situation. They had to move fast to keep the situation under control. It was the right decision but a difficult one. I was proud to have a staff that could act on its own when it had to. I told them so.

We had to move quickly to regain control. In the next days we sent contractor supervisors along with members of our own staff to Helmand. They fired the worst offenders among the contractors. Under the tough leadership of Mick Hogan, a rapid reorganization took shape. They sorted out slightly modified eradication areas, and the contractors returned to work two days later. There was no major attack. While all this was going on, we were also dealing with several different senior visitors, including the vice chairman of the Joint Chiefs of Staff and the head of the White House counterterrorism office, as well as a late-night secure videoconference with Washington.

On February 4, General McNeil took command of ISAF. In Helmand there were ISAF concerns about exactly where the eradication would take place. These were founded on real worries about worsening the situation with the locals, particularly as ISAF had just won a fight not far from the province capital and believed it needed time to stabilize relations with the locals. I suspected the concerns probably incorporated a good deal of lower-level resistance to doing eradication at all when they had their hands full with a war.

I sympathized, but we had a policy agreed to by NATO, Washington, and the Afghan government. Occasionally I had to go to General McNeil for support, and I always received it when the going got tough.

I leveled with him on my bottom line: we needed to show we could cut ten thousand hectares of poppy. If we could make that target, I would pack up the AEF and call it victory. This paralleled discussions I was having with senior Afghan government officials. President Karzai was being attacked in the Afghan press for being tougher on eradication than the foreigners. This was completely untrue but put him in a politically vulnerable position. Nevertheless, he stayed firm on proceeding with eradication in Helmand, realizing that if we backed down it would shred Afghan governmental authority and the next year would be worse. The struggle over the amnesty law was heating up at the same time. It was not a relaxed time in Kabul.

The eradication operation in Helmand continued through February and March. We were getting a lot of criticism for eradicating only in areas of government control, but until we could wage a more successful counterinsurgency campaign we could not get to other areas. The AEF was doing most of the eradication, and by March 30 had cut six thousand hectares (about fifteen thousand acres), but it was a drop in the bucket in an area where the poppy looked like the wheat fields of Kansas.

In addition to the problems of local resentment and trying to operate in the middle of a war, we were feeling gigantic political pressure from Washington to get the cultivation numbers down. This clashed head on with military resentment that eradication was adding to the number of enemy combatants. The arguments were a bit overdrawn on each side, but there was no doubt that we were pushing the edge of the possible without getting our own people killed or having the Afghan government balk.

By late March we were operating day by day, wheeling and dealing, pressuring and compromising. The situation changed on an hourly basis. On one day in the morning I was told our work was completely stopped, and in the afternoon the AEF was able to sort out a local problem, go back to work, and cut five hundred hectares.

With the situation in such flux, one couldn't really micromanage policies from Kabul and certainly not from Washington. I delegated a great deal to the judgment of our people in Helmand and helped sort out specific problems in Kabul when asked. Generally I simply kept up a steady pressure on everyone concerned, telling them that we needed to hit the target of ten thousand hectares and if we did that I would pull the force back. Over and over I argued with different people, American and Afghan, civilian and military, that they had to stop finding what was wrong with every place the AEF wanted to cut and find where we could eradicate. It was a simple approach, sometimes a bit rough and sometimes reasonable, but we continued to make progress.

By the first days of April we reached the limit of the possible. Local villagers in Helmand were starting to demonstrate and to block roads to prevent the AEF from getting to the fields. If we kept up, we risked killing civilians or getting our own people killed in the confrontations. We were just short of our goal, but we had done enough. I agreed with the Afghan command to order the AEF out of Helmand.

Even Iron Men Get Sick

As we worked through the various crises of the spring, I continued to travel. On March 5, I returned to Farah Province in western Afghanistan. I had good meetings, but for the first time in all my travels I did not leave the base. There was intelligence of a suicide bomber somewhere in town. The actual threat to me was low, but we would have had to use the same route in and out to the governor's compound, where we were to meet. The compound itself was small and much of my security detail would have had to remain outside and vulnerable. I stayed inside the base and returned to Kabul uncomfortable with the decision because the logic that caused the cancellation of the move could too easily be extended to many other trips. But it was done and there wouldn't be many other trips.

Two international journalists came with us on the trip. They were veterans of the Afghan scene and reasonable people. We let them have a good deal of freedom to talk to a wide variety of people, including the many Afghans who came for meetings. The stories came out well, and our credibility with the press was high because we had not tried to manage their access. I got back to Kabul to plunge into meetings dealing with Afghan relations with Iran, the amnesty law, a possible kidnapping of a journalist, and several other things.

On March 13, I noticed I was developing a sore throat during the meetings on strategic dialogue, but it seemed minor. Over the next three days it got worse. I saw off the last of our visitors, and the embassy nurse tested me for strep throat. The test was negative. I worked in the office and tried to keep a light schedule but was having trouble sleeping at night because of throat congestion. By March 16, when I went to an embassy staff barbeque for Saint Patrick's Day, I was having trouble swallowing food. For the first time I passed on the afternoon volleyball game.

March 17 was worse. My throat was definitely closing down. Sleep the night before had been impossible. The nurse tried an IV and a combination of stronger drugs, but they caused my blood pressure to drop. I agreed to cancel a trip planned for the next day. The drugs seemed to be helping as I was able to take a small amount of fluid and eat a bit of oatmeal. Then my symptoms started to get worse. In the evening I was moved to the small military hospital at Camp Phoenix. The next morning my secretary, Alene, wrote my wife to tell her I was taking a bit of broth but not much else and if I didn't improve I would be moved to the larger military hospital at Bagram. Alene noted, "The nurse isn't alarmed and thinks his body just needs time for rest and recovery (something both you and I know he resists!)." How well my staff knew me.

I was not having a good time but was cheered by a visit of the defense attaché, Colonel Norton, who drove out to see me despite the well-known dangers of driving on the Jalalabad Road, where all too many suicide car bomb attacks occurred. We reminisced about Vietnam and laughed a bit over how we'd miss our last war when it was all over. It was a good moment even if it did hurt to laugh.

The following day went to hell. My convoy was on the way to get me from the hospital for the trip to Bagram. As they passed a slow-moving car, it exploded into the lead vehicle of the convoy, gravely wounding the guard in the passenger seat and destroying the heavily armored Suburban.

My special assistant, Suzanne Inzerillo, and the embassy nurse were in the second vehicle. It managed to continue through the bomb site but then stopped as the radiator had been holed by bomb fragments. For a time they were isolated. The radio was dead; no one else was in sight. Suzanne took a pistol and kept watch on one area while the driver and embassy security officer watched in other directions. They wondered if they were the only survivors. In fact, the Blackwater reaction team was moving quickly to the site, and the medic who always traveled with the team was administering first aid to the wounded guard.

At the time I knew none of the details, only that the convoy had been hit. Soon enough the survivors and wounded were evacuated to the hospital at Camp Phoenix, where I was. It was a bit like a scene out of *M*A*S*H* as the doctors cut away blood-stained clothing and performed emergency treatment. I stood around watching and talking about the incident with the security detail. I felt proud of the convoy's performance but personally quite useless. Intermittent rain was falling out of a dismal sky and dribbling onto the canvas roof of the hospital tent. Helicopters were called to evacuate us to Bagram.

For some reason that I do not now recall, I became concerned that my rank would get me evacuated ahead of the wounded. I don't know exactly what I said, but the security detail reported to the acting DCM, Carol Rodley, that I was refusing evacuation. Carol told them to tell me that if I didn't get on the helicopter, she'd come out and do an emergency tracheotomy on my throat with a pocket knife. At least that produced a laugh among the rather tense command group at the embassy. I relented.

The helicopters arrived. We were driven out to the landing pad. The stretcher with the guard was loaded onto one helicopter, and I squelched out through the mud to climb onto the second. At Bagram the guard was rushed to surgery, and I was seen by a qualified ear, nose, and throat specialist who correctly diagnosed my problem and put me on antibiotics. I started to recover quickly and had time the next day to spend with my guard since we were in the same ward. Many of the details of the attack I learned from him. He was flown out the next day. We hoped his leg could be saved but learned later that it had to be amputated.

By March 22, I was back in Kabul meeting with the UN on police enlargement, holding a budget review with USAID and a night meeting with President Karzai, and fussing with NATO Brussels about an uncoordinated press conference. It all seemed preferable to the previous week.

10
Wrap-Up

On March 26, I sent my letter of resignation to the president. This is another diplomatic ritual. I made it very simple, thanking the president for allowing me the honor to serve. The farewell parties had started, and the calendar was getting crowded. Often such celebrations are sterile—too many toasts with too much flattery. But I had made some real friends, and some of the regrets were sincere on all sides. The German ambassador hosted a lunch with the European ambassadors. They seemed to appreciate the efforts I had made to collaborate closely. Each of the farewells brought a measure of nostalgia, but most reminded me that I was leaving behind real friendships with first-class professionals. As the days passed, I had a constant desire to "finish" projects in which I had invested so heavily but understood that there was to be no finishing: I could only do what I could and pass the rest on to my successor.

We were pushing forward ideas for building the foundations of a functioning Afghan state, namely bureaucratic and management skills. In the developmental world this has the vague title of "capacity building." Since 2005 a consensus had emerged regarding the need to shift economic strategy from emergency reconstruction to long-term development that could become sustainable. Having capacity—Afghan officials with knowledge of what policies to pursue and the tools to pursue them—to manage and move forward such work was clearly a central element to improving the effectiveness of foreign assistance and encouraging donors to channel more money through the Afghan government. Without improvements in capacity, we would be unlikely to move beyond expensive foreign-financed and foreign-run projects.[1]

Six major foreign donors had jumped into the effort.[2] However, different donors' programs often targeted the same problems and sometimes the same ministries, leading to overlap, confusion, and difficulties in planning and execution.[3] The JCMB semiannual report published in November 2006 highlighted the need to remove bottlenecks in project implementation particularly by focusing on capacity development efforts. In consultation with embassy staff, we decided to attack the coordination problem much as we had the electrical energy issue. We pulled together our own ideas into a single strategy white paper, which we discussed with other donors and with the Afghan government under the auspices of UNAMA, seeking a coordinated approach.

When we had addressed the energy issue, we needed to bring ambassadors and international agency heads to the UNAMA table to secure agreement. In the case of capacity building, we were able to draw on the growing international and Afghan awareness of the problem to make progress in bringing the parties at the technical working level together around our white paper. Still, the overall process of building consensus through the coordinating vehicle, UNAMA, was the same. Key Afghan government stakeholders responded and proposed a capacity-building and development framework and challenged the rest of the government and the donors to respond.

The framework that was developed identified four key areas, or pillars, with a ministerial counterpart responsible for each: justice/Ministry of Justice; public service/Independent Administrative Reform and Civil Service Commission (IARCSC); private sector and NGOs/Ministry of Economy; and Afghan society at large/Ministry of Education. Particular attention was given to the Afghan government's ability to execute its own development budget. The donors responded to this white paper process by agreeing that the World Bank and the Ministry of Finance would be the lead partners for this effort.

Building Afghan capacity to run a truly efficient government not only would be a work of years but also would be a central element of efforts to build real Afghan governance. Without capacity there could be little improvement in delivery of public services, even if progress was made in addressing the corrosive issue of corruption. It would be slow going because education takes time, especially when there is a very limited base of educated people—in a country with 80 percent illiteracy—to move into specialized training.

The slowness of the effort is frustrating—not least of all to the millions of Afghans still waiting for normal governmental services. But there is also frustration in capitals, which gives rise to repeated efforts to find some new policy that will speed results. In April 2007, Washington was thinking about striving for a "year of governance" and a new strategic plan somehow to make a breakthrough.

Metrics and Strategy

Part of the problem was that it was difficult for donor-state capitals to understand just how much work was already going on or how complicated the effort to move from concept to achievement was. Simply establishing a real civil service commission that was neither corrupt nor without influence (both problems of the existing institution) would take at least a year and very possibly longer.

Creating an inventory of projects ("so we have a full picture") and a central plan is a common first call. This approach is not so much wrong as simplistic. I noted in an e-mail to Washington that two of my officers had independently tried after their arrival to work on an inventory of governance-related programs and gave it up as more labor intensive than it was beneficial. UNAMA made a new start, but it was labor intensive and required an ever-increasing staff to compile information. Little of that informational work was actually advancing anything on the ground. Thus we decided to move forward on coordinating tangible progress in certain key areas rather than attempting a comprehensive plan for the economy.

Metrics—collecting statistics to measure how programs are performing—often actually retards real work. While there is no doubt that there must be some standard of what is expected against which to measure progress and while capitals do need periodic assessments of actual progress, the process has gotten out of hand. Sometimes an informed judgment from the field is as good as any seemingly sophisticated PowerPoint data matrix. DCM Norland and I inherited a massive data collection exercise from our predecessors, coordinated by the DCM on a weekly basis with the help of a dedicated handful of military officers loaned to the embassy for this purpose. The data was eagerly received by equally dedicated number crunchers in Washington, whose appetite seemed insatiable.

It was never clear that the hundreds of man-hours that went into this effort contributed anything to policy success. I cannot recall an instance in which the data reported in this process told us of a problem of which we were unaware by other means. While we continued to faithfully produce numbers each week, we drastically scaled the effort back as time went on, and it was never seen as anything more than a distraction. What was far more important was to insist on honest reporting from every level of our staff and the military commands and to transmit our evaluations of what we learned to Washington in clear language.

Likewise, I was suspicious of the idea that a strategic plan for governance was going to be of nearly as much value as many believed, although it might make sense as a marketing and fund-raising tool. I was suspicious because what we were talking about in governance amounted to the basic social and political transformation of Afghanistan, including its cultural norms—that is, how people deal with each other, repay favors, and cultivate influence to protect themselves and their families and retainers. Making significant changes in all this would take many years. Therefore I was reluctant to call for a "year of governance" unless we were going to be explicit that it would be a year of starting (or invigorating) a process that would last for decades. Massive advances in a year were unlikely.

Further, even if a year could produce complex change in the civil service commission organization and rules, it would take far longer to make sure the rules were actually enforced. Afghanistan is not a country that pays any attention to strategic plans, which govern very little of what actually happens. Nor is it yet a country where rule of law prevails. The laws that exist are frequently flouted even by senior officials. Strategies are left unimplemented, and overworked ministries ignore action plans unless there is constant follow-up from the top and harassment from the international donors.

I am not wholly dismissive of plans and strategies, and there are times when a full review of strategy must be undertaken. But such reviews and the plans they produce often have less value than is usually assumed. As with metrics, one needs constantly to consider the trade-off: how much value is gained versus how much time is spent developing the plan and not getting on with the actual work. Some planning is essential for direction. But comprehensive planning is not only time-consuming but takes the efforts of the people who would otherwise be implementing work in the same sector. This is part of the difficulty of not having enough indigenous capacity, but the lack of staffing and its consequences is extremely difficult to understand for those coming from developed countries with vast reservoirs of educated, trained manpower.

Strategy Begins with the First Step

Where building strategies *can* be useful is in helping the donor community and the Afghan technocrats to advance the complex interrelated process of working with the various pieces that have to go into the strategy. But what one needs to understand is that prioritization is the key: after a strategy is agreed to, one must identify whatever part needs to be done *first*, then work on it absolutely as hard as if there had been no agreement on a strategy at all. That decision needs to be forced through the upper levels of government with international support and sometimes pressure, for without agreement and action on the first step, nothing will follow.

After that, there will be a separate process of enforcing respect for the rules that have been agreed to in order to produce results. Some retribution against senior officials who have violated the rules must take place to instill respect for the rules. And after that, one takes the next piece of the strategy and the whole process begins over again. This is an effort that must and can be driven only by those on the ground, but to do so they must themselves have adequate staffing to keep after priorities in many different areas. Washington's slowness in providing staffing requested from Kabul before, during, and after my tenure cannot be made up for by new strategies and plans. It seemed we had our own capacity problem: for a country at war, only the military parts of the U.S. government appeared to have truly been mobilized.

Rather than adopt an entirely new governance strategy, I advocated moving forward with what we were already doing in capacity building—itself a plan but on a more limited scale. We had worked out a large new program named Afghans Building Capacity (ABC) and needed to fund it. Our white paper and the drive of our staff started the focused intergovernmental effort on capacity building. The white paper focused the consensus-building process within the international working group on governance, comprised of donors and Afghan officials. My advice was to focus on how we could extract a few key elements from existing plans, popularize them, and drive the various planning operations already under way in Kabul. Progress would be slow and sometimes crabwise. Each day would bring new challenges. But keeping a steady course would do more in the long run than repeatedly breaking off to search for a new course. However, I was leaving and others would have to make these decisions.

We Can Take ... But Not Hold

Meanwhile, ISAF was shaping a counteroffensive for Helmand. The decapitation strategy—removing insurgent leaders—was disrupting Taliban plans, but it was neither public nor well understood by the Afghans. They were used to movements of large bodies of men, often without much organization or planning, that had marked the back-and-forth waves of combat over the years. To Afghans, ISAF was not doing much because they were not taking territory. But the reality was that without more troops, ISAF forces in the south could not hold, in the sense of making Afghan civilians secure in their homes and work, more land than they already had. There were no extra Afghan security forces to fill in behind them, and offensives had to be carefully managed to achieve any useful result.

Later in the summer, using a new U.S. battalion to reinforce existing forces, ISAF moved part way into northern Helmand to take the important district capital of Sangin. The operation went quickly with minimal Taliban resistance despite the fears expressed by some that the operation would provoke a major battle with large civilian casualties. Stabilizing Sangin would be much harder and longer than taking it, particularly in the absence of qualified Afghan administrators and some way of reconciling the feuding tribes.

After my departure ISAF continued on to take back Musa Qala. However, progress remained spotty. ISAF could capture population centers at will but really securing the population was often impossible. Taliban control of the countryside's population could be maintained by showing up occasionally to threaten individuals, kill government and development workers, and burn schools. Protection, on the other hand, needed to be full-time if Afghan civilians were to take the risk of supporting the government. As a result, the threatened Taliban offensive of 2007 never really took place, but neither was ISAF able to create an environment that seemed to the populace any more secure than that at the beginning of the year. For Afghans, this did not look like progress, and many of them were left sitting on the fence when it came to committing to either ISAF or the Taliban.

Back in Kabul, my Blackwater protective detail held a dinner for me at its camp. One of the team members had run an Italian restaurant, and he produced an extraordinarily good meal that was accompanied by a lot of good fellowship. Unlike our U.S. military colleagues who, under General Order Number One (a restriction imposed by army officers who had seen abuses during Vietnam), could not drink alcohol, we at the embassy were able to have a drink once in a while. My detail deserved one. It had done very well in the convoy bombing when it was coming to get me from the hospital, and the men were still pumped up and justifiably proud of how well they had handled everything from security after the incident to patching up the wounded.

There has been much criticism of private security contractors in general and of Blackwater in particular after an incident in Baghdad in which Blackwater allegedly opened fire on civilians. I can say only that those who protected me in Baghdad and later in Kabul were fine professionals. They constantly interposed their bodies and vehicles to make sure I stayed safe. They did their utmost to avoid injury or insult to

Afghans and to find the balance between keeping me secure and letting me accomplish tasks I felt essential to my mission. One of my team members lost his leg performing that duty. Perhaps some day our nation will find another way to handle security, but that is for the future. I remain proud of my association with these men and of their work.

On March 30, Elaine arrived to spend the final days in Kabul with me and to be part of the final farewells. We had been a team in so many postings that it seemed natural to have her in Kabul. The day Elaine arrived, President Karzai had us and my senior officers to the palace, where he presented me with a medal and some very complimentary remarks. Elaine was able to pay a call on President Karzai's wife. Secretary Rice visited a few days later and greeted Elaine warmly.

Together Elaine and I flew to visit the Hungarian PRT in Baghlan Province. It was the twenty-seventh province of Afghanistan's thirty-four that I had visited. We had a dramatic flight up through the rocky and snow-covered hills with razor-sharp ridges that rose out of the snow around us into the clouds. We tried to fly in the Black Hawk helicopters straight up over the mountains, but the clouds were too low to get over the pass. We turned around and flew west to Bamyan, refueled, and made it to Baghlan. It was a longer and colder flight than we had planned, but the countryside was spectacular. Coming back we flew for miles over green fields with white, flowering fruit trees.

The Hungarians were enthusiastic about their mission and happy to work with our USAID officer stationed at the PRT. They did not have large resources of their own, but without the Hungarians we could not have replaced the Dutch forces that had redeployed southward. USAID was able to provide some project funding. Together we had a team. Later a particularly violent suicide bomb attack killed a number of Afghan parliamentarians who were visiting the province, but the Hungarians have maintained their presence and their work.

On April 7, I sent in a final report summing up my conclusions about where we stood in Afghanistan. I had worked on the message for several days and sought the views of my staff. Dick Norland helped trim the message from twenty paragraphs to a taut fourteen. I wanted to make my final report as honest and clear as I could, trying to analyze where we stood, to acknowledge our accomplishments, but to explain once again the dangers and the need for more attention and more resources.

The telegram again made the case for more troops, particularly more training personnel for the army and police, without which we would not get the payoff from the funding decisions already made.

Our efforts with Pakistan were not producing needed results. In Helmand, security control needed to be a precursor to counternarcotics efforts. We were pushing eradication as far as we could, but essentially we were trying to make the counterdrug policy work before the counterinsurgency policy had taken hold. Staffing of the civilian mission was still insufficient to cover gaps caused by leaves and transfers.

Overall, I said that we were "on solid policy grounds but we are still on a very, very thin margin. We do not need new policies; we need the resources and support to implement effectively what we have decided to do." If we lost focus, we could still tumble. The situation, I said, was fragile and time was not necessarily on our side. "The state does not yet have sufficient political legitimacy to endure on its own; achieving this is the simple definitional objective of justice, governance and security reform and may pass for success for decades before a liberal democracy may emerge." I believed what I wrote. Various analysts in Washington liked the message, but it did not produce new resources.

In the final week there was one more videoconference with President Bush and senior officials in Washington. Again I made the point that we needed to find the training teams to go with the increases in Afghan forces we were proposing to equip. It seemed to me that the issue was somehow getting pushed aside. Iraq was soaking up the available forces. If we could not fill all the needs, it was nevertheless important to understand the consequences of what we could not do. Schedules for producing new, trained Afghan battalions would mean little if we could not put the advisers with them to continue training, to assist them in combat, and to link them to the support and logistics that only we could provide.

Friends told me that my intervention had kept the issue from getting shoved aside, but the effect was temporary. That we did not appear to have the forces, I understood. But it was wrong to hide from ourselves the consequences for actions we could not take.

The last day arrived. The packers had taken the pictures off the walls, and the apartment had that barren and impersonal look that buildings acquire when all the personal touches have been stripped away. I worked after dark finishing up the last papers and odds and ends while Elaine held dinner. The next day I had a chance to say farewell to the entire embassy staff, including the hundreds of Afghan employees who loyally provided the continuity to our operations in Kabul. The front office staff all gathered to shake hands and hug one last time. As I walked out the door, I could not resist a sudden impulse to use the corny line from the old Bugs Bunny cartoons, "That's all, folks."

Epilogue

Elaine and I left Kabul on April 10 for the return to Washington. I spent most of my last weeks in Washington seeing members of Congress and making calls on senior administration officials. In the Congress I found continued solid bipartisan support for sticking with Afghanistan. I was frank in predicting more bloody fighting ahead. Great patience and resolve would be needed from us and others, and the Afghans would have to find the political will to make fundamental changes. Nevertheless, I believed we were on the right track in Afghanistan if we could find the needed troops and continue substantial funding.

Within the administration I focused on the same things, especially troops. The need for additional military and civilian trainers had not been met. Repeatedly I stressed that if we did not have the troops to meet all the needs, then we had to look at the need for combat battalions and trainers as a single resource problem. We needed to avoid continuing to consider the two requirements on separate decision tracks. We should decide where the greatest need lay and make appropriate decisions. I was heard but made little impact; the troop requirements for Iraq were stretching our forces too thin for an adequate response either in trainers or fighters, and NATO nations were not filling the gap.

On funding there seemed to be more willingness to continue heavy expenditures. The congressional support was solid, but the initiative would have to come from the administration. I remained concerned that we would flinch because of overall budget pressures. In my final meeting with President Bush, he told me that he believed congressional support for another supplemental was strong. I agreed but said that I was more concerned that OMB would cut the request before it came to him.

In May, I made a final official trip, visiting several Central Asian states to shore up support for Afghanistan and to discuss several pending issues. Whether the trip did much good or not, it was fun to see new nations along the Great Silk Road. On my return there was a nice ceremony in which the director general of the Foreign Service presented me with a flag. It is standard for retiring ambassadors but a nice moment with a few friends and close colleagues who had supported and mentored me over thirty-seven years of service. On May 31, I gave my last official speech and my retirement was official.

Back home in the United States, I am often asked the question, Am I an optimist or a pessimist about the future of Afghanistan? My reply remains that I am optimistic about *the possibility of success* but do not believe that there is any certainty about the outcome.

The challenges to success in Afghanistan are huge. The state is fragile. Years of war have reinforced historical tendencies to look to tribes and family networks for protection even as the fighting has broken down the cohesion of tribal leadership. Local commanders have ruled through force but offer no unified power that can stand up to insurgents without foreign backing. Militia leaders are too often engaged in feuding with each other and maneuvering for position rather than in securing local peace from the Taliban. To build long-term security on local commanders is contrary to all progress in building a state that can someday stand on its own.

The economy is a bustling shambles, trading with little investment or job creation. Corruption is massive. Both are made worse by the narcotics problem. Some call for a Marshall Plan–style relief effort, but the educational base, trained bureaucracy, and infrastructure that existed in Europe at the end of World War II will take decades to create in Afghanistan. The issue in most of Afghanistan is not "*reconstruction*" so much as it is *con*struction in the first place. On the security front, the army is small and lightly equipped and the police force is a weak reed at best. The problems emanating from Pakistan have grown larger.

Against these manifold problems there are some assets. While the Taliban and their local and foreign allies are becoming more feared, they are not gaining popularity. The Afghan National Army is respected and fighting reasonably well. It now has a solid professional and multiethnic foundation on which to build a larger edifice.

There is also an enormous reservoir of popular support for better governance and a better life. Development is chaotic and inadequate, but a great deal has been done and many more projects are coming to fruition. Eight years after the mission began, international support remains stronger than many predicted. Seeing the flags of some thirty-seven nations blowing in the wind when you pull into the military side of Kabul International Airport is a reminder that the entire international community has a stake in success. It is not certain such broad engagement will continue or that adequate troops and international willpower can be maintained, but certainly NATO and the other international donors—if they have the will—have vast potential to pit against a still weak if determined enemy.

A new Afghan generation of trained managers, bureaucrats, and entrepreneurs is emerging. Training and education are slow. Small numbers of trained modern men and women cannot remake traditional, inefficient, entrenched, and often corrupt bureaucracies in a year or perhaps even a decade. The process of social transformation is more like a nuclear reaction than a steady climb: for a long time nothing visible happens because the numbers of those advocating new ways are too small. But once a certain critical mass is achieved, the results can be large and startlingly rapid. There is no certainty that such results will be obtained. But before we become too discouraged we should remember, for example, the many years that went by after the Korean War before development began to take off in South Korea—and we are far from done with the war in Afghanistan.

Security has clearly gotten worse since I departed from Afghanistan. But much of the insecurity that is so troubling in areas close to Kabul or along the major roads is a function of insurgents pushing into areas that have few or no security forces. We and the Afghans are paying a heavy price for our late start in building adequate security forces. Too often we have been pushed to use short-term expedients to fill gaps. Nevertheless, it is critical to understand that we are facing the problem of a weak state far more than a strong domestic insurgency.

There is little evidence of any massive expansion of those joining the insurgency. Instead there is expansion of the insurgency coming across the Pakistani border to reinforce those Afghan tribal elements already in the insurgency.

We are in trouble. But nothing is happening that exceeds our capacity to respond, first with our own forces to buy time and later with the development of larger Afghan forces. As we confront increasing areas of instability, we should not lose sight of the fact that much of Afghanistan is still relatively calm. We must find the capacity to work faster and better in calm areas to strengthen the Afghan state even as we fight harder where the insurgency is growing. This will be hard, but it is not impossible.

Books are poor places for detailed policy prescription; too many things change in the lengthy time between writing and publication. Yet there are a few principles that are worth keeping in mind.

Principle: Build the Afghan State

The first principle is that success in Afghanistan depends on helping Afghans to build a stronger state. The Afghan government must ultimately find the will to make some of the large changes required for success. If it fails, we will fail no matter how many troops and how much money we pour in. The Afghan government at various levels will often come up short of our expectations because what is asked of it demands so much vision and courage. As we work through these difficult days, two cautions are worth remembering:

First, sometimes the Afghans will be right not to move too fast in the process of social and political transformation. The Afghan Communists who took over in 1978 failed and brought on the Soviet invasion not because of ideological resistance to communism but because they tried to change too many Afghan social and economic practices too quickly, particularly at the village level, and provoked massive popular resistance. There is a lesson there for outsiders who want to move quickly on every facet of creating a liberal state.

That does not mean that Afghan officials will always be right. Social conservatism and fear of destabilization can simply be an excuse for not making hard political choices to reform corruption or threaten political friends with accountability. If too much protection of old ways and old friends prevents progress toward effective Afghan governance, then Afghanistan will remain a fragmented state unable to withstand an insurgency driven and reinforced from outside. Rather the point is simply a caution that we need continually to listen to Afghan points of view and think deeply about which changes are important enough for our strategic objective to insist on pressing quickly. The answers will have to be practical and worked out with a considerable knowledge and judgment of Afghan conditions.

The second caution in building an Afghan state is that great care is needed not to let our frustration with the slow pace of change lead us to try to take charge too directly, to override a government and a parliament and dictate new directions. Their history has made Afghans deeply suspicious of foreign intentions. Foreigners have repeatedly tried to rule through surrogates and just as repeatedly failed. If Afghans in large numbers become convinced that our purpose is to rule rather than to help them build, then we will fail. This fact should make us cautious in forcing large constitutional and organizational changes, even if our own poor record of decision making is not enough to teach us some humility.

Principle: Build Credibility and Patience at Home

How long must we remain?.

We face difficult years. There are very long lag times from decisions to actions. A decision to build a larger Afghan army will take several years to show any effect: equipment must be ordered and built, soldiers trained, and organizations put in place to coordinate the individuals. While all this is happening, there is likely to be little improvement to point to on the battlefield, and fighting may get worse. The same problems are true in every facet of social and economic development. We need to be much more explicit and detailed in explaining these facts to the American people.

It is tempting to tout major decisions as solutions and to refer only generally to the need for time. This is the road to political failure at home. In an age of twenty-four-hour news cycles and daily stories of bombs and casualties, there is an inevitable impatience when time passes and nothing seems to improve or even seems to get worse. By that point, detailed explanations in response to criticism are all too likely to be brushed off as merely excuses.

When that happens, pressures build either to develop new strategies or to consider the enterprise a failure. This cannot be wholly avoided, but it can be mitigated by starting early to explain what people realistically should—and should not—expect to see in a given period. Underpromising and overfulfilling is always a better way to retain long-term political credibility than the reverse. But with two-year U.S. election cycles and a noisy public, it is hard to keep this lesson in focus.

③ Principle: Develop Pakistan and Afghan Policies in Parallel

The situation in Pakistan has changed but not yet improved. The weaker the pressure from the Pakistani state on the frontier areas, the freer the extremists will be to throw more force into the fight in Afghanistan. This fact is increasingly, if belatedly, being understood. Calls for a regional strategy have finally led to new attention to Pakistan even as the odd dual government of Pakistani civilian and military authorities seems to be showing new determination. All this is good. The problems in the no-man's-land of northwestern Pakistan, which serves as a safe haven for the Taliban and al Qaeda, are similar in nature to those of undeveloped Afghanistan and call for similar military, political, and economic solutions to be applied in ways to integrate these areas into their respective states, yet allow populations that straddle the almost invisible frontier set by the Durand line to continue to interact.

In pursuing a regional approach, we should try to bolster the UN's ability to play the kind of constructive role that UNAMA has played in Afghanistan. The United States cannot and should not lead this effort alone, in part because many Pakistanis view us in an intensely negative light. We should also broaden our scope to assess how others among Afghanistan's immediate neighbors in Central Asia can help. This will require more effective engagement with former Soviet states than has been achieved thus far.

My experience and this book have been about Afghanistan. A few short paragraphs that will not be read for months after they are written are not the place to prescribe future policy for Pakistan. However, as the policy debate unfolds with the inevitable demand for resources, it is important to bear in mind that we need not one policy but two. One is the much discussed regional approach that includes Pakistan. But there is no guarantee that it will succeed, and even if it does it may require many years, perhaps more years than American domestic political support for the Afghan war can be sustained. Thus if we depend on only a regional strategy for success in Afghanistan, we are building on hope. And as my military colleagues always remind me, hope is not a plan.

Therefore, we need a parallel strategy of armed state building in Afghanistan that does not depend on success in the regional effort.[1] Succeeding that way would be much harder. But to underresource the Afghan effort in the hope that regional policy will save us makes failure on both fronts more likely. Further, the degree to which we appear to be determined to stay and to win in Afghanistan is directly related to whether Pakistani authorities can be persuaded to maintain their own struggle with extremism and break whatever ties remain with the Taliban. If it appears that the United States is planning a quick exit from Afghanistan, there will be little appetite in Pakistan to take on a full-scale conflict with the Taliban. From the Pakistani point of view, such an effort would constitute a two-front war (India being the other front). The Americans will have left them in the lurch once again.

Principle: Focus on Implementation as Much as on Strategy, and on Civilians as Much as on the Military

Finally, the time is long past to add to our strategic discussions far greater attention to better implementation of the strategies we choose. If the short period covered in this memoir has done nothing else, I hope it has clarified how much depends on local decision making and effective use of resources in the complicated endeavor of building a state while fighting a war. Policy and plans are important, but implementation is equally so. To illustrate the point, consider the possible outcome if policymakers were to decide to use tribal elements (militias) to help secure roads.

The result could be that groups take our money and use our equipment to fight other tribes and commanders for local power and do nothing to enhance local security. This is what happened for several years with efforts to secure oil pipelines in Iraq by hiring tribes. We spent a lot of money on "local security," and the pipelines were still blown up and repair crews attacked. The policy was a failure.

On the other hand, the policy could be successful. We could pay only for real results, chose the tribes and commanders to work with carefully, tighten their relationship with the central government, and take action against those who default on their promises. The difference between success and failure would be entirely a matter of how the policy is implemented by those trying to assess complex situations firsthand and move forward each day.

Therefore the quality of the people who make decisions on the ground and the broad strategies they try to pursue are equally critical. So too are the tools they have to work with.

It has become common wisdom to say that counterinsurgency is as much a matter of civilian success as of military action. Yet we have consistently underresourced the civilian part of our effort. We need more diplomats trained in languages and with area expertise. They must have the protection to tend to their work. USAID needs the personnel to implement technical projects, not just sign megacontracts. It needs a senior-level staff big enough to manage one of the largest USAID programs in the world but cannot get the needed staff because the agency has shrunk to 10 percent of the size it was during the Vietnam War.[2] Department of Agriculture advisers in Afghanistan, a phenomenally effective resource for rural Afghanistan in the eyes of Afghans and U.S. military commanders alike, are limited to a dozen because the department has no money in its budget to send more. The Department of Homeland Security has not sent the numbers and quality of Customs and Border Service experts needed because DHS has no funds to do so.

I did receive some increases in staff but too few, and they were slow in coming. When compared to the massive staff increases in Iraq, our meager increases made it far from clear that Afghanistan was at the epicenter of the struggle with extremism. I may have been too modest in what I requested, but it hardly mattered since recommendations to increase the numbers of State and USAID officers in the PRTs went largely unanswered and even maintaining one officer from each agency in each PRT was a struggle as the numbers of PRTs expanded. Some additional resources have been sent to my successor, but it has taken months to get them in place. The problem is far less a lack of willingness in the State Department and USAID to respond but, rather, the failure at the highest levels to recognize that the staffing of these agencies must be dramatically increased to meet the needs of war. This requires permanent increases in the budget, not just year-to-year supplementals.[3]

Civilian trainers and mentors for the police need to be massively expanded if we are to get serious value from the money we are spending on equipment. But so too do the supervisory personnel in Afghanistan if there is to be coherent management of the overall program with its many contracts. Some of the above changes are happening as I write in mid-2009. We have yet to see that the supervisors will be given the authority to manage the programs in the field without constant application of the "six thousand mile screwdriver" from Washington that dominates policy and holds the purse strings and contracting authority. In every area, personnel need to stay long enough to put to use the knowledge they acquire of a complex society where personal relationships are essential to getting things done. The civilian "surge" may take a year to even be fully developed because we do not have the necessary personnel or skills in the numbers needed in our government. As we pay for these errors of the past, we need to educate the American people about the time needed for change less new policies be condemned as failures before they have actually begun to operate.

In 2007 the Bush administration began to finance some of the needed increases but not enough.[4] We are still moving too slowly to get the resources to the field because that is the nature of our cumbersome system, and we have yet to demonstrate that we can combine new policies and resources with sophisticated understanding of the nature of the problems we face.

We need to understand and accept the need to apply to the civilian side of armed nation building the same ability we have given our military to mobilize resources and adapt to what we learn. The military and civilian sides of the equation are not alternatives. Both are essential. We have the capacity to make progress in both areas. The price tag for the civilians is almost trivial next to the military costs.[5] What is at issue is American political will, the same commodity whose lack we are so ready to criticize in foreigners.

Any number of things could yet go wrong. NATO could collapse if the political will of individual states falters. Pakistan could melt down even further. Quarrels with Iran could see a flow of weapons to the insurgents to offset U.S. military strikes. None of these developments would necessarily be conclusive, but each would reduce the margin for success. Being too parsimonious reduces our ability to react to surprises in a part of the world where surprises are the norm.

We cannot guarantee that time is on our side or that we will have the opportunity to repair tomorrow the mistakes we make today. This is even more the case when we face the fact that a year or more generally elapses between funding decisions and any change on the ground. Diplomats and military commanders in Afghanistan generally recognize that they will not win the war on their watch. Therefore, they have a responsibility to anticipate requirements two to four years into the future and to ensure relevant requests for resources are submitted and strongly pushed. By the same token, leaders in capitals have an obligation to push forward the necessary resources, to keep the pipeline of resources flowing. The difficulties we encountered in getting each year's budget adequately funded probably retarded our looking out as far into the future as we might have done, although I think we did not do badly. But the need for longer-term planning for resources will continue as will the need for honest explanations to Congress and the American people of how much progress is possible in what time frames. Simply put, we need significant resources for people as well as for projects, and we must maintain the flows consistently over time if we are to plan intelligently.

These decisions will be difficult in times of economic and budget stringency. As I write, we are facing the worst U.S. financial crisis since the Great Depression. We will be told again, as I was told, that these are difficult days for the budget. The desire to postpone decisions will be strong. We need to recognize that we are already paying dearly in blood and time for the money we saved earlier. We should not make the same mistake again.

⑤ Principle: Remember 9/11

As we confront those decisions, it is well to remember what is at stake. If we fail in Afghanistan, the state will fragment; there is no power center yet standing on its feet and capable of taking our place. If Afghanistan fragments, then parts of the country will again become the natural base for those who have attacked not only us but also London and Madrid and who have planned to blow up planes over the Atlantic.

And a fragmented Afghanistan will become the strategic rear and base for extremism in Pakistan, a nation of 155 million people that is armed with nuclear weapons. This will allow and facilitate support for extremist movements across the huge swath of energy-rich Central Asia, as was the case in the 1990s. We need to keep in clear view the size of the stakes for which we are playing.

Success is an audacious dream, but it is not impossible. We live in the era of globalization, and this problem is too big to ignore. The West has huge resources, and publics who by and large want those resources applied wisely for meaningful causes. The overwhelming majority of the Afghan people are moderate Muslims who want only a better life, not one of medieval practices and perpetual war. We have made many mistakes. Perhaps I have made a few of them myself. But we have also learned much, if we choose to use the knowledge gained, and we have a great deal yet to work with.

The Afghan people and government will also need to find the political will to build a state in the midst of war. With adequate resources and force, we can shield the Afghan nation while the many reforms, projects, and forces that we and the Afghans have put in motion take shape. We can learn from our mistakes and find good people from many nations to carry forward the work. We will need to pursue stability realistically, in forms acceptable to Afghans and, perhaps, set somewhat less millennial goals than rapid achievement of a twenty-first-century Western liberal democracy in that long-troubled land.

I still believe that success is possible if we have the vision to persevere and the will to resource our vision. America can lead the international effort if it does so with patience, an understanding that it cannot make all the decisions come out our way, and a willingness to fill the gaps that allies will not cover. We will need the honesty to report accurately what is happening, the good and the bad, if we are to maintain credibility over the long run. And it will be a long run. But it can be done.

Notes

Prologue

1. My previous posts included Yemen, where a small insurgency was raging; Algeria, which had a large insurgency and a blanket death threat against all foreigners; Bahrain, which was normally quiet but where we experienced multiple mob attacks against the embassy; and Iraq.
2. I served in Iraq from February to June 2004 under CPA and remained with the embassy as counselor for political-military affairs until June 2005.
3. How much risk I didn't know since only later did I learn he had been ambushed while out with a police convoy. Still, I knew he'd been willing to tour polling stations during the Iraqi elections, and I had seen his pictures of the body of a suicide bomber who didn't make it past a checkpoint.
4. Afghan Dari and Iranian Farsi, which I had learned to some extent when I was in Iran (1971–73), are the same written language, although they are spoken with very different accents and with some regional differences in vocabulary. When I started studying Arabic in 1980 it simply extinguished my Farsi within two months.
5. June 22, 2005, testimony of Assistant Secretary of Defense for

International Security Affairs Peter Rodman, Lt. Gen. Walter Sharp, Director of Strategic Plans, JCS/J5, and Assistant Secretary of State of International Narcotics and Law Enforcement Affairs Nancy Powell. General Sharp testified that the Afghan army was at a strength of 29,000 troops and would reach 70,000 by September 2007 and that the police, then at 24,000, would reach 62,000 by the end of 2006. None of these goals were met.

Chapter 1: First Days

1. Technically an embassy includes both the office, which is called the chancery although it can be several buildings, and the residence of the chief of mission.

2. Secretary of Defense Rumsfeld wanted to limit NATO's mandate in Afghanistan. So did some of the allies. The name ISAF was one fall-out, a matter of diplomatic wording to deal with political objections based more on form than substance. See James F. Dobbins, *After the Taliban: Nation-Building in Afghanistan* (Washington, DC: Potomac Books, 2008), 102–103, for a detailed account.

3. The "south" in operational terms included the provinces of Kandahar, Helmand, Uruzgan, and Zabul. Farah and Nimruz to the west were under the command of Regional Command West (RC-W), which was controlled by an Italian general in Herat and included Spanish and Italian forces and a small U.S. PRT in Farah.

Chapter 2: Elections and More

1. The Bonn agreement is properly titled "Agreement on Provisional Arrangements in Afghanistan Pending the Re-establishment of Permanent Government Institutions." This agreement established a provisional government and scheduled conferences to appoint a transitional administration, a constitutional convention, and elections. The specific, presidential form of government was decided on during the constitutional convention.

2. Austin Bay, "Afghanistan Ballot Battle," *Washington Times*, September 2, 2005.

3. International Crisis Group, *Political Parties in Afghanistan*, Asia Briefing no. 39 (Kabul/Brussels, June 2, 2005).

4. Counting in districts was ruled out owing to fears that armed groups would impose their will on the count.

5.   In total, USAID spent $170 million on support for the constitutional *loya jirga* and elections for the president, National Assembly, and provincial councils.

6.   Ronald Neumann, transcript of remarks, September 1, 2005, http://merln.ndu.edu/archivepdf/afghanistan/State/1sep05.pdf.

7.   Massoud, the "Lion of the Panjshir," was assassinated two days before the 2001 terrorist attacks in America. His picture was displayed in Kabul as much as that of President Karzai.

8.   Like many Afghans, Abdullah has only one name. Sometimes listed as "Abdullah Abdullah," he once joked that this arose when a journalist ask for his full name and he answered "Abdullah."

9.   Taniwal was a gentle but effective governor who had left a comfortable life in Australia to return to Afghanistan. I liked him and was especially happy when months later I was able to assure him that we would pave a road he considered especially important between Gardez and Khowst. It was very sad when in 2006 he was assassinated by a suicide bomber.

Chapter 3: Fall 2005

1.   The U.S. budget or fiscal year runs from October 1 to September 30. Thus the budget for fiscal year 2007 would be sent to the Congress in February 2006. Any supplemental budget for the fiscal year already in progress would go to the Congress at the same time. The complicated schedule of budget preparation and presentation to Congress drives much time in the federal government.

2.   Arnold Fields, *Special Inspector General for Afghanistan Reconstruction: Quarterly Report to the United States Congress* (Washington, DC: Office of the SIGAR, October 30, 2008), 12.

3.   The regular budget under congressional rules must identify how increases will be paid for. Supplementals are not required to explain how they will be funded. On the one hand, this leads to fiscal indiscipline and deficits, arousing periodic congressional complaint. On the other hand, cutting programs or raising taxes are politically painful and despite their protestations, many in Congress are not averse to avoiding such obnoxious responsibilities by agreeing to supplementals. In the end the Rice strategy of raising the base budget to incorporate everything needed in supplementals never came about.

4.   The strategy referred to had been presented to the Deputies Committee

(DC) in 2004 and approved by Deputy Secretary of State Robert Zoellick in 2005. The DC is composed of the deputy secretaries of state, defense, and treasury, the vice chairman of the JCS, the deputy administrator of USAID, and their equivalent numbers from CIA and other departments as needed. Undersecretaries often replace the relevant deputies. The main function of the DC is to coordinate actions already decided on and shape large decisions to be made at the cabinet level.

5. In these days of fascination with e-mail it is important to understand that as outmoded as the cable is often seen to be, it remains the document of record for U.S. foreign policy operations overseas. It is much more widely distributed and read than informal e-mails are and still serves as a useful vehicle for bringing all actors onto the same page of information.

6. The Office of Management and Budget is a part of the White House operation that has the unenviable task of putting together the full federal budget to be presented to Congress. OMB ultimately decides on the division of the budget pie across cabinet departments. Its initial decision can be challenged (a "reclama" in Washington speak), but its reply to the reclama is final unless the cabinet secretary takes his or her case personally to the president. Such appeals require great persuasiveness to overturn the balances constructed by OMB and are, accordingly, rare and highly political.

7. Ronald Neumann, unclassified telegram to OMB, December 5, 2005. At the time this telegram had little impact. Over many months and with some changes it laid the groundwork for a substantial supplemental budget in 2007.

8. Authorizing committees such as Foreign Affairs only propose spending money. The funds actually come from the appropriations committees, so the various subcommittees, such as State, Defense, etc., are the real fiscal powerhouses of Congress.

9. Almost certainly sura 5:32, although I did not note it at the time.

10. The original idea was that a wholly U.S. military effort at customs collection would show the Afghan government how to proceed. The demonstration failed to have the desired effect. Instead the Finance and Interior ministries locked up in a bureaucratic battle over who had authority, a fight probably instigated by local officials who wanted to protect their ability to obtain bribes. We planned to restart the effort with broad international and Afghan support and with agreed-to terms for a trial project to be followed by general application of the

lessons learned. We made some headway but were greatly hampered by the painfully slow progress in getting the Department of Homeland Security to send us the required customs and border experts.

11. Ronald Neumann, unclassified memo to Rep. Jon Porter, February 7, 2006.

Chapter 4: Wake Up, Washington

1. Lieutenant General Eikenberry had an office in the embassy, but there was no space for his staff. As that staff enlarged, it became more and more difficult for him to operate without organizational support, and this eventually compelled him to locate a short distance away. This was very different from Baghdad, where the huge Republican Palace allowed a substantial staff section to be reserved for the military. Some have portrayed Karl's move as a breakdown in our communications, but such a take is silly, mistaking form for function. Karl and I both traveled frequently and maintained extremely busy schedules, so communication was something we worked at very actively. We were in constant touch by classified phone and e-mail, met frequently, and had a weekly private working lunch or dinner to review all pressing civilian and military issues.

2. Jim VandeHei and John Lancaster, "Bush, on Way to India, Stops in Afghanistan," *Washington Post*, March 2, 2006; and "Bush Makes First Afghan Visit," CNN, March 2, 2006, http://edition.cnn.com/2006/WORLD/asiapcf/03/01/bush/.

3. Article of Lt. Col. Les Kodlick, then at Georgetown's Institute for the Study of Diplomacy, for placement on the institute's website.

4. Philip Dine, *St. Louis Post Dispatch*, March 19, 2006.

5. South and Central Asian Affairs (SCA) was our mother bureau. Boucher was a very creative officer and a great help throughout my tour.

6. Hayder Mili and Jacob Townsend, "Afghan Drug Trade and How It Funds Taliban Operations," *Terrorism Monitor*, May 10, 2007, estimates drug funding to the Taliban from taxes and direct involvement at as much as $20 million per year. This figure is also used in the Senlis Council, *US Policy in Afghanistan: Senlis Council Recommendations*, February 18, 2008.

7. Because it has expanded enormously in recent years to handle new programs and because there are few traditional diplomats with the requisite background, INL, sometimes called the Office of Drugs and Thugs, has had to move into large-scale contracting. Doug Wankel was hired on a direct contract by INL, but despite his extensive

background as a contractor, he was not permitted by regulation to directly supervise and rate State officers. Consequently he ran a separate office that coordinated with INL. Such are the wonders of implementing policy in the U.S. government.

8. John Abizaid, e-mail to Ronald Neumann, May 2006.

9. Editorial, *Washington Post*, May 24, 2006.

10. The insurgency was always a collection of different groups, but in general command and control in the south was exercised by a Taliban central control from the Quetta area in Pakistan. The resistance in the east was coordinated to some extent by a Taliban group in Peshawar, but most of the fighters were in the groups controlled by Gulbuddin Hekmatyar and Jalaluddin Haqqani.

11. The Commanders Emergency Relief Program makes flexible funding available to deal with a broad variety of emergency noncombat relief needs.

12. See specifically Ahmed Rashid, *Descent into Chaos: The United States and the Failure of Nation Building in Pakistan, Afghanistan, and Central Asia* (New York: Viking, 2008), 362.

Chapter 5: Afghan Institutions and Donor Cooperation

1. The final membership of the JCMB was as follows: On the Afghan side were the senior economic adviser to the president plus ministers of foreign affairs, finance, economy, rural rehabilitation and development, and justice and the national security adviser; on the international side were the special representative of the secretary general (head of UNAMA) plus the United States, the UK, Japan, Germany, the EU, India, Pakistan, Iran, China, Saudi Arabia, Turkey, Russia, Canada, the Netherlands, Italy, France, the World Bank, the Asian Development Bank, NATO, and CFC-A.

2. The recommendations included a partial privatization of bill collecting to reduce bribery and to supply the government enough money to keep providing electricity from the new projects and an agreement to replace Kabul's antiquated distribution system that lost over half the power that was sent into the city's power grid.

3. Joint Declaration of the United States–Afghanistan Strategic Partnership, May 23, 2005

4. Department of State, *On the Record Briefing on U.S.-Afghanistan Strategic Partnership*, March 21, 2006.

5. The FY 2006 supplemental included funding for the Afghan military and

police, embassy operations, and counterdrug operations, and funding for Iraq. It was a large bill, over $2.4 billion, that was strongly debated.

Chapter 6: Where Is the Margin for Victory?

1. For a description of anti-Soviet fighting in the same area, see Ali Ahmad Jalali and Lester W. Grau, *The Other Side of the Mountain: Mujahideen Tactics in the Soviet-Afghan War* (Fort Leavenworth, KS: Foreign Military Studies Office, 1995), 123–125.

2. There was a great deal written on the fighting. See in particular Adam Day, "Operation Medusa: The Battle for Panjwai," *Legion Magazine*, September 1, 2007, November 1, 2007, and January 26, 2008; "NATO Hails Afghan Mission Success," BBC News, September 17, 2006; and numerous ISAF and NATO Brussels briefings.

3. "NATO Chief Warns Afghan May Switch Allegiance to Taliban," *CNN World*, October 8, 2006; "NATO Forces Insufficient for Early Victory: British General," *The News*, November 1, 2006; and Daniel McKivergan, "NATO in Afghanistan," *Weekly Standard: The Blog*, November 1, 2006, http://www.weeklystandard.com/weblogs/TWSFP/2006/11/.

4. See for example, "NATO Military Chief Calls for Afghan Reinforcements," Agence France Presse, September 7, 2006, quoting one of many statements by NATO commander General Jones.

5. "We Are Not Going to Evacuate. We Are Not Going Anywhere," *Spiegel*, September 26, 2006.

6. Renée Montagne, *Morning Edition*, National Public Radio, October 23, 2006.

7. Rachael Morarjee, "Envoy Urges Kabul to Use Lull in Fighting," *Financial Times*, November 24, 2006.

8. The ANAP received considerable and often skeptical discussion. See for example, *Reforming Afghanistan's Police*, Asia Report no. 138 (Kabul/Brussels: International Crisis Group, August 30, 2007); and Andrew Wilder, *Cops or Robbers? The Struggle to Reform the Afghan National Police* (Kabul: Afghanistan Research and Evaluation Unit, July 2007).

9. The six provinces were Farah, Ghazni, Helmand, Kandahar, Uruzgan, and Zabul.

10. In the failed attempt at a 2006 supplemental, we had recommended approximately $400 million for a "southern strategy" of road building. By the middle of calendar 2006, our proposal for a supplemental,

now for FY 2007, involved roads connecting province and district capitals in both the south and east, plus money to rehabilitate 385 kilometers of all-weather provincial roads.

11. Since these proposals were put forth, there have been some additional roads built in northern and western Afghanistan, but there has not been an integrated donor effort such as we had hoped for.

12. Jason Burke, "Taliban Town Seizure Throws Afghan Policy into Disarray," *Observer*, February 4, 2007; and Michael Smith, "British to Leave Taliban Hotspot," *The Australian*, October 2, 2006.

13. Tom Coghlan and Damien McElroy, "US Envoy Attacks British Truce with Taliban," *Telegraph*, October 25, 2006.

14. Ibid.

15. Rashid, *Descent into Chaos*, 360, refers to "open conflict" between us.

Chapter 7: Progress, Not Victory

1. NATO, press release, November 28, 2006.

2. The idea in 2008 to appoint Lord Paddy Ashdown as the UN coordinator was borrowed from the same Balkan playbook as the idea of the contact group. With Lord Ashdown's Balkan background, reputation for using strong-arm tactics, and press play about things he would coordinate (with no reference to coordinating them with the Afghan government), it appeared to Afghans as an attempt by the outsiders to give orders. That was why President Karzai refused the appointment at the last moment. It was a predictable outcome.

3. At the governor's request, I tried to find auxiliary police to provide local security but did not succeed. No Afghan security forces were added to the valley. Slowly the insurgents, most of whom were local, returned. The governor fell out with Kabul and was fired after making very public criticisms of President Karzai. ISAF had to work elsewhere, and troops were drawn off for other missions. By 2008 most results of the operation were lost, and the valley was again a base for security problems in Kabul.

4. A National Security Council meeting (referred to simply as "an NSC") is at the cabinet level and chaired either by the national security adviser or the president. The NSC can make decisions, although if they are made without the president they will often go to him for ratification. If the president chairs the meeting, it is referred to as either a cabinet meeting or a full NSC.

5. Bureau of South and Central Asian Affairs and Embassy Kabul,

"Afghanistan Reclama to OMB: FY 2007 Supplemental and FY 2008 Base," November 28, 2006, 1.

6. Ibid., 3.

7. Tests we had done showed that the amount of eradication done by individuals with spray and hand-cutting was roughly similar per day. The difference was that spraying could start earlier, when the poppy plants were still too small to be cut, and thus extend the time available for eradication.

8. The Food and Agricultural Organization (FAO) was opposed to ground spraying. The UN Office of Drug Control (UNODC) was in favor. There was no apparent mechanism to reconcile these views to allow a strong UN voice.

9. There were many frictions between ISAF troops and Wafa, and much later he too was replaced.

10. Ismail Khan and Carlotta Gall, "Pakistan Lets Tribal Chiefs Keep Control Along Border," *New York Times*, September 6, 2006; and Arthur Bright, "Pakistan Signs Peace Deal with Pro-Taliban Militants," *Christian Science Monitor*, September 6, 2006.

11. The Durand line was negotiated by the British in 1893. Pakistan held that because it is a successor state to British India, the border is established and not open for discussion. The Afghans claim the line was accepted under duress, that it was an administrative agreement and not a border, and have never recognized the line. Afghanistan voted against Pakistan's entry into the United Nations because of this disagreement. Pushtuns do not recognize the border, and tribesmen move and trade freely across it, sometimes even owning land on both sides. The issue is politically extremely sensitive in Afghanistan. In turn, the Afghan refusal to recognize the border and past Afghan political actions have nurtured Pakistani concerns that Afghans may someday make territorial claims on the area. There are many scholarly articles on the subject. For a more political treatment see Ronald Neumann, "Borderline Insanity: Thinking Big about Afghanistan," *American Interest*, November–December 2007, 52–58.

12. Mark Mazzetti and David Rhode, "Amid U.S. Policy Disputes, Qaeda Grows in Pakistan," *New York Times*, June 30, 2008, describes this effort in some detail.

13. Ahmed Rashid, "Accept Defeat by Taliban, Pakistan Tells NATO," *Telegraph*, November 29, 2006.

14. Ali Muhammad Jan Orakzai was the governor of the NWFP from May 2006 until his resignation in January 2008. He was a career soldier.

15. Gretchen Peters, "Is the U.S. Ambassador to Afghanistan on the Way Out?" *Blotter*, October 11, 2006, http://blogs.abcnews.com/theblotter/2006/10/us_ambassador_t.html.

16. The phrase is attributed both to Napoleon's foreign minister Talleyrand and Police Chief Joseph Fouché on being informed of the 1804 kidnapping and execution of the Duke d'Enghien: "C'est pire qu'un crime; c'est une faute." The quotation has become a favorite of diplomats and of those who sometimes describe them as practical cynics.

17. If a single senator objects to a nomination for any reason or even without giving a reason, the senator can put a hold on the nomination that prevents a vote from taking place. The hold can be confidential. There is no way to overrule a hold. The author of the hold must first be discovered and then persuaded to lift the hold.

Chapter 8: Force, Money, and Decisions

1. Greg Jaffe, "In Afghanistan, Commanders Ask for Money in Lieu of Troops," *Wall Street Journal*, January 17, 2007.

2. "Heavy Afghan Fighting Expected: US Ambassador," Reuters, January 22, 2007; and "Spring to Bring Heavy Fighting in Afghanistan, U.S. Ambassador Says," Associated Press, January 22, 2007.

3. A brigade combat team consists of three battalions plus artillery, engineers, and other attached units—over eight thousand soldiers.

4. The term "political director" is a European usage. For us it meant the undersecretary for political affairs, Nicholas Burns. At the last moment he had to attend to other pressing matters, and the U.S. delegation was led by the assistant secretary for South and Central Asian Affairs, Richard Boucher.

5. The large turbine essential to the dam project reached the dam only in September 2008. It was with a great deal of satisfaction that I read the newspaper accounts of the hundred-vehicle convoy that we had so often discussed making its way successfully to the dam using a decoy route carved out of the hills by sappers. The American press did not notice.

6. One recurrent frustration was finding time for our congressional delegations to meet with the Afghan parliament. Visits were usually compressed into a few hours, the delegation wanted to see President Karzai and visit troops, we needed time for at least a short embassy briefing,

and the trip to Parliament required a half-hour drive each way. This was usually more time than we could fit in. The parliamentarians began to object to coming to the embassy for a meeting, saying it was their country and the congressional delegation should visit them just as they would call on Congress if they went to Washington. We managed various solutions: sometimes we held a social event at my residence, sometimes we had a meeting at the presidential palace, and occasionally the schedule permitted a trip to Parliament. Congressional visitors usually went away impressed by the parliamentarians they met, particularly the women members, but we never found a permanent solution to the protocol problem.

Chapter 9: Final Days

1. See, for example, Anne Applebaum, "Ending an Opium War: Poppies and Afghan Recovery Can Both Bloom," *Washington Post*, January 16, 2007; and Senlis Council, *Poppy for Medicine* (London: May 2008).

Chapter 10: Wrap-Up

1. Many Afghans and foreign economic development specialists argue strongly that costs could be cut, coordination enhanced, and Afghan government performance improved if more funding were channeled through the Afghan government rather than through donor-run projects using expensive foreign contractors. There is validity to the argument, but it runs up against a lack of existing Afghan capacity that was reflected in the problems Afghanistan had in spending its development budget. The issue is too extensive to be fully treated here, but, very generally, our approach was to try simultaneously to increase capacity while gradually expanding the funds channeled through the Afghan government. It is possible that we could or should have moved faster, but real operations are always more complicated and more bureaucratic than theory.

2. The primary donors were the World Bank, the Asian Development Bank, the European Commission, the British Department for International Development (DFID), the UN Development Program (UNDP), and USAID.

3. Many of the details here are re-created from an unclassified summary telegram prepared by Thomas Johnson and Lane Smith in the USAID

office in Kabul, with the cooperation of officers in the Economic Section, the treasury attaché, and other officers, that was sent on January 27, 2007.

Epilogue

1. I am indebted to Dr. Anthony Cordesman for the phrase "armed state building," which captures what we are about far better than either the words "counterinsurgency" or "nation building."

2. In the past ten years the USAID budget has grown 60 percent while its worldwide staff has shrunk by one-third.

3. American Academy of Diplomacy and Henry L. Stimson Center, *A Foreign Affairs Budget for the Future: Fixing the Crisis in Diplomatic Readiness* (Washington, DC: October 1, 2008), http:// www.academyofdiplomacy.org/publications/FAB_report_2008.pdf. This study proposed detailed staffing increases for all agencies under the authority of the secretary of state totaling 4,500 additional personnel to meet worldwide needs. Full disclosure: the author is president of the academy.

4. In remarks of President George W. Bush on September 9, 2008, at the National Defense University, there is explicit mention of fielding increases in State and USAID personnel as well as other civilians, but agricultural assistance is being expanded by using U.S. Army reservists rather than civilian resources. This is an effective short-term measure but one that misapplies scarce military resources.

5. American Academy of Diplomacy and Stimson Center, *Foreign Affairs Budget for the Future*, estimates that over five years, the budget for personnel under the authority of the secretary of state needs to be increased by $3.5 billion to meet the identified shortfalls in worldwide staffing capacity—a small amount when compared to the totals of the defense budget.

Index

About the Author

Amb. Ronald E. Neumann, now president of the American Academy of Diplomacy, served previously as a deputy assistant secretary of state for Near Eastern Affairs and three times as ambassador, to Algeria (1994–97), Bahrain (2001–4), and finally to the Islamic Republic of Afghanistan (2005–7). Prior to his stint in Afghanistan, Neumann, a career member of the Senior Foreign Service, served in Baghdad from February 2004 with the Coalition Provisional Authority and then as the embassy's principal interlocutor with the Multinational Command. He was an infantry officer in Vietnam (1969–70). He lives in Arlington, Virginia.